Social Studies as New Literacies in a Global Society

Routledge Research in Education

For a complete list of titles, go to www.routledge.com

Social Studies as New Literacies in a Global Society

Relational Cosmopolitanism in the Classroom

Mark Baildon and James S. Damico

Routledge
Taylor & Francis Group
New York   London

First published 2011
by Routledge
270 Madison Avenue, New York, NY 10016

Simultaneously published in the UK
by Routledge
2 Park Square, Milton Park, Abingdon, Oxon OX14 4RN

Routledge is an imprint of the Taylor & Francis Group, an informa business

© 2011 Taylor & Francis

Typeset in Sabon by IBT Global.
Printed and bound in the United States of America on acid-free paper by IBT Global.

Library of Congress Cataloging-in-Publication Data

Baildon, Mark.
  Social studies as new literacies in a global society : relational cosmopolitanism in the classroom / by Mark Baildon and James S. Damico.
      p. cm.
  Includes bibliographical references and index.
  1. Social sciences—Study and teaching. 2. Social sciences—Research. 3. Social science teachers—Training of. I. Damico, James S. II. Title.
    H62.B264 2011
    300.71—dc22
    2010018619

ISBN13: 978-0-415-87367-3 (hbk)
ISBN13: 978-0-203-84000-9 (ebk)

This book is dedicated to our parents
Charles Baildon and Carol Baildon
Floyd Damico (1934–1999) and Carol Damico.
We continue to learn about the depth of their
capacity for giving.

Contents

PART III
Synthesis and Implications

Figures and Tables

FIGURES

TABLES

Foreword
Walter Parker

This is a book for social studies education in "new times." It addresses the buzzing present—a moment loaded with new technologies and media, new power dynamics, new affinities, new migrations, new human relations, new complexity, new hope and fear; in sum, new scapes at new scales. Mark Baildon and James Damico describe a social studies education that invites teachers and students to dive in thoroughly and intelligently.

Three ideas are key: *social studies*, *literacy*, and *inquiry*. The authors unpack and repack these categories, deconstructing and reconstructing them so that curriculum, instruction, and learning are opened for examination and then aimed at transformation. This is a book about education, not testing, standardization, and accountability. It is about innovation, but it is tied to discourses of caring, justice, and democracy rather than economic competitiveness and national security. All of this makes for a breath of much needed fresh air in an otherwise narrow and constricted "school reform" literature.

Baildon and Damico define social studies as inquiry with an eye toward critical reading of all sorts of texts, from documents to films and multimodal web-based texts. Paulo Freire's literacy—reading worlds as well as words—is championed, and classroom examples are provided to illustrate what this can mean in elementary (chapter 4) and secondary schools (chapters 5 and 6), and in teacher education courses (chapters 7 and 8).

Inquiry, recall, is the methodical building of evidence-based claims (explanations, theses), which involves evaluating the strength of others' claims as well as developing strong claims oneself. It also involves serious consideration of rival hypotheses and perspectives as a first order of business. This is key democratic work, scientific work, and authentic intellectual work at the same time. Importantly, it surpasses the primary document fetish at which inquiry too often stops in social studies curriculum and instruction. In the context of inquiry, primary sources are not ends in themselves but data sets—sources of information—useful for building and evaluating claims. They must be analyzed, of course, but in service of a larger purpose. Reasoning with evidence, discerning the credibility of sources, and argumentation are key activities, and this means revising theories as evidence, experience, and logic require.

This revision work is an iterative, spiraling process, what John Dewey called "the double-movement of reflection" in his 1910 book *How We Think*. It is both a mundane activity and a scholarly practice. We humans observe things, and we reflect on—theorize—what they mean. We then test our theories in new observations, and then we use these new experiences to revise our theories again, whether we are looking for ripe peaches at the market, sitting on a jury, testing a hypothesis in a laboratory, or trying to figure out whether a particular 'conspiracy theory' has any merit. We engage in this double-movement continuously, until we stop for whatever reason: we've "made up our mind," the theory is no longer challenged by new evidence, our resources dry up, we get lazy. Baildon and Damico insert three critical reading practices into the process—multiple traversals across a problem space, dialogue across difference, and perspective building. Each of these invites additional, intelligent claim-building and revision.

"Intelligent." I've used the term twice already. William Stanley (2010) describes Dewey's approach to inquiry as a "method of intelligence." Stanley is probing a long-standing disagreement among persons interested in curriculum—disagreement over the relationship between social studies education and society: *Should schools cater to the status quo or transform it?* Should they strive to conserve society more or less as it is or to change and improve it? Stanley locates Dewey on a middle course. Rather than indoctrinating students with a particular theory of the good society, whether conservative or transformative, "Dewey believed schools should participate in the general intellectualization of society by inculcating a method of intelligence. This would provide students," Stanley continues, "with the critical competence for reflective thought applied to the analysis of social problems" (p. 21).

On this view, which I support, students should be helped to learn content by studying historical and contemporary social problems and narratives and, in tandem, by being taught to use their minds well—to think critically, to value and participate in the double-movement of inquiry, and thereby to invent, experiment, and cut through conventional dogma. But they are not to be told to what end they should use these competencies. They are not to be indoctrinated but left free to use their minds as they see fit. It is up to them—well-educated democratic citizens, trained thinkers—to engage in the ongoing work of knowledge construction, intellectual development, and government of, by, and for the people. Of course, this requires sensibilities that are often absent in the contemporary "school reform" literature: trust in teachers, belief in democracy, and faith in inquiry (Kridel & Bullough, 2007).

"Method of intelligence." This is for me the core meaning of inquiry. Raymond Boisvert, the author of the best Dewey primer I know, uses this term along with a synonym: "intelligence in operation" (1998, p. 31). Both convey a rigorous yet flexible and adaptive way of applying the mind to problems. It is not a content-less way, certainly, for inquiry is a meaningless process without information (evidence, experience, listening, reading); without it, there can be no double movement. Nor is it a neutral way, for it favors intelligence, experimentation, and an open future. Yet, it does not prescribe where students should end up. This is the wave Baildon and Damico ride in this book. It is the method they want to teach, and it is the method they have explored in their own inquiries with students in Michigan, Indiana, Taipei, and Singapore.

I welcome this book. It is infused with a practical spirit of inquisitiveness, collaboration, and exploration—exactly what "new times" require.

REFERENCES

Boisvert, R. D. (1998). *John Dewey: Rethinking our time*. Albany: State University of New York Press.

Dewey, J. (1910/1985). *How we think, and selected essays* (Vol. 6). Carbondale: Southern Illinois University Press.

Kridel, C., & Bullough, R. V. (2007). *Stories of the eight-year study: reexamining secondary education in America*. Albany: State University of New York Press.

Stanley, W. B. (2010). Social studies and the social order. In W. C. Parker (Ed.), *Social studies today: research and practice* (pp. 17-24). New York: Routledge.

Acknowledgments

The frontiers of a book are never clear-cut; beyond the title, the first lines, the last full stop, beyond its internal configuration and its autonomous form, it is caught up in a system of references to other books, other texts, other sentences: it is a node within a network. (Foucault, 1973, p. 23)

In many ways, this book is part of a network of ideas and influences within a "system of references" that extends far beyond its covers. For us, a cherished set of colleagues, mentors, and friends comprise this network: relationships with the people who have helped us think through, work out, and put into practice ideas we have found particularly compelling.

Many of these ideas took hold during our time as graduate students at Michigan State University, and we are indebted to the many people who shaped our thinking during these formative years. In particular, we want to acknowledge Laura Apol, Gina Cervetti, Cleo Cherryholmes, Karen Lowenstein, Wanda May, Ernest Morrell, Michael Pardales, P. David Pearson, Cheryl Rosaen, Kaustuv Roy, Avner Segall, and Steve Sharra for their many contributions to our thinking. We also wish to express our gratitude to Betsy Ashburn, John Bell, Bob Floden, Bonnie Garbrecht, Marcia Leone, Barbara Markle, Mike Roessler, Shari Rose, Rand Spiro, and Brian Vance who supported and guided us in a range of ways as we worked on Project TIME (Technology Integrated for Meaningful Learning Experiences). We will always be grateful for this opportunity to merge each of our developing interests and explore the many facets of inquiry-based social studies and literacy education using technology. We remain especially grateful to Betsy Ashburn for her leadership on Project TIME and for the space and support she provided us to grapple with pressing and persistent issues of classroom practice.

We are also grateful for the opportunity to develop the *Critical Web Reader* project at Indiana University. We have learned a great deal about technology, inquiry, social studies, literacy, and research with and from our colleagues Gerald Campano, Stephanie Carter, Anne Elsener, Marisa Exter, Max Exter, Ruth Riddle, and Tarajean Yazzie-Mintz, along with a number of others who made important contributions at key moments during the project, including Kathleen Allspaw, Rindi Baildon, Serafín Coronel-Molina, Shiau-Jing Guo, Michelle Honeyford, Daehyeon Nam, Becky Ruppert, and Lenny Sanchez, among many others. The *Critical Web*

Reader project now extends to the National Institute of Education in Singapore and we have been extremely fortunate to work and learn with Suhaimi Afandi, Agnes Paculdar, Lena Teo, and Sharmila Singaram as part of the research team in Singapore.

Indiana University and the School of Education also deserve special thanks. Our work on the *Critical Web Reader* project has received generous financial support from a number of funding sources, including the Maris M. & Mary Higgins Proffitt Endowment, the Kempf Trust Fund, the Faculty Research Support Program, the School of Education Diversity and Equity Research Initiative as well as the Pathways Initiative, and the Faculty Global and International Education Grant program. Several colleagues also played key roles working with or shepherding us through the grant writing process, and we would like to especially thank Cathy Brown, Carthell Everett, Mary Beth Hines, Larry Mikulecky, Bob Sherwood, and Josh Smith for their mentorship and support.

We also extend our deepest gratitude to Keith Barton, Jerome Harste, and Li-Ching Ho along with several anonymous reviewers for their careful and critical reading of our manuscript. Their invaluable feedback and suggestions significantly strengthened the final outcome. We also want to thank several colleagues who provided feedback on parts of the manuscript we found especially challenging. Tracey Alviar-Martin, Agnes Paculdar, and Jasmine Sim all offered important suggestions at a critical time in the project. And Walter Parker deserves special thanks for his sage advice and his ongoing support for our work and the ideas in this book. We are especially delighted and grateful that his voice in the Foreword helps launch the book.

We also wish to thank the editors and staff at Routledge for their patience, assistance, and support through this process. We also acknowledge the publishers who granted us permission to draw from material initially published in the following academic journals:

Baildon, M., & Damico, J. (2009). How do we know? Students examine issues of credibility with a complicated multimodal Web-based text. *Curriculum Inquiry*, 39(2), 265–285. Blackwell Publishing.

Baildon, R., & Baildon, M. (2008). Guiding independence: Developing a research tool to support student decision-making in selecting sources of information. *The Reading Teacher*, 61(8), 636–647. Copyright 2008 by the International Reading Association.

Damico, J., & Baildon, M. (2008). Reading web sites in an inquiry-based social studies classroom. In D. Rowe, & R.T. Jimenez (Eds.), *National Reading Conference Yearbook* (204–217). Oak Creek, WI: National Reading Conference. Reprinted with permission of the National Reading Conference.

We, of course, have also had the good fortune to work with many teachers and students, especially in Michigan, Taipei, Singapore, and Indiana.

Confidentiality rules prohibit us from listing their names, yet we remain grateful for the many ways they taught us about collaboration, inquiry, and the potential of understanding social studies as new literacies.

Finally, we reserve a very special thanks to Rindi Baildon and Gabrièle Abowd Damico, our models and mentors for understanding and embodying compassionate, critical, and artful ways of being in the world each and every day. We can feel their influence in every page of this book.

Introduction
Social Studies as New Literacies in a Global Society

This book draws on our experiences as teachers, curriculum developers, technology designers, and researchers. For the past ten years we have been working together, merging our interests and expertise in social studies education (Mark) and literacy education (James), to develop web-based curricula and tools to guide teachers and students to become more vigilant and critical readers and writers of web-based texts. Each of us has worn a number of hats in doing this work—classroom teacher, researcher, teacher educator, consultant, professional development coordinator, and university-school liaison, to name the most prominent ones—and we have been fortunate to learn a great deal with and from a wide range of students and teachers across grade levels (elementary through graduate school) and contexts (classrooms in Indiana, Michigan, Taiwan, and Singapore).

Throughout our work, a core set of questions has continued to tug at us, inviting deeper investigation and inquiry, questions like: What are different facets of critical reading when it comes to web-based texts? How should social studies content and classrooms be conceptualized when the Internet is the only curricular resource? How can teachers and students work together to discern the credibility of complicated websites? What strategies do students use to adjudicate among conflicting perspectives on websites? In what ways might students develop deeper understandings about societal problems through web-based inquiry approaches? *Social Studies as New Literacies: Living in a Global Society* takes up these questions with explicit attention to challenges and possibilities related to teaching, learning, and schooling in the 21st century.

In this book we define social studies as *inquiry-based social practices for understanding and addressing problems, especially complex, multifaceted problems.* We recognize that social studies education in the United States is typically configured as a loose confederation of social sciences and humanities courses intended to promote civic engagement and competence. We also realize that the term, social studies education, is not commonly used in some countries. Thus, we adopt a broad definition of social studies education, one that encompasses academic subjects within the humanities (history and geography) and the social sciences (economics, psychology, sociology, political science) in ways that seek to help students understand society (e.g., in time and space) and become prepared to be engaged citizens. *Social Studies as New Literacies in a Global Society* conceptualizes social studies teaching and learning in ways that will help prepare students to live in "new times"—prepared for new forms of labor in the post-industrial economy, equipped to handle new and emerging technologies and function in the new media age, and prepared to understand different perspectives to participate in an increasingly diverse, multicultural global society. In the context of new educational imperatives precipitated by far-reaching changes of globalization, we explore and examine the ways teachers and students use technology tools in ways that can promote a critical and global conception of what it means to be a citizen in the 21st century.

BUILDING ON RICH TRADITION: SOCIAL STUDIES, PROGRESSIVE EDUCATION, AND CRITICAL LITERACY

Our emphasis on *inquiry-based social practices for understanding and addressing complex, multi-faceted problems* is situated in issues-centered social studies education with a noteworthy historical lineage. The 1916 Report of the Committee on Social Studies of the National Education Association's Commission on the Reorganization of Secondary Education advocated a broad interdisciplinary "Problems of Democracy" course emphasizing the study of social problems and current issues that were relevant to students. From the 1920s to the 1940s, Harold Rugg called for and created curriculum and a textbook series that helped students "understand the roots, dimensions, and concerns of contemporary life—locally, nationally, and globally" and empowered youth "to wrestle with controversial issues as informed, deliberative, and tolerant citizens" (Boyle-Baise & Goodman, 2009, p. 275). Since the 1950s, Hunt and Metcalf (1955/1968), Massialas and Cox (1966), Oliver and Shaver (1966), Engle and Ochoa (1988), and others have advocated problem-solving and decision-making approaches to deal with controversial issues and persistent modern problems (e.g., racism, conflict, war, poverty, etc.). To some extent or another each of these social studies scholars conceptualized intelligent inquiry as absolutely necessary to solve society's most pressing issues. Edwin Fenton fostered inquiry-focused "New Social Studies" in the 1960s and 1970s which required students to identify problems, collect and analyze data, and formulate their own conclusions. More recently, scholars such as James Banks, Walter Parker, and Diana Hess, among others, have articulated how multicultural and citizenship education must be rooted in deliberation and dialogue around complicated texts and controversial issues. Avner Segall, Elizabeth Heilman, and Cleo Cherryholmes (2006) have called for the infusion of critical postmodern perspectives, such as feminist, poststructural, and postcolonial theories and pragmatist perspectives (Cherryholmes, 1999) into social studies education. From the

1916 Committee on Social Studies report nearly 100 years ago to the 1996 *Handbook on Teaching Social Issues* published by The National Council for the Social Studies and now moving into the second decade of the 21st century, many scholars and educators have helped cultivate inquiry-based, issues-centered social studies.

The tradition of issues-based social studies education also recognizes that the academic disciplines themselves are issue-laden. According to Walter Parker, the way curriculum is traditionally construed may give teachers and students the idea that:

> the academic disciplines are settled and devoid of controversy. Nothing could be further from the truth. The disciplines are loaded with arguments, and expertise in a discipline is measured by one's involvement in them . . . Argumentation is authentic disciplinary activity. Social scientists argue about everything they study—about why Rome fell, what globalization is doing, why slavery lasted longer in the U.S. than in England, why poverty persists, how the nation-state system developed initially, and why it is maintained today. (2010, p. 254)

Parker helps us see the salience of guiding students to deliberate the controversies within an academic discipline because this involves students in the substantive (content and ideas) and syntactic (methods of investigation) dimensions of an academic discipline. This prepares students for the argumentation that both democracy and inquiry require.

This historical lineage can also be situated within the broader progressive education tradition in the United States, which took root in the late 1800s and early 1900s with pioneer leaders like Jane Addams and John Dewey. This tradition developed in response to monumental immigration, bewildering technological change, and basic questions about civic responsibility: all of which have present-day parallels (Bruce & Bishop, 2008). Although progressive educators have long debated what progressive education has meant or means definitively, they have, in general, shared a set of values, such as, community, collaboration, holistic learning, social justice, active learning, intrinsic motivation, and deep understanding (Kohn, 2008). The cornerstone of these values has been a concern and commitment to producing engaged citizens who possess the ability to cope with complex problems and participate actively in social, economic, and political decisions (Bruce & Bishop, 2008).

Within the progressive education tradition, some educators, who came to be called social reconstructionists, argued that schools and teachers needed to assume more active roles in social critique and transformation. Harold Rugg (1921), for example, a leading social reconstructionist, believed the root cause of many social problems was economic, and he developed his textbook series to guide teachers and students to investigate the ways the current social, economic, and political systems marginalized or exploited certain segments of the population, especially the poor (Stanley, 1992). The social reconstructionists believed that students should "directly study poverty, crime, political corruption, unemployment, and abuse of power as the themes that would prepare them for adult society" (Shannon, 1990, p. 13). Critical reading of texts and contexts was deemed essential to this effort:

> No longer was it sufficient for the literate to read accurately or to write clearly and expressively. What was needed for the educational frontier was the ability to read beyond the text to understand how the author and the ideas connected with various political, economic, and social arguments concerning the future of America . . . [What was needed was] an expanding definition of literacy—one that encouraged readers and writers to see the ideological basis of any text. (Shannon, 1990, p. 97)

In this sense, conceptions of what it meant to be literate were tied to critical understandings of society and, in turn, to what it meant to be an engaged citizen.

Through the latter decades of the 20th century, scholars and educators working within the field of critical literacy have also contributed to the ideals of progressive education and to goals of social reconstructionism. Paulo Freire, one of the most influential critical literacy educators, offered a concise description of the role of literacy in progressive and social reconstructionist efforts with his view that critical literacy entails learning to "read the word" through "reading the world" (Freire & Macedo, 1987). Put another way, children and adults learn to be literate through engaging in ongoing critical analysis of social conditions in the world. In the 21st century, reading the word and the world increasingly requires "new literacies" (Lankshear & Knobel, 2003; Leu, Kinzer, Coiro & Cammack, 2004), what we define as the practices (the range of practices associated broadly with reading and writing) that are necessary to work with new technologies and texts, especially the Internet. This includes facility with technology tools (knowing how to send and receive electronic mail, upload photos, compose and manipulate digital texts, conduct effective web searches, etc.), the ability to critically engage with content and ideas vis-à-vis new technology tools (e.g., discern the credibility of a website), and the know-how to use tools like the Internet to promote critical literacy goals (e.g., create and distribute a digital video to a wide audience to marshall support for a cause).

Social Studies as New Literacies in a Global Society builds on this rich tradition in social studies and literacy education with a similar intention: to better understand, describe, and promote ways that teachers and students can cultivate a critical and creative "method of intelligence" (Dewey, 1935; Stanley, 2010) to address complex, multi-faceted problems. We proceed with the view that the scope of these problems is global and that we need to move the center of global education from imperial views that divide the world (Willinsky, 1998) to helping students engage multiple viewpoints, develop perspective consciousness, embrace hybridity, and manage complexity (Merryfield, 2001). Such a move makes it possible to organize social studies curricula and integrate literacy practices in ways that enable students to understand how various social, economic, political, historical, and contemporary issues and problems are interconnected—in ways that help them integrate local dimensions of human experience with global conditions and concerns.

We believe this orientation to curriculum calls for teachers and students, along with administrators, parents, and policymakers, to embrace and enact a *relational cosmopolitanism*. A *relational cosmopolitanism* integrates progressive values, such as, open-mindedness, a commitment to public deliberation and dialogue, capacity for critical reflection (including self-reflection), and willingness to skillfully act in the face of injustices. *Relational cosmopolitanism* recognizes that our common humanity transcends borders and boundaries (Appiah, 2006) while also remaining "rooted" (Appiah, 1997), situated deeply in and through particular daily struggles of time and place. A *relational cosmopolitanism* is nurtured and sustained by a feminist ethics of care, concern, and connection (Martin, 1994), the forging of alliances and coalitions as a "lived process of ongoing political and ethical action and education" (Mitchell, 2007, p. 717). A *relational cosmopolitanism* helps frame the challenges of living in a global society and the ways social studies and literacy educators, along with their students, can critically and creatively respond to these challenges.

OUTLINE OF THE BOOK

Social Studies as New Literacies in a Global Society is divided into three sections. *Part I, Reconceptualizing Social Studies: Frameworks and Tools* offers an integrated theoretical framework to guide a reconceptualized social studies education. *Part II, Exploring and Examining Challenges and Possibilities: Windows into Classrooms,* provides concrete examples of teachers and students wrestling with core challenges involved in doing inquiry-based investigations of complex topics with web-based texts. *Part III, Synthesis and Implications,* synthesizes key findings across the book and offers a six dimensions model to help guide educators interested in enacting and researching social studies as new literacies for living in the global society.

Part I– Reconceptualizing Social Studies: Frameworks and Tools

A critical, global conception of social studies requires understanding of and facility with new and critical perspectives and practices in literacy because our experience is increasingly mediated textually vis-à-vis new mediascapes, technoscapes, and ideoscapes (Appadurai, 1996). We elaborate on these new global landscapes in the first chapter and make a case for social studies reconceptualized as new literacies for living in the global society. We also consider Singapore as a case study. All nations, to different degrees, are redefining their relationships with their populations, with other countries, and with international institutions and transnational organizations, and we use Singapore to illustrate how one government is using education and educational reform to manage the transnational flows and forces of globalization (Koh, 2007). As a contextual space that straddles East-West, North-South, developed-newly developed-underdeveloped, colonial-postcolonial, national-transnational, local-national-global, and traditional-(post)modern, Singapore offers a compelling example of the complex ecologies of globalization. In this opening chapter we also make a case for seeing the teaching and learning of these complex ecologies through a lens of *relational cosmopolitanism*.

In Chapter 2 we outline an integrated theoretical framework for thinking about social studies as new literacies. This framework draws on disciplinary, interdisciplinary, and transdisciplinary perspectives to fuse work in new literacies and social studies education. We outline a five-phase inquiry model and identify five corresponding teaching and learning challenges: 1. Defining purposes and launching an inquiry; 2. Discerning credibility of textual sources; 3. Adjudicating among conflicting claims and evidence in a range of texts, especially complex multimodal texts; 4. Synthesizing findings; and 5. Communicating new ideas. We also discuss three sets of practices to respond to these challenges: multiple traversals across problem spaces, dialogue across difference, and building of perspective. We then introduce two metaphors—*excavation* and *elevation*—to help map the landscape of these inquiry-based social practices.

In Chapter 3 we consider how a range of web-based tools and resources can help teachers and students engage in social studies inquiry and grapple with the five epistemological challenges outlined in Chapter 2. We then describe a set of web-based technology tools, the *Critical Web Reader*, designed to guide a reconceptualized social studies education aligned with new literacies perspectives.

Part II—Exploring and Examining Challenges and Possibilities: Windows into Classrooms

Undoubtedly, the approaches we describe in Chapters 1–3 call for "ambitious teaching" in which teachers understand both their subject matter and their students and remain "willing to push hard to create opportunities for powerful teaching and learning" (Grant, 2010, p. 49). Such work, though challenging for teachers and students, is possible as well as necessary. In Chapters 4, 5, and 6, we consider the ways groups of students—a class of fourth graders in Singapore and two groups of ninth graders in

Taiwan—grappled with core epistemological challenges of inquiry-based social education: the challenge of discerning credible and useful resources in Chapter 4; the challenges of evaluating claims and evidence and discerning the credibility of a complicated multimodal text in Chapter 5; and the challenge of synthesizing findings during an inquiry project in Chapter 6. Chapters 7 and 8 then consider the ways a group of undergraduate pre-service social studies teachers in the Midwestern United States and their instructor worked through the five epistemological challenges. Chapter 7 focuses primarily on the first three challenges, while Chapter 8 addresses the fourth and fifth challenges. These two chapters also provide an important window into the work of prospective social studies teachers at a crucial time in their professional training and development. We document the ways this group of future educators experienced these core challenges as students themselves, with a goal for them to build on these experiences to envision and enact comparable inquiry-based work with their own middle-level and secondary school students.

Chapters 4–8 in *Part II* help instantiate our definition of social studies as *inquiry-based social practices for understanding and addressing problems, especially complex, multi-faceted problems,* and the range of pedagogical and curricular approaches evident in these chapters highlights the diverse ways teachers and students can bring life to this definition. There are whole-class and small group inquiry projects, ones that move swiftly through the inquiry phases and ones that progress methodically, as well as inquiry projects launched and completed in one day (Chapter 5), a week or two (Chapter 4), several weeks (Chapter 6), and up to two months (Chapters 7 and 8).

Part III– Synthesis and Implications

In the final chapter, we have two aims: to synthesize key ideas across the previous chapters and to encourage social studies as well as literacy educators to rethink content, curriculum, teaching, and learning in our global age. We offer two figures in Chapter 9 to depict and discuss our ideas. The first figure synthesizes key features of a conceptual landscape marked by transnational flows and forces. With the second figure, we identify six dimensions of *inquiry in use*, what we define as the multi-faceted work that students and teachers in a classroom community can do with complex texts and technologies.

Globalization is changing the way people live their lives, creating new opportunities for global communications and interactions, and making people more aware of pressing global issues, such as global climate change and environmental degradation, social injustice and human rights, the impact of multinational corporations, militarization and terrorism, and global diversity and interconnectedness. We believe the time is ripe for reconsidering what should be taught, why it should be taught, how it should be taught, and how these decisions get made (Eisner, 1997). And we appeal to social studies and literacy educators to reconsider conceptions of teaching and learning, curriculum, and classroom practice. With Pinar (2004), we believe curriculum should be a "provocation for students to reflect on and to think critically about themselves and the world" (pp. 186–187) and that "to become ever more critically aware of one's world leads to one's greater creative control of it" (Hall, 1998, p. 186). *Social Studies as New Literacies in a Global Society* is intended to enlist social studies and literacy educators and leaders in the task of taking greater control of education in the global age and to further cultivate and deepen understandings about the challenges and possibilities of doing so.

Part I

Reconceptualizing Social Studies

Frameworks and Tools

1 The Role of Social Studies in "New Times"

Social Studies as New Literacies in a Global Society is based on two powerful, interrelated ideas: 1. Social studies and literacy education are about reading the word and the world (Freire & Macedo, 1987) and 2. Our knowledge and understanding about the world are increasingly mediated through texts. This is especially apparent in our global society and the new work-order of fast capitalism (Agger, 1989, 2004; Holmes, 2000) as emerging digital technologies, multimedia, and multimodal texts (images, graphics, sound, print, etc.) are part and parcel of transnational flows of people, goods, and ideas. To function in an increasingly complex and relentlessly changing world, students need to learn and be able to use new sets of literacies that will prepare them for new economic realities and workplaces and diverse communities and cultures. The myriad and uneven changes accompanying globalization have significant implications for work, citizenship, and education.

Social studies, in particular, can play a pivotal role with preparing students to live in an increasingly complex world. Social studies can help students develop the knowledge and the interpretive, reflective, and deliberative practices necessary to make sense of new historical realities. This includes helping students develop the capacities to continually interrogate their experience, engage intellectually in public life to address pressing issues of the 21st century, and rediscover in their daily lives what active freedom means (Roy, 2005). Social studies can guide students to have greater control over the means of production, communication, and participation made available by new technologies, media, and social contexts. For this to happen, however, it is necessary to understand the many changes accompanying globalization and their implications for educational practice. This is no easy task, as our social philosophies consistently lag behind new and emerging global realities (Sachs, 2008). Reconceptualizing social studies to empower students to live, work, and participate in "new times" (Hall, 1996) requires new ways of thinking about globalization and how it is shaping work, education, knowledge and knowing, teaching and learning, and civic life.

This chapter maps the terrain of global flows and forces and their effects to situate an overall argument about the need to envision and enact more robust and responsive social studies curricula and instruction. The chapter begins with a consideration of contemporary contexts of globalization and draws on the influential work of Appadurai (1996) to frame the processes shaping the complex systems in which people learn and live. We offer Singapore as a case study for understanding these processes and examine some of the ways Singaporean educational policy is responding to new global imperatives and local "sociopolitical and cultural-ideological needs" caused by changes brought about by globalization (Koh, 2004). Next, we conceptualize global citizenship education as *relational cosmopolitanism*. The chapter concludes with an initial consideration of how social studies conceptualized as new literacies for living in a global society can help address the many challenges facing educators living and working in these "new times."

THE CHALLENGE OF UNDERSTANDING "NEW TIMES"

Because globalization is complex, contradictory, and paradoxical (Kellner, 2002), its history, significance, scope, and effects are heavily contested. Sen (2002) and Wallerstein (1999) argue that there is a long history of cross-cultural exchange and global economic interaction, while others suggest that the acceleration and intensity of recent global forces constitute a fundamentally new global age (Albrow, 1996). Some celebrate globalization as bringing about greater free trade and prosperity, international integration, and the spread of technology, goods, and ideas (e.g., Fukuyama, 1992; Friedman, 1999), while others argue that it is resulting in widespread environmental degradation, cultural homogenization, and increasing inequality (e.g., Mander & Goldsmith, 1996; Eisenstein, 1998). World polity theorists (e.g., Boli & Thomas, 1997) see the emergence of a world culture and new global consciousness while others, such as Huntington (1993), argue that globalization is creating civilizational fault lines rather than a common culture. Other perspectives focus on the complex interdependence of nation-states and transnational institutions (Keohane & Nye, 2001), the neoliberal policies of economic globalization (Greider, 1997; Stiglitz, 2006), and postcolonial histories of globalization as a continuation of imperial forms of power and domination (Krishna, 2009; Said, 1993). In short, globalization is a polarizing force; it divides and unites simultaneously (Bauman, 1998) and it contains democratizing and anti-democratizing tendencies, constituting "contested terrain with opposing forces attempting to use its institutions, technologies, media, and forms for their own purposes" (Kellner, 2002, p. 301). At the same time, it is remarkably resilient, able to neutralize and absorb these contradictions and oppositions (Hardt & Negri, 2000).

While there is disagreement about the causes and consequences of globalization, there is little debate about the need for educators (and citizens alike) to better understand the complex and contradictory social, cultural, economic, and political realities shaped by globalization. Transnational flows of goods, people, and ideas, new identity movements and cultural politics, the information society and knowledge economy, new technologies and fast capitalism, and increasing inequality and uneven development are just a few of the transformations associated with processes of globalization that are "restlessly transgressing boundaries and dismantling oppositions" (Eagleton, 1996, p. 133). Not surprisingly, the bewildering array of hybridized changes, structural transformations, and technological-social revolutions of globalization has been difficult to grasp or resist (Castells, 1999). Such rapid shifts typically distance or "disembed" people from their traditions and communities; as a result, community members can lose "their meaning-generating and meaning-negotiating capacity and are increasingly dependent on sense-giving and interpreting actions which they do not control" (Bauman, 1998, p. 3). In turn, such widespread transformations shape new ways for people to think of themselves, their communities, and their experiences. Likewise, educational systems are caught up in these transformations and seek to cultivate capacities deemed necessary to help people participate in the types of intellectual work and shifting social practices accompanying these changes.

NEW GLOBAL LANDSCAPES

Appadurai (1996) identifies five dimensions of global flows to frame these transformations. He labels these dimensions *technoscapes, financescapes, mediascapes, ideoscapes,* and *ethnoscapes* and argues that they cut across nation-states, diasporic communities, localities, and identities to construct new social realities as well as "imagined worlds." *Technoscapes* refers to rapid transfers of technology across national borders. *Financescapes* refers to the flows of global capital and investment. *Mediascapes* refers to the ways information is produced and distributed electronically. *Ideoscapes* are ideological flows (typically transmitted through various media) and counterideologies that comprise the political content of a country or region. *Ethnoscapes* refers to the shifting populations of tourists, diasporic communities, immigrants, exiles, refugees, and workers. These "scapes" are building blocks of identities and imagined communities (Anderson, 1983) and are produced by both private and state interests.

These transnational "scapes" create new forms of identity and belonging. They create new possibilities for social relationships and provide resources, such as electronic and digital media, for constructing meaning. In particular, these "scapes" provide resources for constructing imagined selves and imagined worlds as "a form of negotiation between sites of agency (individuals) and globally defined fields of possibility" (Appadurai, 1996, p. 31).

These resources allow people to meld the global into their local practices because "it is the imagination, in its collective forms, that creates ideas of neighborhood and nationhood, of moral economies" (p. 7). These imagined communities develop from notions of constructed pasts and imagined futures, elements drawn from tradition and commitments to change, visions of belonging and views of "the Other"; they offer a sense of continuity amidst change or mobilize populations to challenge tradition and bring about change. In other words, globalization shapes local communities and identities through the use of resources provided by transnational flows; new media and texts and available technologies, ideas, and cultural resources are used to construct new imaginaries or reformulate existing ones.

These new affiliations and formations of identities and communities are fundamentally "postnational," framed by "principles of finance, recruitment, coordination, communication, and reproduction" (Appadurai, 1996, p. 167). These postnational social formations, however, should not be confused with the numerous international organizations that are typically intergovernmental, such as the International Monetary Fund, the World Bank, the European Union, NATO, or Interpol. Rather, postnational social formations constitute a potentially new global civil society and provide spaces for people to come together around shared interests, values, or purposes. These new social formations include the World Social Forum which brings together native peoples, peace and anti-globalization activists, and fair trade organizations to counter inequities stemming from globalization. These new formations also include non-governmental organizations (NGOs), transnational philanthropic movements, activist groups, international terrorist and anti-terrorist organizations, and online communities. These organizational forms are "more diverse, more fluid, more ad hoc, more provisional, less coherent, less organized" (p. 168) and they provide a range of opportunities for civic engagement.

To examine these transnational flows and "scapes" it's useful to consider a specific example and we selected Singapore as our example for several reasons. Singapore is immersed in many social, economic, and cultural transformations. Due to its location, Singapore also has a history of being in the crossroads of people, goods, and ideas. As a trading emporium and colonial port city under the British, geography provided the impetus for its growth and development, despite the natural shortcomings of its size and limited natural resources (Ooi & Shaw, 2004). Its free trade policy, outward orientation, and cosmopolitan mix of Western, Arab, Malay, Indian, and Chinese residents also ensured its success as an entrepôt under colonial administration. This has continued in recent times with its well-resourced economic and technological infrastructure and its commingling of ethnic groups. Singapore is also a relatively smaller country in population and size (e.g., compared to the United States, China, India), and this significantly helps contain and manage this task.

SINGAPORE: A CASE STUDY OF NEW GLOBAL LANDSCAPES

Since independence from Malaysia in 1965, the ruling People's Action Party (PAP) has industrialized Singapore by pursuing a strategy of infrastructure modernization to attract multinational corporations and foreign investment (Ooi & Shaw, 2004). The government's pursuit of economic development strategies has resulted in Singapore being seen as the prototypical developmental state able to gain legitimacy through its ability to promote and sustain economic development (Castells, 1996). The government was able to skillfully manage the many uncertainties and challenges posed by its abrupt independence and geographic shortcomings and orchestrate the country's emergence as a global business hub by integrating global trade and capital investment (Ooi & Shaw, 2004). This entrepreneurial city-state enacted favorable business laws; enforced strict codes of social discipline; provided basic social services such as housing, health care, and transportation; diversified its economy; and invested in human capital to increase labor productivity. In particular, due to limited resources, labor supply constraints, and the emphasis on connectivity with the global economy, Singapore allocated major investments in the education of its workforce, especially in mathematics, science, and technology. The state education system also produced "the national subjectivities necessary for affiliation to the state's modernization project" (Gopinathan, 2007, p. 57). That is, the state education system aimed to provide students with the necessary skills to modernize Singapore and "to inculcate in them values that will ensure their loyalty and commitment to the nation" (Quah, 2000, p. 78).

These efforts helped Singapore's economy make the postindustrial transition from a manufacturing-based economy to a service- and knowledge-based economy, one that emphasizes greater use of information and communication technologies and multimedia, and more diverse, flexible, and specialized approaches to production, distribution, and consumption. Singapore is a highly networked society where information, ideas, social and commercial exchange, and all sorts of social relationships are electronically mediated. It serves as a transnational hub for multinational corporations, financial services, telecommunications, and a range of high tech industries. In sum, Singapore has taken advantage of its geographic location and its strategic management of global flows of people, ideas, capital, and goods to become fully integrated into global economies. Its pragmatic, forward looking governance and its ability to capitalize on global developments have made it a success story other nation states emulate.

With Appadurai's model, we can begin to better understand the extent of global flows of people, finance, culture, media, and technology in the Singaporean context.

Technoscapes

Supported by investment from multinational corporations, government policy promoting technology transfer and innovation, and a highly skilled and technologically proficient labor force, Singapore has benefited from the consistent deployment of new technologies in its industries and services. For example, Singapore's government built a US$300 million research park in 2003 that houses the Genome Institute of Singapore and the Institute of Bioengineering and Nanotechnology. They have recruited top-level scientists and researchers from all parts of the world to support research and development efforts. (Chan, 2005, http://www.iht.com/articles/2005/09/19/blommberg/sxsing.php) In 2009, Singapore's National Research Foundation allocated US$300 million to develop a strategic Interactive Digital Media (IDM) research program that would make Singapore a global IDM capital. Singapore's tech savvy population, combined with heavy investment in research and development in telecommunications, IDM, and new technologies in the emerging fields of biotechnology and nanotechnology, make its technoscape quite diverse. In turn, these new technologies require a population able to effectively keep abreast of technological change to use new technologies in ways that further promote economic growth and development.

Financescapes

Due to favorable government policy, a relatively corruption-free government and business environment, and a highly educated and disciplined workforce, Singapore has consistently attracted foreign investment. By encouraging savings and investment among its populace through the Central Provident Fund (a mandatory savings and retirement plan), Singapore created the capital assets for wide-ranging government expenditures and investments. Not only were these funds used by the government to develop Singapore's infrastructure to handle emerging flows of people, finance, technologies, and media, they were invested in international financial markets. As a result of its prudent financial policies, Singapore's financescape has drawn comparisons with Switzerland as a financial hub. Singapore's finance ministry has also engaged in ongoing efforts to promote the growth of legal and financial services and other "producer services" that coordinate, manage, and service global economic flows (Sassen, 2001).

Singapore continues to attract foreign investment, as evidenced by the recent influx of private equity money that has caused local property rates to soar, making Singapore a haven for transnational companies and wealthy elites. Singapore also uses its considerable assets to invest outside the country. The government's investment arm, Temasek, invests heavily in Singaporean companies that do business mostly outside of Singapore, especially in the rapidly developing economies of China and India. For example, Singapore has set up industrial parks, development zones, and other development projects in several locations in China. Singapore's Government Investment Corporation (GIC) invests in overseas interests and has recently come under scrutiny as one of the world's most wealthy sovereign wealth funds. With offices located in several key financial capitals around the world, GIC has drawn attention by investing in major Wall Street financial firms such as Merrill Lynch, Morgan Stanley, and Citigroup. What is unique about the transnational legal, accounting, public relations, management, and consulting services that make up this global infrastructure of finance is the extent, speed, and ease of their ability to cross national borders. It's also important to note the ways this financescape shapes transnational flows of technology, labor, and media to create mutually reinforcing relationships with the other "scapes" described by Appadurai.

Mediascapes

Singapore, envisioning itself as a "global media city," launched Media 21 in 2003 to nurture local media and attract direct foreign investment in the media industry (Media Development Authority, 2003). With an eye on the global media market, the plan seeks to establish Singapore as a media hub, deploy digital media, and internationalize Singapore media enterprises. As with other sectors of Singapore's economy, the government has taken an active role in managing and developing this mediascape. Although most local media is state-owned (by MediaCorp) and Internet services are regulated by the government's Media Development Authority, blogging and podcasting have become important new media for expression, including expression that has crossed "out-of-bounds markers" in Singapore's conservative political climate. Although the government claims to have eased censorship policies, they continue to carefully monitor new media, claiming: "Our people are still largely conservative. Hence, the Government needs to balance between providing greater space for free expression and the values upheld by the majority" (Bhavani, 2005). To what extent Singapore's government can manage the transnational flows coursing through its mediascape remains to be seen.

Ideoscapes

As with most nation-states in the global economy, neoliberalism holds sway in Singapore. Neoliberal ideas "furnish the concepts that inform the government of free individuals who are then induced to self-manage according to market principles of discipline, efficiency, and competitiveness" (Ong, 2006, p. 4). These market principles are then embodied and internalized in ways that make it very difficult for individuals to question their "taken-for-grantedness" (Allen, 2003, p. 87). Alongside these neoliberal policies and practices, "Asian values" are also deployed in Singapore's ideoscape, such as "Orientalist essentialisms" (Ong, 1999, p. 81) and "Confucian cultural triumphalism" (p. 135). Ideals of meritocracy and Confucian values of hard work and harmony are used to create a disciplined society and workforce that is appealing to global capital, as Ong (1999) points out: "By raiding the rich storehouse of Asian myths and religions, these discourses can find legitimization for state strategies aimed at strengthening controls at home and at stiffening bargaining postures in the global economy" (p. 77). By emphasizing a moral economy of neoliberal values combined with government paternalism and Confucian respect for authority, hierarchy, and order, Singaporean officials are able to cultivate disciplined individuals attractive to global capital.

Ethnoscapes

In Singapore, a tourist hub, there are flows of expatriate "foreign talent," imported labor from South and Southeast Asia, and multiracial and diasporic communities of Chinese, Malays, and Indians that extend far beyond Singapore's borders. A transnational class of managers and entrepreneurs works in multinational and Singaporean businesses while approximately a quarter of Singapore's labor consists of unskilled or semi-skilled foreign labor that comes from countries such as India, Bangladesh, Sri Lanka, and the Philippines. Meanwhile, Singaporean Chinese have guanxi connections (Chinese social contacts or networks) with Chinese business leaders all over the world, Singaporean Indians have business connections in India, and Singaporean Malays are able to foster business relations with international Malays and Muslims.

Because of its geographic location, Singapore has a long history of global flows of people and a corresponding history of governmental attempts to manage this diversity through a nationalist agenda. After Singapore separated from Malaysia in 1965, the founding generation was committed to a "depluralizing" form of multiracialism and the development of a Singaporean identity (Tan, 2004). The many dialect, religious, and caste groups from varied geographical backgrounds were subsumed by four ethnic categories (Chinese, Malay, Indian, Other) and four official languages were adopted (Chinese, Malay, Tamil, and English, which became the unifying language of commerce and government). Ethnic identity also came to be considered secondary to being Singaporean.

However, recent immigration from China and India seems to be making Singapore's traditional ethnic categories (Chinese, Malay, Indian, Other) less relevant. As new flows of people enter Singapore and numbers of highly educated Singaporeans leave to live and work in other countries, Singapore's government is trying to manage new tensions inside and outside of its borders. For example, while noting that "a Chinese-Chinese is different from a Singapore-Chinese [and] an Indian-Indian is different from a Singapore-Indian," Prime Minister Lee Hsien Loong (2006) called for a "big-hearted approach" (p. 9) to ensure that all talent feels welcomed in

Singapore. In addition to promoting immigration into Singapore as a way to attract new talent, Singapore's government is also attempting to harness the talent of Singaporeans who live and work outside the country. Variously referring to "quitters and stayers" (Goh, 2002) and the need to bond "cosmopolitans and heartlanders" (Goh, 1999), recent rhetoric has called for the need to maintain "strong links with the Singaporeans who are abroad, with our overseas network so that they become a strength for us and not a loss" (Lee, 2006, p. 7).

Summary

Each of these five "scapes" intersect and interact in mutually reinforcing ways. New media and technologies are financed by private and public investment, new ideas are transmitted by new media and technologies, and people are continually brought into contact with new ideas and cultures in increasingly diverse social relationships. Appadurai's "scapes" help paint broad brushstrokes of the larger terrain, providing a sense of the intersections, multiplicities, and hybridities that comprise this ever-shifting global landscape. These scapes help illuminate transnational flows that run through and across nation-states, making analytical models that focus solely on the nation-state less relevant. Locality becomes a "socioscape" in which multiple co-existing flows and social realities are possible (Albrow, 1996). This results in tremendous diversity at the local level as individuals and groups of people respond to globalization in a variety of ways.

As "an example par excellence of a contextual space to understand the discourse and operation of globalization" (Koh, 2007, p. 180), Singapore also helps us consider several challenges and tensions individuals and groups of people face in the midst of transnational flows.

Looking across the five "scapes" illumines the ways nation-states like Singapore are attempting to respond to several dilemmas as traditional notions of national citizenship are being destabilized by forces of global capitalism, secularization, new technologies and media, and democracy (Parker, Nonomiya, & Cogan, 1999). We consider four of these dilemmas here: diminishing capacity to control information flows, the escalating impact of hyper-consumerism, the conflicting relationship between a nationalist and a strategic cosmopolitan identity, and inequitable consequences and conditions across populations.

Diminishing Capacity to Control Information Flows

Transnational movements of ideas and media are increasingly beyond any government's (or school's) capacities to filter and control them. New media, technologies, and texts that can convey a wide range of perspectives and meanings "outside the frame of reference set by the nation-state" (Albrow, 1996, p. 58) continue to proliferate. As Albrow (1996) argues, "the state has one huge disadvantage as the generator of privileged meanings, namely that they are always conveyed and received by individual human beings, who in principle can always, and in practice frequently do, differ in their interpretations" (p. 60). The decentered nation-state in an age of transnational flows loses some of its capacity to adjudicate meanings for its citizens. New forms of meaning-making, civic participation, and affiliation are made possible by transnational flows of media, technologies, finance, communities, and ideas. Children and youth have access to technologies that are fundamentally social in nature and make transnational communication, expression, and mobilizations possible. Young people, of relative affluence, live increasingly digital lifestyles with opportunities to develop identities and communities in gaming environments, through blogging, in online chat rooms, through popular websites like YouTube and in social networking websites such as Facebook and My Space. In these spaces they can share and create content that has the potential to challenge official discourses (Baildon & Sim, 2009). Youth in Singapore, for example, can access information about transnational human rights groups such as Reporters without Borders, who have challenged Singapore's crackdown on bloggers, cyberdissidents, and defamation suits that challenge press freedoms (Reporters without Borders, 2007). Gay rights and alternative lifestyle movements also challenge more traditional conceptions of identity and community. How Singapore's government will engage these oppositional or alternative identities and communities represents a core challenge to the governance of a more globalized civil society.

Escalating Impact of Hyper-consumerism

As neoliberalism extends its reach and deepens its impact across the world, conceptions of citizenship (and education) are also being shaped by a cultural landscape of burgeoning consumption (Baildon & Sim, 2009). In the postindustrial society, consumption has become a new form of social discipline, as Appadurai explains:

> The labor of reading ever-shifting fashion messages, the labor of debt servicing, the labor of learning how best to manage newly complex domestic finances and the labor of acquiring knowledge in the complexities of money management. This labor is . . . directed at producing the conditions of consciousness in which *buying* can occur . . . This inculcation of the pleasure of *ephemerality* is at the heart of the disciplining of the modern consumer. (1996, pp. 82–83)

Similarly, Baudrillard (2001) argues that consumption has become a form of social labor requiring individuals to manage flows of signs and codes that operate within a logic of consumerism. According to Baudrillard, commodities act as symbols that cultivate desire, create systems of meaning, and communicate ideological values. Citizens must be increasingly savvy to operate in the all-pervasive ecology of signs and codes that penetrates all forms of social experience. Although consumerist signs and codes are experienced as sources of pleasure, citizens must be critically aware of how signs and codes function ideologically to represent the values, perspectives, and interests of particular groups. As the social historian, Christopher Lasch, argued, citizens must be aware of how mass consumption and rampant consumerism

> tend to discourage initiative and self-reliance and to promote dependence, passivity, and a spectatorial state of mind both at work and at play . . . The state of mind promoted by consumerism is better described as a state of uneasiness and chronic anxiety. The promotion of commodities depends, like modern mass production, on discouraging the individual from reliance on his own resources and judgment: in this case, his judgment of what he needs in order to be healthy and happy. The individual finds himself always under observation, if not by foremen and superintendents, by market researchers and pollsters who tell him what others prefer and what he too must therefore prefer . . . (1984, pp. 27–28)

If citizens view themselves first and foremost as consumers, they are more likely to cultivate allegiances, forms of identity, and habits of mind aligned with consumer culture rather than with activist and critical, global conceptions of citizenship. Some argue that this is the case in Singapore, considered by many to be a consumers' paradise. Seah (2005), for example, has noted that Singaporean citizens seem generally disinterested in politics and are willing to defer to the government so long it gives them the good life.

Conflicting Relationship between a National and a "Strategic Cosmopolitan" Identity

Nation-states like Singapore remain committed to the preservation and maintenance of a national identity. At the same time, there are calls for the cultivation of more "strategic cosmopolitans" (Mitchell, 2003) where the driving goal is motivated by ideals of global competitiveness and the need to skillfully adapt and excel as workers, managers, or entrepreneurs in the global marketplace (p. 387). The educational implications of commitments to develop both national identities and strategic cosmopolitans are evident in escalating pressures for more curricular standardization and accountability through testing. This helps ensure that students have a common curricular experience to learn the official national history of Singapore (the "Singapore Story"), for example, while learning the skills deemed necessary for individual and national success in the global economy.

Global flows and landscapes, which produce new forms of identity and community, exacerbate this tension. In a recent acknowledgement of the powerful combination of mediascapes and ideoscapes, Singapore's Education Minister Tharman (2004) declared: "Ideologies and events that threaten to polarise communities are now instantly spread and instantly accessed globally, via both traditional media and the Internet." The variety of Appadurai's "scapes" provides new opportunities for individuals and communities to construct identities that may challenge the subjectivities desired by nation-states and schools as instruments of national policy. As a result of globalization, "identities are up for grabs" (Koh, 2004, p. 338). Singapore's social studies curriculum strives to manage this tension by making the idea of "being rooted and living globally" a centerpiece of the curriculum.

Inequitable Consequences and Conditions across Populations

The effects of global intersections and interactions in a place such as Singapore, of course, are not uniformly positive for everyone. There are disjunctures; some people and groups reap benefits while others are marginalized as globalization compels people to either accommodate or resist its forces (Morris-Suzuki, 2000). A more integrated global economy produces or reinforces asymmetrical dependencies within nations and between rich and poor nations. Global forces and flows are much more likely to enrich wealthy countries and create financial dependency and debt loads that can paralyze poor countries (Stiglitz, 2006).

Different mechanisms contribute to these inequities and asymmetrical dependencies. Governments in wealthy countries, for example, heavily subsidize some of their farmers, enabling them to artificially reduce prices in the global marketplace, which places an economic stranglehold on farmers in poor countries. International organizations, such as the International Monetary Fund (IMF) and the World Trade Organization (WTO) have also been criticized for monitoring and regulating trade in ways that primarily serve the interests of corporations and wealthy nations. The rise of corporate power in the last few decades has coincided with and contributed to the diminishing authority and vitality of labor (e.g., unions and other collective efforts and arrangements for workers' rights) leaving nation-states more likely to overvalorize capital and undervalorize labor, especially immigrant labor. This reproduces existing inequalities within and between nations (Sassen, 2005).

Basch, Schiller, and Szanton Blanc (1994) demonstrate that the internationalization of capital and the economic liberalization promoted by the IMF and World Bank exacerbated existing disparities within and between countries. They point to how liberalized flows of transnational capital created large pools of displaced labor that disrupted local economies and necessitated the movement of labor to respond to the needs of global capital. Or, as Doreen Massey (1994) argues, various social groups have differentiated relationships to capital: "some people are more in charge of it than others; some initiate flows and movements, others don't; some are more on the receiving-end of it than others; some are effectively imprisoned by it" (p. 149).

Remittances tend to be transfers between private parties and while they may be a major source of income for poorer communities and families, they seldom get channeled into public or social investments, such as infrastructure development, technology transfers, public education, or health-care programs in ways that investment capital does in wealthier countries like Singapore. In Singapore, for example, maids come from the Philippines and construction workers come from South Asia, and while remittances flow from Singapore to families and communities in both, capital in Singapore flows into investment and research and education where the benefits accrue primarily to the educated class and further reinforce asymmetrical relationships, such as those between the well-educated and those with less education or between those who have the social capital and wealth to take advantage of new technologies and those who do not.

EDUCATIONAL IMPERATIVES OF "NEW TIMES": FROM THE NATION-STATE TO RELATIONAL COSMOPOLITANISM

Transnational flows necessitate new relationships among a government, its markets, and its population, as well as its relationships with other nations/governments. A government needs to be more flexible, agile, and adaptive in response to relentless and accelerating change of all kinds and diminished control over this change as the conditions affecting nations increasingly originate outside of national borders (e.g., new flows of people, capital, ideas, disease, climate change, terror, etc.). In essence, transnational flows and forces are requiring new modes of governance and "a new conceptual architecture" (Sassen, 2001, p. xviii) marked by greater flexibility, agility, and responsiveness. Singapore's government provides a good example of this; it is anticipatory, always scanning the horizon to safeguard its population from shocks that are part and parcel of transnational flows (e.g., its program to inoculate the nation from H1N1, attempts to contain the adverse effects of the financial meltdown in the United States).

Education is a primary way nations can mediate and manage new and shifting relationships to capital and the global economy as well as greater diversity of people and ideas/perspectives. For the most part, nation-states have adopted an educational platform focused on protecting and advancing purely national interests. This platform is committed to neoliberal, instrumentalist outcomes to ensure that education and labor are able to meet the shifting demands of global capital and is committed to conceptions of national citizenship that are tied to goals of economic competitiveness. Educational reform, particularly in the areas of literacy and social studies education, has become ever more essential in the never-ending drive for competitive advantage in a global, innovative information economy. Because "all curriculum narrates, projects, 'trajects' imagined human subjects into future pathways" (Luke, 2002, p. 3), in an era of intensified global flows these future pathways are aligned with the needs of chaotic global capital, always shape-shifting and following the flows of profit, quick to adjust to new global conditions and imperatives. Educational systems, likewise, are expected to respond continually, quickly, and with agility to changing conditions, requirements, and trajectories (Baildon, 2009).

In response to asymmetrical, unpredictable, and fragmentary consequences of global capitalism (Brown & Lauder, 2001; Stiglitz, 2006; Tan & Gopinathan, 2000), the rhetoric of educational reform across nation-states is strikingly similar. Reform proposals accentuate the need for higher order thinking, more effective technology integration in schools, new approaches to assessment, and more emphasis on processes (Gopinathan, 2007). In Singapore, for example, Prime Minister Goh Chok Tong (1997) launched *Thinking Schools, Learning Nation (TSLN)* reforms by calling for an educational system that would "better develop creative thinking skills and learning skills required for the future . . . bring about a spirit of innovation, of learning by doing, of everyone, each at his own level, all the time asking how he can do his job better." With an eye toward the future, *TSLN* set forth a plan for lifelong learning. These national learning goals were prefaced by Goh declaring that a nation's wealth would increasingly depend on the capacity of its people to learn, change, and innovate. By creating new sets of skills and capacities for globalization and the information age, commitments to lifelong learning, and greater flexibility and adaptability, *TSLN* reforms were designed to retool the productive capacity of the system (Gopinathan, 2007, p. 59)

In this book, we argue for a shift away from strictly neoliberal, instrumentalist conceptions (and narrowly conceived outcomes) of education and educational reform and toward conceptions and programs that more directly confront pressing 21st century problems. While global capitalism has proven to be a remarkably productive and resilient engine for economic productivity and growth, it has also engendered remarkable inequalities (e.g., of wealth, power, and educational opportunity), injustices (e.g., poverty, inadequate access to health care and education, etc.), tensions (e.g., diminishing capacities to control information, hyper-consumerism, etc.), and exploitation (e.g., of labor, the environment, etc.). As Drèze & Sen (2002) note, in the last few decades high rates of economic growth have been combined with "the persistence of widespread poverty, illiteracy, ill health, child labour, criminal violence and related social failures" (p. 72). In the effort to respond continually and with agility to constantly changing global landscapes, nation-states, like Singapore, have largely adopted a framework of "human capital ideology and a competitive nationalism" (Koh, 2002, p. 255) to ensure that national education systems are aligned with transnational flows of global capital. Unfortunately, this framework has established misguided priorities that fail to adequately address the multitude of multifaceted problems that confront humanity. National education approaches to address what are perceived to be national problems are inadequate because the problems are no longer solely "national" (Alexander, 2008). Similarly, citizenship education that promotes national history, collective memory, and national identity formation through the transmission of a common cultural heritage and a set of national ideological commitments fails to adequately prepare young people for a complex interconnected world in which they must comprehend the motives and choices of people different from themselves.

In the face of mounting pressures on nation-states and populations to address global problems in ways that are equitable and just, national education systems that promote narrow national self-interest and allegiance are no longer sustainable. National citizenship education prevents young people from understanding that identity does not need to be singular (national), from knowing that there is a range of social bonds that can be formed for effective social and political participation, and from understanding that common aims and aspirations can exist among different groups of people both within and outside of the nation-state. Drawing on Hill (2002), we argue that rather than solely focusing on national citizenship and privileging the prerogatives of the nation-state, social studies education should emphasize commitments to social justice and equity, empathy and compassion for others, respect for diversity, dialogue across difference, concern for the environment, inclusion, solidarity, and informed collective action. These are commitments that transcend national borders and must be enacted across local, national, and global levels. It is necessary for individuals and groups of people, including national governments, to fundamentally rethink their relationships to each other—to their communities, to the nation-state, and to global society. We need to understand ourselves in *relation* to others—as being in relationships and having responsibilities that extend beyond national borders.

SOCIAL STUDIES AND NEW LITERACIES AS RELATIONAL COSMOPOLITANISM

Living in the 21st century necessitates a conception of citizenship education that is global and critical. We believe this global, critical citizenship education can be conceptualized as *relational cosmopolitanism*, a multidimensional view of civic education that builds from a particular stance toward knowledge; embraces core progressive values, such as open-mindedness, public deliberation, dialogue, and critique; and remains committed to active collaboration in a range of communities and struggles to forge alliances and coalitions as a "lived process of ongoing political and ethical action and education" (Mitchell, 2007, p. 717).

Relational cosmopolitanism begins with an integrated view of knowledge within the social studies. Rather than understanding knowledge as segmented, disjointed, and fragmented, an integrated perspective helps frame social studies content and curricula in ways that understand various social, economic, political, historical, and contemporary issues and problems as interconnected and shared. This greater recognition of interconnectedness means that, in some fundamental way, "all essential problems have become world problems" (Jaspers, 1955, cited in Albrow, 1996, p. 75). One particular way to promote a stance of interconnectedness is to integrate local dimensions of human experience with global conditions and concerns. For instance, a complex and multifaceted issue, such as poverty, pollution, immigration, income inequality, war, or climate change, can and needs to be investigated as it occurs in a particular place and it needs to be investigated as an issue that cuts across the globe in comparable and distinct ways.

Relational cosmopolitanism also calls for a critical and relational view of knowledge that continually considers the role of different contexts (e.g., historical, ideological, cultural, etc.) and power in shaping how knowledge is constructed, legitimated, and disseminated in various communities (Segall, 2006). This critical and relational stance toward knowledge includes the ability to observe oneself and others in relationship to different contexts and power (McIntosh, 2005) and understand all knowledge, especially one's own, as historically and socially situated. It is an orientation to knowledge that emphasizes making connections between different perspectives and forms of knowledge (Kincheloe, 2001) and exploring connections, interactions, and patterns across time and space (Dunn, 2010). A critical and relational view of knowledge is grounded in concern about injustice and the well-being of others (Noddings, 2005) and a "caring reasoning" that seeks out and values difference as necessary for better knowing oneself and the world (Thayer-Bacon, 2003).

Relational cosmopolitanism is also rooted in core progressive values, such as open-mindedness and a willingness to engage different perspectives through public deliberation and dialogue. This involves participating with others in a "community of reason" (Nussbaum, 1997, p. 25) in ways that "subject the prevailing beliefs and alleged reasons to critical examination" (Sen, 2009, pp. 35–36). Citizens, along with teachers and students, need to be able to skillfully interpret a range of texts, consider multiple perspectives, and deliberate to make informed decisions (Parker, 2006).

Engaging in this process involves critical self-examination, a willingness to question one's beliefs, values, and traditions. As Martha Nussbaum (1997) reminds us, "attaining membership in the world community entails a willingness to doubt the goodness of one's own way and to enter into the give-and-take of critical argument about ethical and political choices" (p. 62). This requires that we see our beliefs and values in relation to others' beliefs and values as we understand that all beliefs and values are contextual, contingent, and necessarily limited in certain ways. Differences across beliefs and values, in turn, promote pluralism and enable us to create new understandings. Jane Roland Martin (1994) describes this as a "relational epistemology" because "we learn more about our own situatedness by having ourselves reflected back to us by others not like us. The more variety and differences in the others we are exposed to, the more perspective we will be able to gain on ourselves" (p. 252).

Engaging and deliberating different perspectives in a "community of reason" is also the primary pathway to enacting substantive social and political change. Strident forms of partisanship are replaced by an ethic of care, concern, and connection (Martin, 1994) and this comes with a commitment of all members of a community to embrace complexity, understand global interconnections and patterns, and to act skillfully and judiciously in the face of pressing problems and injustices.

Relational Cosmopolitanism in the Real World

New postnational social formations and the use of new technologies and media encourage forms of participation and communication that can foster *relational cosmopolitanism*. These global formations and movements originate among people with shared interests and value commitments to address what are increasingly seen as issues and problems that transcend national boundaries. New technologies and media, especially the Internet, connect localities and struggles across the world, including struggles for human rights, environmental initiatives, worker strikes, and AIDS campaigns against pharmaceutical companies (Sassen, 2005). The alternative globalization movement, the global justice movement, and organizations like the World Social Forum are examples of postnational social formations in which activists use new media to creatively and critically challenge neoliberal and corporate-dominated globalization discourses. For example, at the Copenhagen climate change summit in 2009, groups engaged in a range of symbolic and textual actions; they displayed an illuminated cube to visually depict the amount of carbon dioxide produced by an average person in an industrialized country in one month; they created art installations and sculptures showing the consequences of global warming; and NGO groups patrolled the summit wearing alien and tree costumes and carrying signboards calling for a climate treaty.

Relational Cosmopolitanism in the Classroom

The scope of our focus in this book is confined to several classrooms, yet this broader perspective and mention of the work of some global justice advocates does provide a backdrop for understanding how the groups of students and their teachers in this book moved toward *relational cosmopolitanism*. In broad strokes, *relational cosmopolitanism* is evident in classrooms where students and teachers engage in a range of literacy practices to participate as "reflective, moral, and active citizens in an interconnected global world" (Banks, 2004, p. 298). This means that teachers and students collaboratively deliberate over which issues are significant, relevant, and worthy of investigation and action; determine which texts and sources of information are of most value for fully understanding particular issues; critically analyze and evaluate selected texts, information, and issues; and develop shared criteria and standards for guiding their work. These are classrooms where multifaceted issues provide opportunities for rigorous investigation, deliberation, and action and where classroom activities ensure that multiple and competing views about multifaceted issues are acknowledged, fairly considered, and critically evaluated (Hess, 2009). These are classrooms that make full use of the range of meaning-making resources offered by new transnational flows of media, technologies, texts, and ideas and students are guided to continually make connections between their own lives, subject matter, and broader social, historical, cultural, and global contexts as well as consider social responsibilities with significant issues (Goodman, 1992; Giroux, 1988).

SOCIAL STUDIES AS NEW LITERACIES IN A GLOBAL SOCIETY

There is an increasing recognition that contexts of new transnational flows and global landscapes call for new literacies. With widespread computerization, the Internet, and the new media of the "network society" (Castells, 2004), different modes of meaning-making are made possible with greater emphasis on language, texts, and discourses and the ways they shape knowledge and social practices. In other words, the social relations, interactions, engagements, and cultural practices required to participate in these global flows are increasingly symbolic and textual.

We believe new contexts and directions of globalization necessitate a tighter integration of new literacies with social studies education. Rather than view social studies and literacy education within a framework of "human capital ideology and a competitive nationalism" (Koh, 2002, p. 255), as many current educational reforms do, we believe social studies reconceptualized as critical practices with new literacies can better promote *relational cosmopolitanism* in ways that can empower students and teachers.

Social Studies as New Literacies in a Global Society emphasizes the goal of students learning to become careful, critical readers of all texts, from textbooks, trade books, magazines, and newspapers to maps, videos, websites, music, and architecture (Segall, 1999; Werner, 2002). A reconceptualized social studies education makes strategic use of digital technologies and new media to support students in inquiry-based learning, the critical analysis of texts, and the composition and production of their own texts to construct knowledge and share their learning as they make sense of and participate in the world. In order to do so effectively, students need curricular opportunities to reason, discuss, and critically engage with the range of texts they encounter or are likely to encounter in their lives. Chapter 2 moves us in this direction by framing several core pedagogical and learning challenges associated with living and learning in new global contexts.

2 Teaching and Learning in New Times
Challenges and Possibilities

Learning to read the word and the world and navigate the complex landscapes of globalization requires new forms of knowledge and social practices. New media and communications technologies require media and digital literacies; transnational flows of people necessitate abilities to understand different cultures and perspectives; postindustrial labor relies on new kinds of cognitive, communication, and social skills; symbolic and image-based mediascapes and ideoscapes suggest the need for new spatial logics and visual literacies; financescapes and global flows of capital require critical and quantitative literacies.

Since these flows and our understandings about the world are mediated through texts (increasingly produced and disseminated through digital networks), social studies education must seriously consider the literacy practices central to social education in the global society. Moreover, transnational problems and issues, such as global warming and pollution, disease, poverty, war, and terrorism, are drawing the attention of all societies. These challenges require transnational efforts, solutions, and new types of knowledge produced within, across, and outside of academic disciplines.

In this chapter we outline a definition of social studies education as *inquiry-based social practices for understanding and addressing complex, multifaceted problems.* With an understanding that "the workings of the world" cannot be neatly divided into discrete categories, such as academic disciplines (Segall, 1999), we develop an integrated framework for thinking about social studies as new literacies. This framework draws on disciplinary, interdisciplinary, and transdisciplinary perspectives to fuse work in new literacies and social studies education. This helps identify five core 21st century teaching and learning challenges as well as three sets of practices to respond to these challenges. We then introduce two metaphors—*excavation* and *elevation*—to help map the landscape of these inquiry-based social practices.

NEW LITERACIES AS SOCIALLY SITUATED, CRITICAL PRACTICES

In the last few decades what it means to be literate has undergone significant change. Moving from psychological models to sociological models of literacy (Luke & Freebody, 1997), work in the New Literacy Studies (New London Group, 1996) has led a shift away from an autonomous model of literacy, which posits that literacy (reading and writing) are sets of technical, context-independent, neutral skills, toward an ideological model of literacy, which views literacy as culturally and historically situated social practices (Street, 2003). Pioneer literacy researchers, such as Shirley Brice Heath (1983) and Brian Street (1984), have demonstrated how the ways people work with texts is connected intimately to specific contexts and that the literacy practices people engage in differ across time and place. There are, for example, personal, home, community, work, and school-based literacy practices and these vary across contexts (Hagood, 2000). The type, quality, and quantity of texts that readers are called upon to negotiate are also shaped by technological advancements and changes, such as the accelerated growth of networked information and communication technologies (ICT), especially the Internet with its varied text formats and structures, such as interactive texts, non-linear hypertext, and multimedia texts (Coiro, 2003). Web 2.0 and digital internetworked technologies, which combine audio, visual, and print-based texts (e.g., blogs, wikis, and podcasts), are changing mindsets (Lankshear & Knobel, 2006), altering how we think about literacy, learning, teaching, and knowing (Web 2.0 is dealt with in more depth in Chapter 3). A highly contextualized understanding of literacy helps us see that meaning-making is multimodal because the texts people engage with are increasingly integrated by multiple modes, including print, visual, gestural, aural, and spatial modes (Cope & Kalantzis, 2000) and that literacy practices are fluid, dynamic, and responsive to the new ways texts (e.g., e-mail, text messaging, hyperlinks, and images) are being produced, distributed, exchanged, and received (Lankshear & Knobel, 2006). What it means to be literate is undergoing constant change as new technologies make their way into our lives. A key implication, as Don Leu (2000) has argued, is that educators should not be concerned primarily with teaching students to be literate. Rather, they need to be concerned with teaching students how to be *continuously* literate, helping them learn new literacies called for by new technologies as they continuously develop.

A view of new literacies as culturally and historically situated also means that understandings of literacies are always embedded and contested in relations of power. Questions about whose literacies are privileged or dominant and whose are suppressed or marginalized in any given context remain of crucial importance (Street, 2003). Literacy practices "are shaped by social rules which regulate the use and distribution of texts, prescribing who may produce and have access to them" (Barton & Hamilton, 1998, p. 7). Considering who benefits and who doesn't from particular conceptions and practices of literacy forges a link between new literacy studies and critical literacy, which understands literacy as facility with textual practices in the service of identifying and transforming unjust and inequitable social conditions (Freire & Macedo, 1987)—where being literate requires an ability to critically analyze and evaluate as well as produce a range of texts and other representational forms as well as an "ability to engage in the social responsibilities and interactions associated with these texts" (Anstey, 2002).

Critical literacy has a rich theoretical history (Cervetti, Pardales, & Damico, 2001; Janks, 2000; Lankshear & McLaren, 1993; Luke & Freebody, 1997; Morgan, 1997). Some major influences include the work of Paulo Freire; critical linguistics; feminist, postcolonial, and critical race theory; cultural and media studies; and poststructuralist models of text and discourse (Luke & Woods, 2009). Critical literacy also continues to make inroads in classrooms (e.g., Ball, 2000; Christensen, 2000; Comber & Simpson, 2001; Edelsky, 1999; Lewison, Leland & Harste, 2008; Morrell, 2004, 2008; Vasquez, 2004). These classroom enactments of critical literacy demonstrate how teachers and students can examine language in a range of texts in ways that align with broader socially transformative goals, such as identifying, reducing, and eliminating injustices to sustain a more just and equitable world. Critical literacy provides a way for teachers and students to "reconnect literacy with everyday life and with an education that entails debate, argument, and action over social, cultural, and economic issues that matter" (Luke & Woods, 2009, p. 16). Critical literacy practices engage students in challenging taken-for-granted meanings and assumptions; questioning how knowledge is constructed and used; and examining issues of power, justice, identity, and the ways texts and practices are shaped by ideology. This means understanding that all texts and practices can be interrogated in a number of ways, that some are advantaged and/or disadvantaged by certain power relations, and that certain views, kinds of knowledge, and ways of knowing are privileged while others are marginalized (Segall & Gaudelli, 2007).

In this sense, engaging in literacy practices is connected to envisioning and enacting social change, where readers (teachers and students) see themselves as "active designers" or "makers of social futures" (Cope & Kalantzis, 2000; New London Group, 2000). As social designers, readers investigate "how texts work" (Luke & Freebody, 1997), discerning the ways in which authors and texts position themselves and position readers. Readers also create or produce a range of their own texts (photography, drama, audio, video, multimedia, websites, etc.) to reflect and communicate their own critical insights.

A conception of literacy as socially situated critical practices is foundational to our framework of social studies as new literacies in a global society. The emphasis on literacy as social practices means that individuals and groups recognize their own social and historical locations as readers (i.e., it matters where they read *from* and it matters *why* they are reading) and investigate different texts to generate individual and collective understandings about something, some form or type of content, in ways that can lead to transforming unjust and inequitable social conditions (Freire & Macedo, 1987). What this "something" entails, and the specific kinds of practices that are part of the process of moving toward this something, moves us to three perspectives in social studies education.

SOCIAL STUDIES AS DISCIPLINARY, INTERDISCIPLINARY, AND TRANSDISCIPLINARY PERSPECTIVES

Social studies education is inherently multidisciplinary, drawing on content and methods in, for example, history, geography, economics, sociology, psychology, and political science. Yet what this multidisciplinarity might mean for actual classroom practice in 21st century classrooms merits closer inspection. After providing a historical perspective of how academic disciplines developed, we consider the ways three perspectives—disciplinary, interdisciplinary, and transdisciplinary inquiry—align with a conception of literacy as socially situated critical practices and help fortify our framework of social studies as new literacies in a global society.

Academic Disciplines: A Historical Perspective

Humanities and social science disciplines have historical roots. Based on the work of the Greeks, the Copernican Revolution, and the birth of modern science during the Enlightenment, the disciplines emerged from the work of Sir Francis Bacon and the Royal Society of London in the 17th century (Boorstin, 1985). The rise of a new "experimental philosophy" meant that knowledge should no longer be based on appeals to ancient authorities, but instead needed to be grounded in careful observation and inductive reasoning. New methods and norms regarding the nature, generation, and validation of truth claims became the basis for modern disciplinary knowledge (Hogan, 2007). A new form of discourse based on systematic skepticism, open inquiry, and vigorous debate shaped the following basic steps of disciplinary work, steps that correspond to a five-phase inquiry model we discuss later in the chapter and use throughout this book:

- Recognize a significant problem or question (or the need for certain knowledge).
- Gather as much relevant information or data about the problem as possible.
- Rigorously evaluate, analyze, and interpret evidence (the verification of the authenticity and credibility of sources).
- Synthesize findings to develop claims and conclusions that could be supported by available evidence.
- Share findings (claims and conclusions) in an account that met disciplinary standards (as defined by the disciplinary community of practice).

The empirical and rational philosophy of the Enlightenment, then, resulted in new methods for generating knowledge claims, new standards for evaluating or validating the truth of these knowledge claims, new discursive practices (ways of talking, writing, etc.) for communicating and debating knowledge claims, the development of communities and social identities for sustaining the new disciplines (e.g., scientists, historians, etc.), and institutionalized practices, procedures, skills, norms, and dispositions that focused on explanation, demonstration, prediction, interpretation, representation, expression, and understanding or control of some aspect of human experience, the natural world, or the social world (Hogan, 2007).

As Foucault and others have noted, the scientific or technical-rational discourses that emerged from the Enlightenment produced disciplinary effects that privileged control and measurement, carried an assumption of presumed objectivity, and emphasized "exact measurement, precise predictability, absolute certainty . . . and a detached mode of observation" (Best & Kellner, 1997, p. 202). This new scientism established arbitrary disciplinary boundaries and dualisms that especially separated the humanities and sciences by creating methods that emphasized exclusion and closure (Harari & Bell, 1982). This helped create the modern university system and academic subjects that "systematically direct individual memory and channel our perceptions into forms compatible with the relations they authorize" (Douglas, 1986, p. 92). The isolation of the disciplines from each other and even the isolation of specialized fields within disciplines have shaped the ethos of modern academic life (Damrosch, 1995). Not surprisingly, the impact of this legacy is especially evident when we consider a conception of social studies as disciplinary inquiry.

Social Studies as Disciplinary Inquiry

Organizing curriculum and instruction with a disciplinary perspective is based on the premise that individual academic disciplines have particular ways of structuring content and methods of inquiry. While disciplines often share similar approaches, such as careful scrutiny of claims and evidence, each discipline differs in the ways it structures, creates, and investigates content. Schwab (1978) helped elucidate these distinctions with a description of the differences between substantive and syntactic knowledge. Substantive knowledge includes the paradigms, frameworks, concepts, canons of accumulated evidence, and facts within the disciplinary domain. Syntactic knowledge refers to methods of inquiry, truth procedures for making claims, and norms for evidentiary warrants. Syntactic knowledge in history, for example, differs from syntactic knowledge in biology. The sourcing, contextualizing, and corroborating work of historians (Wineburg, 2001) is qualitatively distinct from laboratory testing procedures in biology.

The classroom implication of a disciplinary approach to curriculum is that teachers induct students into the discipline, guiding them to understand the syntactic and substantive knowledge of the particular discipline. In social studies the academic discipline that has made the most inroads with secondary school curricula has been history, and one inquiry approach to the teaching of history is guiding students to learn to think like historians and immerse themselves in the "doing" of history (Levstik & Barton, 2006). Historians know how to ask significant questions, consider issues of perspective, reliability, and credibility, draw on a range of analytical and interpretive strategies with different types of texts, make evidence-based inferences, and systematically corroborate and contextualize information to develop interpretive accounts made available for public scrutiny (Wineburg, 2001). Historians work like "detectives seeking plausible explanations" based on evidence contained in available sources, texts, and artifacts (Bain, 2006). Wineburg (2001) offers an example of this historical work. In a study that asked historians and advanced high school students to read and evaluate different historical documents about the Battle of Lexington in 1775 during the American Revolutionary War, Wineburg shows how the historians skillfully sourced, contextualized, and corroborated claims and evidence across the documents while the students struggled. Moreover, unlike the students who viewed the school textbook as the most trustworthy source, the historians found this source the most problematic, imbued with contradictions and inaccuracies. The historians displayed the type of thinking reflective of their discipline. Thus, from a disciplined inquiry perspective in history, one implication for the teaching and learning of history in K–12 schools is for students to emulate the reading practices of historians.

Social Studies as Interdisciplinary Inquiry

An interdisciplinary approach proceeds from the premise that different disciplines contribute different concepts, modes of thinking, and findings that can shed light on a particular phenomenon. Integrating different disciplinary approaches, then, can augment what one learns through investigating a topic. Boix-Mansilla, Miller, and Gardner (2000) offer an example pertaining to a common social studies topic, what might be named 'The Rise and Fall of Nazi Germany.' They describe how the disciplines of history and psychology can work in tandem to help students enrich their understanding of how people in Nazi Germany came to accept and obey an authoritarian government. From the discipline of history, students could employ historical inquiry tools to examine the political, economic, and social conditions that allowed Nazi ideology to spread. For example, students could be guided to draw evidence-based inferences when investigating primary sources, further contextualize the rise of Nazi Germany by reading secondary sources (e.g., other historical accounts), and provide explanations based on their findings. From a psychology perspective, students could ground their investigations with key concepts in the discipline to learn social and psychological aspects of obedience to authority (e.g., investigating underlying factors shaping "groupthink" or "herd behavior"). Integrating the disciplines of history and psychology with this type of approach enables each discipline to retain its integrity as students learn how to think like historians in developing historical knowledge and they learn to employ key concepts from psychology to understand the topic.

Calls for interdisciplinary approaches are also bolstered by two related claims about knowledge. The first is that knowledge is increasingly interdisciplinary, due primarily to the need for and results of research that address pressing social, economic, and technological problems. Second, different types of boundaries continue to be blurred and crossed. These include disciplinary boundaries, distinctions between academic and popular knowledge, and the dividing line between science and non-science (Klein, 1996). With respect to these two claims about knowledge, interdisciplinary inquiry has much in common with transdisciplinary inquiry.

Social Studies as Transdisciplinary Inquiry

At the heart of transdisciplinary approaches is an understanding that there are common modes of inquiry that cut across academic disciplines, especially within the humanities and social sciences. All forms of inquiry in the social sciences start with identifying basic problems or formulating questions for investigation, require seeking and collecting various sources of information, involve the careful analysis, interpretation, and evaluation of reliable information sources, and result in sharing findings in ways that involve the use of language and other symbolic systems. The social science disciplines basically use the scientific method, focus on understanding and explaining human behavior, make inferences based on data, and try to verify information and conclusions (Beal, Bolick, & Martorella, 2009).

As with interdisciplinary inquiry, a transdisciplinary approach to social studies centers upon vexing social, cultural, economic, and political problems and proceeds from the premise that new ways are required to understand and explain the workings of an increasingly interconnected world. These new ways involve dismantling disciplinary barriers, which include eradicating the division of knowledge among disciplines, and forging new approaches to frame and investigate problems that lead to tangible results (Polimeni, 2006). This has led to calls for "postdisciplinary conversation," where the goal is not to sustain the stratification of knowledge or scaffold institutional imperatives, but to transform academic work as "reflective, public intellectual activity" (Dimitriadis & McCarthy, 2001, p. 37).

There is also evidence of both interdisciplinary and transdisciplinary approaches being embraced in universities with the emergence and development over the past few decades of academic departments, such as cultural studies, gender studies, media studies, and race/ethnicity studies. Scholars working in these fields employ theoretical constructs and focus on analytical categories (e.g., race, ethnicity, gender, class, religion) to grapple with conceptual and practical problems that are not the province of any singular discipline. While these scholars might draw from individual disciplines, their work does not fit within any one discipline. Their questions, modes of analysis, findings, and implications are inter or transdisciplinary.

Perhaps two related factors differentiate transdisciplinary from interdisciplinary perspectives. Advocates of transdisciplinarity more explicitly aim to address what they see as a "mismatch between knowledge and action," that is, the disconnect between knowledge that is produced in academia and the demand for knowledge that helps solve societal problems (Jäger, 2008, p. vii). The second factor is that the inclusion and actual involvement of a broader array of participants and stakeholders is seemingly more salient for transdisciplinary perspectives (Hirsch Hadorn, Hoffmann-Riem, Biber-Klemm, Grossenbacher-Mansuy, Joye, Pohl, Wiesmann & Zemp, 2008). For example, an investigation of pollution in a local riverbed might include researchers across academic disciplines collaborating with state, regional, and local officials, environmental groups, additional community associations, as well as nearby residents to better understand the causes and consequences of the pollution and to devise ways to solving the problem. Interaction, collaboration, and mutual learning among all these participants are central to this type of inquiry.

Summary

This book is based on two core ideas: Social studies and literacy education are about reading the word and the world (Freire & Macedo, 1987) and our knowledge and understandings about the world are increasingly mediated through texts. Disciplinary, interdisciplinary, and transdisciplinary perspectives help develop these core ideas. Disciplinary perspectives illumine the ways that disciplinary experts (historians, psychologists, economists, etc.) access and employ the methods of their disciplines to work with texts and construct knowledge claims about the world. Teachers and students can, in turn, work to emulate these practices. Interdisciplinary perspectives highlight how the resources of different disciplines can be leveraged in ways that can help students better understand the different facets and deepen their understandings of an important issue. Transdisciplinary perspectives signal the importance of disciplinary experts collaborating and learning with a range of actors or participants in the actual "life-world" (Hirsch Hadorn, et. al., 2008).

Understanding social studies as disciplinary, interdisciplinary, and transdisciplinary inquiry-based perspectives enables educators to view these three approaches as part of a collective set of tools they can use with students. While we believe a comprehensive investigation of a complex, multifaceted problem is likely not best pursued through a single academic discipline, each of these three perspectives is valuable and can guide learners in doing important investigative work with social studies content, which is increasingly complex and transnational. Problems such as climate change, pollution, disease, war, terrorism, financial crisis, public health, poverty, increasing inequality, and injustice affect all corners of the world and, thus, necessitate groups of people working across geographical and professional contexts and within, across, and outside of academic disciplines to address and solve these problems. Looking across the three perspectives also helps us build from our understanding of literacy as critical social practices to name core epistemological challenges and an inquiry-based pedagogical approach to address these challenges.

FIVE-PHASE INQUIRY MODEL AND EPISTEMOLOGICAL CHALLENGES

Preparing students for working with 21st century texts and technologies to address complex, multifaceted problems requires grappling with core epistemological challenges. Building on the work of others (Bruce & Bishop, 2002; Leu, Leu & Coiro, 2004), we outline a five-phase inquiry model as a process of negotiating five of these key challenges. We more deeply consider each of these challenges in subsequent chapters. Phase 1 is *defining purposes and launching an inquiry with a worthy investigative question*; Phase 2 is *discerning useful and credible resources*; Phase 3 is *evaluating resources*, which includes adjudicating among conflicting claims and evidence, especially with complicated multimodal texts; Phase 4 is *synthesizing findings*; and Phase 5 is *communicating new ideas*.

Phase 1: Defining Purposes and Launching an Inquiry with a Worthy Investigative Question

Decisions about what topics to investigate and how to best proceed are governed by curricular expectations or mandates, professional prerogative of teachers, and the interests of students. Our stance in this book is that teachers must do their best to ensure that the curriculum remains grounded in the exploration and examination of complex, multifaceted problems. In other words, the worthy investigative questions that teachers and students identify to launch an inquiry need to focus on these problems. Yet, coming up with generative and meaningful questions that can sustain an inquiry is not an easy or necessarily straightforward task. Which facets of a complex, multifaceted topic or problem should be the focus? Also, the purposes of an inquiry and the focus of an investigation are often dynamic, shifting as new information is examined and new understandings are gleaned. Initial investigative questions are not necessarily set in stone. Instead, they often are revised and clarified as an investigation ensues. So, how can teachers guide students through this process? Appealing to academic disciplines as well as inter and transdisciplinary perspectives can help. Teachers can connect students to existing knowledge along with the methods of the disciplines, such as the ways historians or economists have framed and studied a given topic, to help guide them in the formulation of their own worthy investigative questions.

Phase 2: Discerning Useful and Credible Resources

A second epistemological challenge concerns how students (and educators) discern the credibility and usefulness of information sources, especially multimodal and web-based texts. Incredibly vast amounts of information via the Internet are a mere keystroke or mouse click away, while the traditional, established vetting processes are absent or still emerging, as Burbules notes:

> [T]he referencing and organizational systems that are available, for example, in libraries, do not exist here [on the Internet]. The markers of institutional credibility and authority, the lines of tradition, that allow viewers to judge media sources, or publishers, for example, have not been settled yet; there is an even greater capacity to locate information that will tend to confirm one's existing views and prejudices, rather than challenge them. In all this, the scope of the network, and its deregulated content, overwhelm the ordinary idea that we can comparatively judge different sources (which ones?), or that we can trust popular processes of selection to weed out the less credible, and give status to the survivors. (2001, p. 443)

The Web is also "a self-sustaining reference system," in which readers often rely on other information gleaned within the network to determine credibility (Burbules, 2001). One potential danger of this is an "echo chamber" effect (Hess, 2009; Jamieson & Cappella, 2008) where ideas get reinforced through repetition and remain unchallenged by different perspectives. The sheer volume of information sources at our disposal also makes it more likely that readers will enact the practices of selective exposure (choose sources that align with one's beliefs) and selective perception (interpret events in line with one's beliefs) in an attempt to manage this volume (Manjoo, 2008).

Moreover, with the Web, not only must readers be able to assess the credibility of the source they are reading or viewing, they must be able to assess the associations a source makes, including external references and links and semiotic or textual references (images, sounds, symbols, metaphors, etc.) found within the text itself. Put another way, discerning useful and relevant online resources requires facility with a range of skills, including how to use search engines, evaluating results of search engine queries, initial scanning of a website, and making inferences about information vis-à-vis links on a site (Leu, Zawilinski, Castek, Banerjee, Housand, Liu, & O'Neill, 2007). Moreover, challenges associated with effectively using Internet search engines and evaluating search results are compounded by the increasing commercialization of the World Wide Web. As Bettina Fabos has argued, commercial search engines of leading companies like Google, Yahoo, and Microsoft function in ways highly similar to mainstream news media where "commercially controlled industry sanctioned positions dominate, and dissent is marginalized" (2008, p. 865). If students primarily use commercial search engines without a critical understanding of the way search engines work and without some facility with keyword search strategies to access a range and depth of perspectives about a topic, they are less likely to produce sound, meaningful research.

The superabundance of information at our fingertips also means that perhaps more than ever our most precious resource is our attention (Lanham, 1994). There is no shortage of sources competing for our attention, especially online where the increasingly ubiquitous presence of advertising works to blur boundaries between commercial and more scholastic or academic domains of the Internet. Teachers and students need to be mindful of these broader trends as they work to locate sources for their investigations.

Phase 3: Evaluating Resources– Adjudicating Among Conflicting Claims and Evidence, Especially with Multimodal Texts

A third and related epistemological challenge is adjudicating among conflicting claims and evidence. While the need to systematically evaluate and adjudicate among competing claims and evidence has long been a core practice of social scientists, the near boundless growth of information sources (especially web-based) has intensified this challenge. Technological advances with audio and video recording coupled with increased ease of uploading digital files onto the Web have led to a staggering array of documentary data to sift through. And this is altering the work of social scientists. With the discipline of history, for example, historians are moving from a culture of scarcity to one of abundance; the potential historical record is more immense than ever before as new technologies and digital archives make records and sources more accessible to more people (Rosenzweig, 2003). The greater access to diverse perspectives has also resulted in a proliferation of truth claims and this requires that students have enough background information to contextualize information and authorship, be able to read intertextually across assorted texts and modalities to consider the "vast network of relations of credibility" (Burbules & Callister, 2000), and make sound judgments about claims and evidence.

This is especially vexing with multimodal Web texts because "truth is 'made present' through processes that are closer to rituals and iconographies than propositions in texts" (Lankshear, Peters & Knobel, 2000, p. 35). Literacy practices are increasingly governed by a spatial "logic of the image" rather than strictly a linear logic of written language (Kress, 2003). Students need to increasingly negotiate and create meaning with multimodal texts which possess combinations of linguistic, gestural, aural, visual, and spatial modes through a mix of images, music and other sounds, graphic art, video, and print. Multimodal texts are also inherently intertextual, in that any meaning of a text is shaped by other texts. Kristeva (1980), drawing on Bakhtin (1973), describes how two paths merge within texts: intertextual relationships within texts and outside of texts. For example, images create syntagmatic relationships or sequences within a multimodal text to create meaning, and images are related to other images and signifiers that exist outside of the text. The modes in any one multimodal text, as a whole or separately, communicate particular information that can connect to students' experiences and previous knowledge in different ways and can also reference other texts. Thus, the multiple modes in any one text often need to be analyzed individually as well as examined as a whole. Reading multimodal texts requires an understanding that texts exist in relationship to other texts and that multiple, shifting, and competing readings are possible.

Phase 4: Synthesizing Findings

A fourth related epistemological challenge is synthesizing findings. Different forms or kinds of synthesis include narratives, taxonomies, rules, aphorisms, metaphors, images, themes, theories, and paradigms (Gardner, 2006). Synthesizing findings is especially challenging because most individuals as well as institutions have little expertise in this area due to inadequate training and a scarcity of useful standards to evaluate good syntheses (Gardner, 2006). To create compelling and useful syntheses, students must look across multiple claims, consider different perspectives, decide what is significant, and create a coherent account of findings for oneself and others. This challenge is intensified with web-based inquiry. In addition to having access to an escalating array of texts vis-à-vis the Internet, online readers not only need to assemble an understanding of texts they read, they also need to consider the range of choices they make about which web pages to visit, links to explore, and with whom to communicate as they seek answers to their questions (Leu, et. al, 2007).

Phase 5: Communicating New Ideas

A fifth epistemological challenge is creating texts to communicate ideas and new understandings. After synthesizing findings, students need to decide what text(s) to create as well the audience to which they want to communicate their ideas. Some text options include writing an essay, creating a digital video, composing and performing a piece of music, or creating a pamphlet. Having a wide range of multimodal options to communicate ideas offers opportunities for students to enact more "performative" ways of knowing in which "knowing itself is a kind of doing . . . not had as much as it is done" (Gill, 1993, p. 48). Performative practices include digital remixing, bricolage, collage, and montage and reflect a range of strategies for "assembling, editing, processing, receiving, sending, and working on information and data to transform 'data' into 'knowledge'" (Lankshear, Peters & Knobel, 2000, p. 21). The content and form of the texts created by students also should align with the audience selected to "receive" the text. Potential audiences might include peers, politicians, business leaders, community organizations, parents, and researchers, among others, so students need to deliberate to discern optimal ways of communicating with their intended audiences.

A Note About the Inquiry Phases and Five Challenges

We have presented the five inquiry phases and corresponding challenges in a linear order, yet this is somewhat misleading. While students do progress through these phases, often their journeys are more recursive than linear; they move more fluidly back and forth through the phases rather than proceed in a lock-step fashion. For instance, the process of identifying credible and useful resources (Phase 2) and evaluating them (Phase 3) can often lead to new or refined investigative questions (Phase 1). Moreover, sometimes an inquiry project begins not with a clear question, but with a curiosity, a hunch, or an itch (Harste, 2010).

THE NEED FOR DYNAMIC, INQUIRY-BASED LITERACY PRACTICES

To best address the five epistemological challenges, independently and together, students and teachers embody the values and enact the practices of *relational cosmopolitanism*. Through public deliberation in a "community of reason" (Nussbaum, 1997) and guided by an ethic of care, concern, and connection (Martin, 1994), students and teachers investigate complex, multifaceted issues in ways that understand various social, economic, political, historical, and contemporary issues and problems as interconnected. They also respond specifically to the epistemological challenges, and in our work we have discerned three ways students and teachers can do this. 1. Multiple and varied traversals across shifting problem spaces; 2. Dialogue across difference; and 3. Building of perspective. We describe these three core sets of practices here and further develop each in Chapters 4–8.

Multiple and Varied Traversals Across a Problem Space

Cultivating deep understandings of complex issues requires that learners "criss-cross the landscape" or make multiple traversals across a problem space (Spiro, Coulson, Feltovich, & Anderson, 2004). Learners investigate multiple representations (which are often multidirectional and multidimensional much like the sounds or up and down movement of a calliope), explore interconnections and relationships, and assemble diverse knowledge sources to address persistent problems (e.g., environmental preservation, health issues, genocide, etc). Criss-crossing the landscape, especially with the World Wide Web also involves what Heim (1993) calls "meditative perusal," a "contemplative, meditative meander along a line of thinking" in which "the reader is open to unexpected connections, meaning and interpretation, options that were taken and others that were not, authorial hunches, tensions and contradictions" (p. 25).

This key practice helps address each of the epistemological challenges. Readers often don't know what questions to investigate until they explore the terrain first, reading across a range of sources and bolstering background knowledge. Multiple and varied traversals across the terrain can lead us to "overturn the questions we originally came to ask," thus, making it possible to find "something more important than the discovery we had originally hoped to make" (Heim, 1993, pp. 25–26). The same is true for the second challenge; the more traversals across sources, the more likely readers will be exposed to and encouraged to discern useful and credible resources. In terms of the third challenge, multiple traversals means that readers are more likely to come across competing claims and evidence about a topic, which invites them to adjudicate among conflicting claims and evidence. The fourth challenge, synthesizing findings, necessitates reading across a range of sources. Finally, readers can perhaps best address the fifth challenge, communicating new ideas, if they are more aware of the range of potential texts they could create (video, website, essay, podcast, etc.), an awareness that can be cultivated through multiple and varied traversals across an issue or problem space.

Dialogue Across Difference

Dialogue is not simply a method or technique; it is "at heart a kind of *social relation*" (Burbules, 1993, p. 19). It involves questions, responses, redirections, and building statements as participants collaborate "in the face of likely disagreements, confusions, failures, and misunderstandings" (p. 19). This involves trust, concern, and mutual respect with participants committed to establishing and sustaining social bonds and committed to the intellectual work of collaborative inquiry. Returning to the epistemological challenges, a collaborative inquiry model assumes that enhanced performance and higher-level results for each phase of an inquiry project are more likely when students have opportunities to test ideas, compare and contrast perspectives, and deliberate to identify the best ways of moving through an inquiry (with teachers guiding students to skillfully do this).

Not surprisingly, dialogue across difference can be exceedingly difficult. Research in cognitive science and neuroscience over the past four decades has shed some light on why this is so. This research has shown that how we make sense of the world is shaped by brain structures called "frames" and "metaphors" which form our systems of thought or worldviews (Lakoff, 1996; 2004). We then employ these worldviews (e.g., conservative or progressive) to make meaning with language, images, etc. Or, put another way, different words or images activate different worldviews. Thus, dialogue across difference about a particular issue (e.g., best approaches to curtail climate change) is often inseparable from acknowledging and discussing differences across larger frames from which people operate (e.g., causes of environmental change are man-made or providential from God). So, while the Internet provides possibilities for dialogic encounters across difference, the overwhelming proliferation of sites and media outlets (and corresponding truth claims) can also support insularity: readers can more easily screen what they consume and select sources and sites that align with their own world views. Moreover, media outlets are under increasing pressure to tailor content for increasingly niche audiences (Manjoo, 2008). Viewers of FOX news, for example, expect content consonant with their views. If FOX moved significantly leftward across the political and ideological spectrum, current viewers could easily move on to another news source, one more compatible with their own perspectives.

What remains most significant to our purposes is to ensure that students engage and negotiate different perspectives in their investigations. Because "there can be no escape from plurality" (Bernstein, 1992, p. 329), especially with complex multifaceted problems, teachers and students have an obligation to acknowledge and respond to this plurality, to consider "reasonable perspectives in forums well-designed for deliberation" (Gutmann, 1993, p. 198). Classrooms need to be these forums.

Building of Perspective

Multiple traversals across a problem space and dialogue across difference are vital to the building of perspective. This inquiry-based literacy practice involves probing persistence (Gallo, 1994), being open to unexpected connections, meanings, and interpretations (Heim, 1993), and continually striving to understand and then synthesize diverse perspectives. Building of perspective needs to occur at each phase of an inquiry project.

We contend that this practice also entails a particular "evaluativist" epistemological stance. What it means to know can be viewed in terms of stages, from absolutist to multiplist to evaluativist (Kuhn, 2003). The absolutist stage is characterized by individuals who view knowledge as certain and unproblematic and who are not concerned with issues of justification. With the multiplist stage, individuals view knowledge as idiosyncratic and highly personal. With the evaluativist stage, there are shared norms of inquiry and knowing which leads to an understanding that some positions are more reasonably justified and sustainable than other views. The evaluativist stage embraces the uncertain and personal qualities of knowledge construction, yet situates these qualities within a community that shares understandings and practices of dialogic inquiry, such as students examining and adjudicating among conflicting claims and forms of evidence and considering how their own beliefs and values shape their evaluations of any text. Dialogue across difference and the building of perspective with an evaluative stance resist singular or one-dimensional accounts of complex realities (Kumashiro, 2001) and signal the importance of communities working within (or developing their own) standards of inquiry, which can be rooted in disciplinary, interdisciplinary, or transdisciplinary perspectives.

Engaging different perspectives is also essential for cognitive growth because it requires the negotiation and integration of diverse ideas (Greeno & van de Sande, 2007; Rommetveit, 1987) and the ability to see and evaluate something from distinct vantage points. Dewey (1934) offered the following metaphor to capture this process:

> [It's like] turning an idea around, the way a jeweller might examine a gem, looking at it first from this angle and then from that, examining its depths, testing its instrumental worth, pursuing its connections with other ideas and with the world of action, moving close to it, then backing away for a view from afar, even abandoning it for a time, the way an artist might temporarily lay a work aside, only to return to it with renewed energy on another occasion. (pp. 158–159)

Metaphors, like a jeweler viewing a gem, help conceptualize experience as "one kind of thing in terms of another" (Lakoff & Johnson, 1980, p. 5) and can lead to generative "redescriptions" of phenomena to change the ways we talk, think, and do (Rorty, 1986, p. 9).

To more fully conceptualize a more relevant, robust, and epistemologically sensitive social studies education, we offer two additional metaphors to help educators think about the inquiry and literacy practices central to social studies as new literacies: *excavation and elevation*.

EXCAVATION AND ELEVATION: METAPHORS FOR UNDERSTANDING SOCIAL STUDIES AS NEW LITERACIES

Several years ago, after a session with a teacher inquiry group we were working with in Battle Creek, Michigan, the two of us were struggling to name an ongoing challenge the teachers had identified in their work with sixth and eighth graders in a web-based unit focused on issues of Mexico migration (Ashburn, Baildon, Damico, & McNair, 2006). The teachers were struggling to guide students to closely read and evaluate specific web pages about Mexico migration while at the same time striving to help them keep in mind the "big ideas" of the unit. As we attempted to name this challenge, the song *Elevation* by U2, and the voice of Bono in particular, entered our conversation. In the song Bono moves between the metaphors of excavation and elevation to seemingly describe a romantic or spiritual experience or process. In the refrain, Bono sings how a mole is "digging up" his soul by "going down, excavation" while also making him feel like he "can fly so high, elevation" (Bono/U2, 2000). The song helped coax into our consciousness how we might use these metaphors as a way of understanding the teachers' dilemma—how the metaphors could help us think about Internet-based inquiry practices as dialectical processes that require both careful inspection and analysis of individual texts (*excavation*) along with meta-level framing and evaluation of individual texts within the broader terrain of a text's production, dissemination, and consumption (*elevation*). In other words, excavation could refer to the ways students can be guided to dig into sources, to do the *intratextual* work that is necessary to analyze, interpret, and evaluate sources, while elevation would include the *intertextual*, *contextual*, or *metatextual* sorts of work that are necessary to make meaning.

Excavation Practices

Excavation involves a core set of literacy practices with a primary focus on the careful analysis of individual texts. Excavation begins with getting a sense of the "lay of the land," surveying the information landscape and deciding when to "go in" and "mine" a source or text. Comprehending online texts comes with additional complexities. Readers need to access prior knowledge of search engines and website structures, engage in "forward inferential reasoning," and self-regulate with physical actions (typing, clicking, scrolling, dragging) and with rapid cycles of information-seeking (Coiro & Dobler, 2008). This process involves discerning the credibility of the source (Who is the author? What are her/his credentials, political or ideological allegiances? Who is the sponsor of the text or website? What are its allegiances, etc.?) and determining the relevance of the source for the particular inquiry. Evaluating the credibility of a text requires being able to distinguish fact from opinion, specific information from generalizations (or overgeneralizations), and being able to identify inconsistencies in the text. Within an inquiry approach, all these decisions depend on readers identifying their purposes and needs and then choosing texts to examine more closely.

After a text is selected (or when a text is provided by a teacher), readers employ core comprehension strategies with the text, such as predicting, visualizing, asking questions, determining main idea(s), making inferences, and summarizing (Pearson, Roehler, Dole, & Duffy, 1992). These strategies help readers understand what the author (or illustrator, videographer, etc.) is communicating with the text. Readers also access relevant prior knowledge to help evaluate the claims and evidence in the text and discern whether or not the claims and evidence are convincing. Readers' own experiences are vital to this meaning-making. Readers also analyze arguments and detect errors in logic or reasoning. Through close, careful reading, students can also learn to make inferences about subtexts in which claims and evidence are not explicit or obvious.

In this vein, excavation practices involve more critical investigations of a text, such as locating included and omitted perspectives in the text and identifying techniques used by authors, illustrators, and web designers, among others, to influence readers (e.g., loaded words, use of images, etc.). In addition to this type of critical reading, excavation includes readers inspecting how their own beliefs, views, understandings, and emotions influence their meaning-making with a text (Damico, Baildon, Exter, & Guo, 2009). Someone with politically liberal views, for example, will likely respond more favorably to content distributed by politically liberal media outlets than someone with strong conservative viewpoints; hence, the need for vigilant self-reflective reading. Excavation practices can also extend to more intensive self-exploration and monitoring of subconscious influences or "hidden persuaders" (Packard, 1957) on meaning-making, such as the myriad ways advertisers or public relations specialists endeavor to shape our decisions as consumers and citizens.

Elevation Practices

Elevation practices involve *intertextual, contextual,* or *metatextual* types of work. In terms of intertextuality, readers engage with a number of texts, considering connections and points of divergence across the texts to build understandings of a topic. Elevation practices also focus on situating texts in broader and multiple contexts, such as the disciplinary, cultural, discursive, historical, social, and economic contexts that shape the ways a text or collection of texts is produced, distributed, and consumed by readers. All texts are products of a particular time and place and are inevitably shaped by larger societal events and influences. To understand how this happens in social studies education, we can attend, for example, to the politics of historiography—how and why particular versions of the past are created, legitimated, and disseminated and how these versions serve larger political and social purposes (Segall, 2006). Engaging in these practices, for example, could include analyzing how imperialism has shaped mainstream academic knowledge and, more generally, investigating how the world views of certain groups are marginalized and underrepresented (Merryfield, 2001; Zinn, 1980). Segall (2006) elaborates on the meta-level qualities of this type of practice:

> Rather than ask students whether a historical text accurately reflects the past, a critical perspective poses the following: according to what conventional and methodological practices, whose discourse, whose standards, whose past? As a variety of interpretations are engaged,

students are made to consider why and how different discursive communities produce different truths about a supposedly common past; why different audiences believe different truths; and what makes some genres, some conventions more convincing than others. (pp. 138–139)

From a new literacies perspective, Carmen Luke (2003) refers to the knowledge necessary for elevation practices as "a meta-knowledge of traditional and newly blended genres or representational conventions, cultural and symbolic codes, and linguistically coded and software-driven meanings" (p. 401). Elevation practices, then, entail "lateral cognitive mobility across disciplines, genres, modalities, and, indeed, cultural zones" to cultivate "critical understandings of the *relations* among ideas, their sources and histories, intertextual referents and consequences" and *"connection codes"* (p. 401). With the Internet in mind, Lankshear and Knobel (2006) call for a "raft of meta-understandings" that includes "being able to scrutinize the veracity of texts obtained via networks or online spaces that have very little to do with conventional 'information' or 'truth' criteria and everything to do with discursive understandings of how online practices work" (p. 240). In the context of the Internet, elevation practices include knowing how to avoid being scammed, knowing how to conduct oneself in various online spaces, and being savvy in terms of the social relations central to the collaborative, collective, and creative features of Web 2.0. Such meta-understandings embrace ambiguity, uncertainty, complexity, divergent perspectives, and multiple ways of knowing. A primary goal is for students to be knowledgeable about how texts, especially Internet texts, work.

DIALECTICAL TACKING: EXCAVATION AND ELEVATION

The teachers we were working with in Battle Creek, Michigan helped us better understand that inquiry-focused readers are continually moving back and forth between excavation and elevation practices. Geertz (1976) called this type of movement a "continuous dialectical tacking between the most local of local detail and the most global of global structure in such a way as to bring both into view simultaneously" (p. 239). With his concepts, "experience-near" and "experience-far," Geertz suggested that we need to see the two in "dialectical interplay if we are to come to an understanding of the incommensurable phenomena that we are studying" (p. 90). Excavation and elevation require keeping open the spaces for creating meaning, inviting multiple perspectives and diverse viewpoints, and using our imaginations to try to understand difference.

In subsequent chapters in this book we demonstrate groups of teachers and students engaged in excavation and elevation literacy practices with web-based texts and technologies. At this point, we aim to set the stage for these classroom studies with three brief examples to illustrate the dialectical tacking of excavation and elevation: a written review of a television series, a literary analysis, and an example of two middle school students investigating an issue during an inquiry-based unit on Mexico and migration.

In a piece titled, "TV Panders to the Gilded Age" (http://www.iht.com/articles/2008/09/09/arts/gossip.php), television critic Alessandra Stanley considers the reincarnation of the television series, "Beverly Hills 90210" (a popular early 1990s series in the United States). In terms of excavation practices, Stanley analyzes the plots and characters to demonstrate the ways the series portrays a significant widening of income disparities between the wealthy and the middle or upper middle class. After a critical reading of a specific episode, Stanley concludes that "the wealthy on television are now really, really wealthy, and anyone who doesn't have a beach house and a butler might as well be on welfare."

Stanley also engages in elevation practices. She makes intertextual referents to contemporary shows (MTV's "Hills" and CW's "Gossip Girl" and "Privileged"), and she explores connections to the initial 1990s "Beverly Hills 90210." Stanley also historically situates her analysis in terms of Reagan economics and the Gilded Age along with the current context of "the aspirational age." This type of reading further supports her claim that class distinctions in these contemporary series, unlike their predecessors, are not just between "the haves and have-nots, but the haves and the have-mores."

Martha Nussbaum (1986) provides another example of excavation and elevation in her analysis of Sophocles' *Antigone*. In a demonstration of excavation, Nussbaum writes:

> The lyrics both show us and engender in us a process of reflection and (self) discovery that works through a persistent attention to and (re)-interpretation of concrete words, images, and incidents. We reflect on an incident not by subsuming it under a general rule, not by assimilating its features to the terms of an elegant scientific procedure, but by burrowing down into the depths of the particular, finding images and connections that will permit us to see it more truly, describe it more richly. (p. 69)

Later, she describes an approach to understanding the lyrics from a more elevated position:

> It advances its understanding of life and of itself not by a Platonic movement from the particular to the universal, from the perceived world to a simpler, clearer world, but by hovering in thought and imagination around the enigmatic complexities of the seen particular (as we, if we are good readers of this style, hover around the details of the text), seated in the middle of its web of connections, responsive to the pull of each separate thread . . . The image of learning expressed in this style,

like the picture of reading required by it, stresses responsiveness and an attention to complexity; it discourages the search for the simple and, above all, for the reductive. (p. 69)

Nussbaum argues that excavation is not simply a matter of using an elegant scientific procedure but instead requires burrowing into the depths of the particular, digging into a text in ways that will unearth new insights. Reading, however, must also include "hovering" and being responsive to the various threads that a web of connections might produce. This elevated view encourages one to engage the complexity of a text through a "flexibility of perception" (p. 69).

Our third example is drawn from a discussion with two eighth grade students at the end of an inquiry-based unit on Mexico and migration (Damico & Baildon, 2007). These two girls wanted to investigate the murder of young Mexican women working in *maquiladoras* (assembly plants in Mexico) along the Mexico-United States border. Based on their inquiry question "What is the Mexican government doing to stop the serial killings along the Mexico-United States border?" the girls examined a website news article entitled, "Expert Profiles Juarez Killers" (http://corpus-delict. com/media_juarez_71298.htm). As they read the website, they engaged in a range of excavation practices: the two girls noted the website was a news article which they deemed as credible; they questioned who the author was and noted that much of the article contained an interview with a retired FBI agent; they identified the main claim (the killer of these women resided in the United States); and determined that this claim lacked sufficient evidence. One of the two girls, for example, pointed out that "[the FBI agent] is convinced that someone in El Paso is responsible for more than half those deaths. There's no evidence to support that."

The girls also used important elevation practices to evaluate this website. First, they noted their familiarity with this genre of news reporting and said that they had used other online news articles they had deemed credible. They also corroborated some of the information on the site by saying that the site aligned with what they had already learned about the killings. One of the girls noted that she had "read a little bit of the same stuff on other sites and they were all credible." They also contextualized this website by pointing out that this was the first website they had come across that indicated the killer resided in the United States. Since other information couldn't corroborate the main claim, they questioned the accuracy of the information.

This snapshot of student work also illustrates the importance of dialectical tacking between excavation and elevation practices. To evaluate claims they looked at evidence contained within the website but also weighed claims by corroborating and contextualizing the claims with other sources of information and the knowledge they had developed about their topic.

IMPLICATIONS FOR SOCIAL STUDIES
CONTENT AND CURRICULA

Social studies content and curricula are typically defined and structured by the methods and organization of knowledge in the disciplines that make up social studies. When disciplinary knowledge is translated into an academic subject like history, content is organized in various ways—in terms of causes and consequences, overarching themes (e.g., progress and decline), and defining trends, events, or issues. However, in these situations students often gain little sense of the "epistemological fragility" (Jenkins, 1991) or the social and discursive nature of historical sense-making (or economic, geographical, or sociological sense-making, among others). Students seldom engage in disciplinary, interdisciplinary, or transdiciplinary inquiry to construct their own knowledge. Instruction typically centers on the conclusions of the inquiry rather than centering upon the inquiry itself (Bruner, 1960).

Social studies reconceptualized as inquiry-based literacy practices opens up curricular spaces for students to explore and investigate significant issues. The curriculum becomes more permeable, allows for the merging of different funds of knowledge available in a range of intersecting contexts, and helps us consider the local dimensions of globalization as well as the global dimensions of local experience. The impact of globalization also means that the transnational flows and global landscapes described in Chapter 1 not only provide the contexts of a reconceptualized social studies education, they also inform the content of social studies education. That is, students need to engage with the tensions central to new transnational flows and the new media, ethno, finance, ideo, and technoscapes they are producing. Part of this process entails unlearning assumptions about a divided world (Willinsky, 1998) and embodying a *relational cosmopolitanism* with social studies curricula so that students see various social, economic, political, and historical issues and problems as shared and global (Gaudelli, 2003). A primary goal is for young people to become global learners as "they learn how to relate their knowledge of a particular part of the world to the larger trends and issues that affect all societies" (Gunn, 2006, np), draw on the range of meaning-making resources and tools available to them in the classroom and beyond, and create new blended syntheses of practices and knowledge that help them make sense of the world and their experience in it.

In the next chapter we consider sets of tools and pedagogical strategies for working with social studies subject matter, new texts, and emerging technologies in the ways suggested in this chapter. Drawing on our teaching, research, and work creating, developing, and using web-based technology tools over the past decade, we lay out an argument for the ways tools and practices can be conceptualized and enacted by teachers and students to accomplish a range of goals central to social studies as new literacies in a global society.

3 Web-based Technology Tools to Guide Inquiry

In this chapter we use an ecology metaphor to describe the new technology and media environment as a system consisting of many dynamic and interdependent factors. These factors include the people, information, practices, and media and technology tools that make up the system and which consist of physical (abiotic) and living (biotic) components that interact to form complex relationships that evolve over time (Zhao & Frank, 2003). For our purposes, the physical or abiotic elements of the Web are made up of the hardware and software of existing technologies and media, the infrastructures for interlinked hypertext and interactive information sharing, and the architecture of participation that characterizes social media. These physical elements include Web 1.0 and 2.0 tools as well as previous and new technologies, such as mobile or handheld computing devices that are changing the ecology. The living or biotic components are the users of these technologies and tools and the relationships and communities they foster. Technologies and the data and information they convey represent deep assumptions about ways of knowing and participating, even as they appear to be bias-free tools and representations of the world (Bowers, 2002). People and their values are deeply imbricated with the technologies they create and use and these technologies, in turn, shape social relations, social practices, and the construction of knowledge.

An ecological perspective of new techno and mediascapes helps us see uses of technology more holistically, as a complex web of relationships between the many parts that make up the system. It also helps us understand classrooms as nested in a broader ecology so that relationships between new techno and mediascapes, knowledge, social practices, and teaching and learning might be more fully considered. This ecology consists of many technologies, which can be broadly defined as tools and devices that assist human endeavors (Swan & Hofer, 2008), such as the creation, storage, management, and communication of information. Human activity is mediated through the use of tools and throughout time tools have shaped and transformed the ways we think, act, and interact. Similarly, relatively new technologies such as mobile or handheld computing devices (with an increasing range of tools, such as text messaging, e-mail, web access, maps, video, photography, music, games, and other applications), online gaming platforms, and social networking software are shaping new forms of social interaction and communication. Young people, especially, use technology almost seamlessly as part of their everyday social practices, functioning as "digital natives" (Prensky, 2001) in this ecology, having grown up with a range of electronic, online, and digital experiences. They interact with the world and others through a range of multimedia and communication tools and these new digital, networked communication and information technologies have changed what it means to be literate. The new media and technology ecology is fluid and ever-changing—new social practices, which are fundamentally literacy practices, are called for by new and emerging technologies.

At the end of the first decade of the 21st century, there is no shortage of scholars striving to better understand the substance and impact of the ways new technology tools are transforming our thinking, interactions, and lives. Sociolinguists and semioticians are studying how new media and increased information flows are reshaping understandings of language and sign systems, critical theorists are considering how forms of political participation are cultivated and distributed vis-à-vis networked communication systems, cognitive psychologists are investigating the intellectual demands of comprehending digital texts, and social and cultural anthropologists are exploring how participants in particular contexts enact digital literacy practices (Tierney, 2008). Educators are left with the daunting task of making sense of all these findings to devise curricular and instructional approaches that meaningfully integrate new technologies into classrooms. In this chapter we attend specifically to Internet technologies, the tools and resources accessible via the World Wide Web, and consider how web-based tools and resources might support teachers and students to engage in social studies inquiry and grapple with the five epistemological challenges outlined in the previous chapter: 1. Identifying worthy investigative questions; 2. Discerning useful and credible resources; 3. Adjudicating among conflicting claims and evidence, especially with complicated multimodal texts; 4. Synthesizing findings; and 5. Communicating new ideas.

We begin by describing key features of the ecology by highlighting specific Web 1.0 and Web 2.0 technologies. While we view changes with the Web as more continuous than dichotomous (Leu, O'Byrne, Zawilinski, McVerry, & Everett-Cacopardo, 2009), the binary framework of 1.0 and 2.0 helps orient the chapter and illumine distinctions between reading and analysis tools (Web 1.0) and collaborative writing and discussion tools (Web 2.0). We then draw on our teaching and research developing and implementing web-based technology tools over the past decade to describe ways these tools can be conceptualized and used by teachers and students in ways that align with an understanding of social studies and literacy as *inquiry-based social practices for understanding and addressing complex, multifaceted problems*. We also set the stage for the next section of the book, Chapters 4–8, by introducing the *Critical Web Reader*, a set of web-based inquiry tools for teachers and students.

WEB 1.0 AND WEB 2.0

Web 1.0 is a term used to define and describe a first generation of web design and development. Characteristics of Web 1.0 include websites that are static rather than interactive and web applications that are proprietary rather than open source (where a source code for an application is freely available for users to modify or develop new applications). Much information on websites with a Web 1.0 emphasis, especially in the early years of wider web access and use, was arranged hierarchically and distributed by a small group of content providers (Cormode & Krishnamurthy, 2008), with programming expertise in hypertext markup language (HTML) a prerequisite for content creation. From a classroom perspective, then, teachers were likely to view website content as mostly comparable to traditional sources (books, journals, newspapers) and means of communication (web pages similar to overhead transparencies) (Wallace, 2004). In this sense Web 1.0 embodied a more traditional conception of knowledge as created and disseminated by credentialed experts (Dede, 2008). The expansion of the World Wide Web did come with a significant upsurge in content-related sites that social studies educators could access and consider integrating into their curriculum. These sites have included a range of mostly static web resources to help address the five epistemological changes. In general, however, expectations for teachers and students did not need to undergo any radical change vis-à-vis Web 1.0. If teachers viewed the Web primarily as a repository of additional sources of content to supplement the curriculum, they could access these web resources to help meet a range of goals as they planned curriculum and devised lessons. In sum, Web 1.0 tools emphasize reading and analysis, primarily of individual texts. While some tools are specific to the web environment (ideas about how to determine a credible website), others are more applicable to texts in general (strategies to interpret primary sources). Web 2.0 tools, in contrast, shift the emphasis to composing and production and more possibilities of web-based collaborative inquiry.

Web 2.0 is a common descriptor for a second generation of web design and development. Primary characteristics of Web 2.0 include communication, the creation and sharing of information, and the development of web-based communities and applications, such as blogs, wikis, social networking sites (Facebook, Ning); and media sharing sites (Flickr, YouTube). Web 2.0 tools promote the sharing of content through communal bookmarking, social networking, and the distribution of photos and videos. Web 2.0 also can stimulate thinking through blogs, podcasts, and online discussion forums and promote collaboration and co-creation through wikis, mashups, and online communities committed to different social goals (Dede, 2009). A

Web 2.0 environment enables children and youth to use digital and multimedia tools to communicate across contexts, expressing and expanding their sense of identity (Tierney, 2008). Through participation in different online communities, they can explore and enact a range of social roles, such as peer, learner, technology expert, mentor, collaborator, reader, author, and consultant (Black, 2009). Children and youth play a more vital and collaborative role in generating and distributing content with Web 2.0 tools (e.g., wikis, blogs, VoiceThread), which can lead to the creation of new genres, such as online fanfiction (Black, 2009). Wikis have been one popular approach to using the Web for the collaborative construction of content. A wiki is essentially a website that allows web users to create, edit, and hyperlink web pages with great ease. A wiki often is created for private or select communities, such as an organization, business, or classroom.

In general, content is commonly "remixed" through the practices of photoshopping, music and video remixes (mixter.org, splicemusic.com), remixes of "machinima" (machinima.com) and anime (animemusicvideos. org, newgrounds.com), as well as remixes of television programs, movies, and books (fanfiction.net) (Knobel & Lankshear, 2008). Content is also more easily shared via content aggregation and organization tools, such as RSS, or Really Simple Syndication feeds (Greenhow, Robelia, & Hughes, 2009). Students' greater level of involvement in content creation can also engender more diverse perspectives, representations, and ideas for them to negotiate. Because peers in different communities often establish assessments of validity and knowledge, Web 2.0, in general, moves us toward a conception of knowledge as "collective agreement" where facts are combined with "other dimensions of human experience, such as opinions, values and spiritual beliefs" (Dede, 2008, p. 80).

In sum, Web 2.0 has significantly reduced the barriers to entry for students and teachers to compose, produce, upload, and share a range of texts. Web 2.0 also has facilitated communication and collaboration for groups of people across contexts. Websites are much more interactive, offering many opportunities for comments, questions, and the expression of ideas from readers/viewers.

MAPPING NEW SKILLS

Web 1.0 and 2.0 technologies provide a range of tools and resources that can be used by teachers and students in ways that align with an understanding of social studies and literacy as *inquiry-based social practices for understanding and addressing complex, multifaceted problems*. Effectively using these tools and resources in inquiry-based social studies classrooms requires emphasizing a range of sophisticated skills in social studies curriculum and instruction. The National Council of Social Studies and Partnership for 21ˢᵗ Century Skills (http://www.21centuryskills.org/images/stories/

matrices/ICTmap_ss.pdf) developed a map to lay out these skills, which include:

- *Creativity and innovation* (e.g., demonstrating originality and inventiveness in work, being open and responsive to new and diverse perspectives, acting on creative ideas).
- *Critical thinking and problem solving* (e.g., monitoring one's own understanding and learning needs, demonstrating commitment to lifelong learning).
- *Communication* (e.g., articulating thoughts and ideas clearly and effectively through speaking and writing).
- *Collaboration* (e.g., demonstrating ability to work effectively with diverse teams, making necessary compromises to accomplish a common goal, assuming shared responsibility).
- *Information literacy* (accessing information efficiently and effectively, evaluating information critically and competently, using information accurately for an issue).
- *Media literacy* (e.g., understanding how media messages are constructed, for what purposes, and using which tools, characteristics and conventions; examining how individuals interpret messages differently, how values and points of view are included or excluded, and how media can influence beliefs and behaviors).
- *ICT literacy* (e.g., using digital technology, communication tools and/or networks appropriately to access, manage, integrate, evaluate, and create information; using technology to research, organize, evaluate, and communicate information).
- *Flexibility and adaptability* (e.g., adapting to varied roles and responsibilities, working effectively in a climate of ambiguity and changing priorities).
- *Initiative and self direction* (monitoring one's own understanding and learning needs, utilizing time efficiently and managing workload, demonstrating initiative).
- *Social and cross-cultural skills* (e.g., leveraging the collective intelligence of groups, bridging cultural differences, and using differing perspectives to increase innovation and the quality of work).
- *Leadership and responsibility* (e.g., using interpersonal and problem-solving skills, leveraging strengths of others to reach a common goal).
- *Productivity and accountability* (e.g., setting and meeting high standards and goals for delivering quality work on time, demonstrating a positive work ethic, etc.).

This 21st Century Skills map provides a useful orientation to the kinds of capacities necessary to navigate new techno and mediascapes. Yet, developing this broad range of skills is a daunting task for social studies educators.

The use of new technologies and media in schools has a checkered past (Cuban 1986, 2001). Schools tend to be resistant to change and seldom support pedagogical or technological innovation (Zhao & Frank, 2003). In a literature review about technology use in social studies education, Swan and Hofer (2008) found that technology alone has not moved traditional pedagogies toward more student-centered, inquiry-based approaches. In fact, new technologies often are used to support traditional, teacher-centered instruction. The teacher's orientation and purposes play a pivotal role in determining the use of new technologies in classroom practice (Saye & Brush, 2006; Swan & Hicks, 2007; Windschitl, 2002). Swan and Hicks (2007), for example, found that when history teachers were guided by a pedagogical approach that emphasized historical inquiry, the development of historical thinking, and constructing historical knowledge through the analysis of primary sources, they leveraged technology in innovative ways to support these pedagogical goals.

AN ECOLOGICAL PERSPECTIVE OF TECHNOLOGY AND SOCIAL STUDIES IN A GLOBAL SOCIETY

We believe a more ecological view of the technology environment supports the reconceptualization of social studies as new literacies for living in a global society. In previous chapters we provided an integrated framework for viewing social studies as *inquiry-based social practices for understanding and addressing complex, multifaceted problems*. We also outlined three key practices—multiple traversals of a problem, dialogue across difference, and the building of perspective—to develop a "method of intelligence" for new global and knowledge landscapes. An ecological perspective helps educators consider the web of relationships between new global contexts, one's pedagogical orientations, available technologies as tools to support certain pedagogical approaches, the kinds of social interactions and practices they support, and the kinds of knowledge work they make possible. However, many challenges persist and we organize the next section around the five epistemological challenges we believe are central to inquiry-based social studies education. In doing so, we sample, rather than conduct an exhaustive review of, available technology tools and resources that can be used to manage these challenges.

WEB-BASED TOOLS TO ADDRESS FIVE EPISTEMOLOGICAL CHALLENGES

We consider web-based technology tools and resources in terms of how they support the central goals and practices of inquiry: asking good investigative questions; locating useful and credible information sources;

analyzing, interpreting, and adjudicating among different claims, evidence, and perspectives; synthesizing findings; and effectively communicating ideas. We draw on Larreamendy-Joerns & Leinhardt (2006), who contend that uses of technology need to be guided by an "epistemic-engagement view" of "knowledge and learning as practices both within the structure of a domain and within a disciplinary community . . . [in which] knowledge rests not on facts or isolated skills but on principles of inquiry" (p. 590). This means that "the questions that guide inquiry, the tools that allow inferences and interconnections, and the actions and principles (rules) that validate knowledge" (p. 590) should guide technology design and pedagogy. In learning environments based on these principles, learners engage in inquiry practices to develop understanding in subject matter, engage in sustained knowledge-building activities, and expand their discursive repertoires.

PHASE 1—IDENTIFYING WORTHY INVESTIGATIVE QUESTIONS

To launch an inquiry, students need to develop a sense of purpose for their investigation, identify significant issues or topics that are meaningful to them, and develop good questions that can sustain their research. To develop good investigative questions, students must be able to draw upon their own prior knowledge and lived experience and develop a knowledge base from which their questions might emerge. The Internet provides a rich repository of information that can allow students multiple and varied traversals across a problem or issue and helps them develop some level of understanding to better formulate investigative questions. Web 2.0 tools, such as wikis, blogs, or online forums and discussion boards, can provide online spaces for sharing questions, peer review, and getting valuable feedback within a collaborative community of practice. Utilizing such tools can help students develop learning spaces that provide opportunities for questions to evolve through ongoing review, revision, and refinement. Guided by the teacher, this communal and public exploration could be "done in a critical and rigorous yet sympathetic manner" where questions and ideas "are put forward for the purpose of exploration" (Doll, 1993, p. 142).

One useful website that guides students in asking good research questions was developed by William Cronon, Professor of History, Geography, and Environmental Studies at the University of Wisconsin, Madison. Professor Cronon created a primer for environmental history students (http://www.williamcronon.net/researching/index.htm), which includes a section on how to ask researchable questions (http://www.williamcronon.net/researching/questions.htm) and takes viewers through a process of finding research topics, making questions specific, and provides lists of do's and don'ts as well as tips for asking good research questions.

PHASE 2– DISCERNING USEFUL AND CREDIBLE RESOURCES

Many university libraries include lists of evaluation criteria or guiding questions and suggestions to guide readers in making reasoned judgments about the credibility and reliability of a web page (among other factors). Cornell University (http://www.library.cornell.edu/olinuris/ref/webcrit.html), for example, offers five criteria with sets of questions for evaluating the accuracy, authority, objectivity, currency, and coverage of a web page. Cornell also divides its sets of questions into two categories: initial appraisal and content analysis. The initial appraisal emphasis—author, date of publication, edition or revision, publisher, title—is particularly useful for students or teachers who are working on identifying relevant and reliable resources to read or evaluate. The content analysis section deals more in-depth with the quality of the web page and emphasizes intended audience, objective reasoning, coverage, writing style, and evaluative reviews. The University of California, Berkeley (http://www.lib.berkeley.edu/instruct/guides/evaluation.html) provides a set of web page evaluation questions (e.g., What can the URL tell you? What do others say? Does it all add up?) as well as implications for why these questions are important. For example, the implications for the question "Who links to this page?" include "Sometimes a page is linked to only by other parts of its own site (not much of a recommendation)."

There are also checklists and surveys more specifically for K–12 contexts, such as "critical evaluation surveys" created by Kathy Schrock for elementary, middle, and secondary school students. One particular set of surveys centers upon the technical and visual aspects of a web page, content, and authority. These surveys prompt students to answer a series of "yes-no" questions as well as write a narrative evaluation of a site (http://school.discoveryeducation.com/schrockguide/eval.html). Another website with resources for teachers was developed by Alan November (http://novemberlearning.com/). This site provides guides and tips for reading web addresses, finding out the publisher and history of sites, checking a site's external links, and other useful resources and activities for information literacy (http://novemberlearning.com/resources/information-literacy-resources/).

With more explicit attention to design aspects of web credibility, the Stanford Persuasive Technology Lab (http://captology.stanford.edu/) lays out ten guidelines for creating and evaluating credible websites. These guidelines help readers verify the accuracy of site information by highlighting the expertise of the organization operating the site and whether or not they consistently update the site's information. (http://credibility.stanford.edu/guidelines/index.html).

In addition to resources that support a more comprehensive evaluation of a web page in its entirety, there are tools that guide a close or critical reading of specific genres of texts or web pages. The Center for Media

Literacy, for example, provides strategies for locating and analyzing hidden messages in advertisements (http://www.medialit.org/reading_room/articles.html), and there are some resources that demonstrate how to identify propaganda techniques in texts (http://www.propagandacritic.com/) or to discern media stereotypes and biases (e.g., http://mediawatch.com/about.html).

The resources described above, for the most part, share a common feature: static web pages which can serve as valuable references for teachers as they plan curriculum and for students to guide their web reading. There are also resources that are more interactive, moving beyond providing static sources of support. The University of Maryland offers a web page evaluation checklist that teachers or students can complete online, checking off or typing short responses into boxes, and then printing their work (http://www.lib.umd.edu/UES/webcheck.html). Teaching Tolerance, a project of the Southern Poverty Law Center, also offers a more interactive tool called Site Check on its website (http://www.tolerance.org/teach/web/site_check/index.jsp). Site Check guides readers through a series of questions to help evaluate its appropriateness for classroom use or for research purposes. At the end of the tutorial, readers can print their assessment of the site for future reference. The questions can also be downloaded as a pdf file.

PHASE 3– EVALUATING RESOURCES: ADJUDICATING AMONG CONFLICTING CLAIMS AND EVIDENCE

There are also web-based tools to guide teachers and students to read and engage with social studies content in discipline specific ways, and we consider but a sample of these resources here. Most of these resources are dedicated primarily to developing historical reasoning skills. The National History Project provides historical thinking and analysis guides, background on the habits of mind of historians, and heuristics for doing historical analysis and interpretation (http:www.history.ilstu.edu/nhp/terminology.html). The Library of Congress offers "The Learning Page," which provides guides, activities, and lessons (e.g., a time and place rule, and a bias rule) to help students learn how to analyze and interpret primary sources. (http://1cweb2.loc.gov/ammem/ndlpedu/lessons/psources/pshome.html). Another useful site was created by professor, Bob Bain, for his "Web-Supported World History Course." Bain provides graphic organizers, a "dynamic archive," and embedded scaffolds that support historical thinking. (http://www-personal.umich.edu/~bbain/display/talkingpoints.htm).

The Historical Inquiry: Scaffolding Wise Practices in the History Classroom site http://www.historicalinquiry.com/index.cfm) developed by Peter Doolittle, David Hicks, and Tom Ewing at Virginia Tech University provides a SCIM-C strategy for interpreting history with a set of multimedia tutorials to scaffold students in the historical reasoning skills of summarizing, contextualizing, inferring, monitoring, and corroborating. This site provides information about historical inquiry, inquiry strategies, and resources for understanding the past.

There are also resources that focus on how historians work with different texts or historical documents. The US National Archives and Records Administration's Digital Classroom provides a set of document analysis worksheets for several different primary sources (written documents, photos, cartoons, posters, maps, artifacts, sound recording, and motion pictures) (http://www.archives.gov/education/lessons/index.html). One set of resources that we have found highly useful is the "History Matters" website created by the American Social History Project and Center for Media and Learning (http://historymatters.gmu.edu/). The site is designed for high school and university teachers and students and is divided into three areas: 1. "Many Pasts," a collection of primary source documents in text, image, and audio "about the experiences of ordinary Americans throughout U.S. history;" 2. "Making Sense of Evidence," which provides strategies for analyzing primary texts with interactive exercises and a "Scholars in Action" section which demonstrates, with audio clips, how scholars interpret a range of documents; and 3. www.history, a database of carefully selected and screened websites with an analysis of each site's strengths and weaknesses and utility for teachers. The resources offered on these websites serve as models for document analysis.

Each of these web resources provides a range of tools and strategies that can be used to guide and scaffold students' historical reasoning skills and their work with primary source materials. There are also some tools that address how students might adjudicate among different or competing accounts. The following sites, for example, offer tools to discern facts in competing accounts or to consider alternative accounts:

- Factcheck.org: http://www.factcheck.org/. A project of the Annenberg Public Policy Center, provides information about what it considers inaccurate, misleading, or false claims by politicians and media outlets. FactCheck also offers classroom resources and lesson plans, a five-step process for avoiding deception, and a guide to Internet sources considered reliable and unbiased and those which are not.
- Accuracy.org: http://accuracy.org/. Set up by the Institute for Public Accuracy, this site archives articles that challenge mainstream news accounts. As its website notes, it seeks to broaden public discourse by providing news releases that offer well-documented analyses of current events and underlying issues.
- Dispute Finder: http://disputefinder.cs.berkeley.edu/. Dispute Finder, an experimental browser extension developed by Intel, has to be installed to work. The extension will highlight sections of websites that make disputed claims and provide links to websites that support other points of view.

- Swift River: http://swift.ushahidi.com/. Swift River uses crowdsourcing to validate and filter news. It is a free and open source software platform that uses a combination of algorithms and crowdsourced interaction to evaluate user-generated content in Web 2.0 platforms. By using a range of resources related to trust systems, meme tracking, and other software to track online activity, Swift River seeks to validate information through crowdsourcing and social networking tools.
- Snopes.com: http://www.snopes.com/. Snopes.com is a fact checking site that helps people determine the accuracy of information for a range of subjects. While noting that many sources contain a mixture of truth, falsity, and exaggeration which cannot be accurately described by single "true" or "false" ratings, it evaluates the claims made in news stories and identifies a range of political smears, rumors, hoaxes, scams, urban legends, and misinformation that circulate in online spaces.

While these sites do not necessarily provide students with explicit tools to adjudicate among competing accounts, they help them consider the accuracy of information and provide new types of tools to support students working with different informational accounts.

PHASE 4– SYNTHESIZING FINDINGS

Gardner (2006) argues that the "synthesizing mind" is particularly vital in the global information society. It includes being able to take information from disparate and diverse sources, putting it together in novel and productive ways, and being able to use a range of synthesizing tools, such as narratives, taxonomies, metaphors, themes, and theories. Google Wonder Wheel and Timeline are new tools that might help students look across topics to see relationships or put topics into patterns. Inquiry Chart strategies (see http:forpd.ucf.edu/strategies/stratIChart.html) also support students looking across different sources of information to synthesize what they know about a topic. Mind mapping software can help students visualize relationships among ideas or information. Data visualization is also being used as an approach to analyze and synthesize large amounts of data (e.g., see http://www.smashingmagazine.com/2007/08/02/data-visualization-modern-approaches/; http://www.smashingmagazine.com/2008/01/14/monday-inspiration-data-visualization-and-infographics/).

Concept maps or synthesis charts that help students look across claims and evidence, different perspectives, and information sources are important tools to guide students in synthesizing information. This work can be done inductively by having students make generalizations based on specific information from different sources or students might be given concepts or "big ideas" that can help them organize information. Research on the knowledge of experts indicates that expert knowledge "is organized around core concepts or 'big ideas' that guide their thinking about their domains" (Bransford, Brown & Cocking, 2000, p. 36). Big ideas "help students 'learn their way around'" a discipline by connecting specific content knowledge to larger networks and helping them develop "an overall picture that will ensure the development of integrated knowledge structures and information about conditions of applicability" (Bransford et al., 2000, p. 139). Big ideas can serve as conceptual lenses for seeing, interpreting, and synthesizing ideas in the social world and can help students organize their knowledge and make connections between social studies content and lived experiences. Some of the big ideas we have used with middle school and high school students include *knowledge is subject to change and interpretation*, which helped students think about different perspectives and knowledge as tentative; *history as story*, which helped students understand that authors create history and that there are different histories of events; *space becomes place*, which encouraged students to examine how different spaces are shaped by issues of gender, race, class, nationality, and power; and *culture as a human creation*, which helped students explore how humans create culture, why cultures change, and how individual and cultural identities are intertwined (Ashburn, Baildon, Damico, & McNair, 2006; Segall, 1999). Yet more work needs to be done to explore how such conceptual lenses might be developed to guide and scaffold this synthesizing work.

PHASE 5– COMMUNICATING NEW IDEAS

Web 2.0 facilitates participatory, interactive, and collaborative communication through social networking sites (e.g., Facebook), media sharing sites (e.g., YouTube, Flickr), collaborative knowledge spaces (e.g., Wikipedia), and places for creative works and the remixing of content (e.g., podcasting, videocasting, blogs) (Dede, 2009; Greenhow, Robelia & Hughes, 2009). Using these Web 2.0 tools and resources, the validity of knowledge produced and shared in these online spaces tends to be determined through peer review in communities of practice and social networks. Web 2.0 makes it possible for students to produce a greater range of products and performances to demonstrate learning, the potential to share their learning with multiple audiences, and opportunities for greater interaction with and feedback from different audiences. Yet, the standards and criteria used to judge these new forms of intellectual work are still emerging, as Zhang (2009) argues:

> When opposing views are presented, a knowledge community needs to examine them critically and evaluate them in light of their underlying reasons and values. The process is not to vote for the favourite but to

determine which view has the greater explanatory power or how the
views complement each other in formulating a higher-level ideas complex. (p. 276)

Using these new forms of communication raises important assessment
issues. Determining what counts as valid, legitimate, or desirable knowledge production and creativity in current contexts is an ongoing challenge
(Greenhow, et al., 2009). There is also "a lack of explicit, coherent knowledge spaces and representation tools for indexing, tracing, monitoring, integrating, and advancing ideas" (Zhang, 2009, p. 275) in distributed social
networking spaces. Web 2.0 supports a community of practice approach
to knowledge but doesn't necessarily sustain a commitment to the progressive advancement of knowledge or the community (Zhang, 2009). Creative
knowledge work requires deep and focused inquiry, progressive and collaborative problem solving, and expansive learning opportunities (Engeström,
2008) that allow learners to develop the necessary practices and knowledge
to adequately address problems. As a result, important questions remain
about the extent to which Web 2.0 can support these knowledge creation
goals (Zhang, 2009). One starting point to address these challenges is to
focus on and perhaps work to revise the standards developed by different
communities of practice to provide authentic standards and criteria that
can be used in the various communities in which students do or might
participate. These communities include disciplinary, interdisciplinary, and
transdisciplinary communities, the world of work, civil society, and peer
and popular culture.

An example of how new media and social networking sites can be used
to powerfully communicate content, David Darts, an Assistant Professor
in Steinhardt's Department of Art & Art Professions at New York University has developed an ongoing project of contemporary art, emerging
technologies, and new social practices. Called *CT4CT: Creative Tools for
Critical Times* (http://ct4ct.com/index.php?title=Main_Page), Darts has
created a repository of projects "that exist at the intersection of contemporary culture, critical theory, and civic engagement." This site provides
evidence that new media and technologies can be used to "provide powerful lenses for perceiving and understanding the technological, cultural,
economic and environmental transformations happening around us." The
"strategies and tactics" section on the site includes examples of critical
design, culture jamming, data visualization, DIY, pranks, remixes, and
projects that use historical research in media projects. Some of the issues
and themes on the site focus on capitalism, the environment, free speech,
homelessness, human rights, public space, surveillance, war, and terror.
These projects demonstrate the potential of new media and technologies
to communicate new understandings about complex multifaceted issues
using a range of disciplinary, interdisciplinary, and transdisciplinary tools
and resources.

SITES THAT SUPPORT WEB-BASED INQUIRY

There are also web-based tools that support the entire inquiry process. Perhaps the most popular is WebQuest (http://webquest.org), which supports teachers in designing highly structured and scaffolded inquiry tasks for students. WebQuests are based on prescribed procedures that guide students in analyzing, evaluating, and synthesizing information found on the web. The WebQuest site provides easy-to-use templates for teachers, a range of scaffolds for students, rubrics for evaluating student work, and many useful resources, including research studies on students using WebQuests.

Web Inquiry Projects (http://webinquiry.org/overview.htm) were introduced "as inquiry roadmaps" for teachers (Molebash, Dodge, Bell, Mason & Irving, http://webinquiry.org/WIP_Intro.htm). Unlike WebQuests, which provide students with step-by-step procedures and online resources needed to complete a predefined task, Web Inquiry Projects allow students to determine their own task, define their own procedures, and locate needed online resources (Molebash, 2004). Web Inquiry Projects follow a "spiral path of inquiry" and outline six inquiry stages that require students to: reflect on previous or new material; ask questions related to their topic; define procedures they will use to investigate their topic; gather and investigate data; analyze and manipulate data; and report findings, draw conclusions, and support conclusions with data.

The W.I.S.E. project (Web-based Inquiry Science Environment) is an example of how a reliable technology infrastructure coupled with carefully designed curricular units can promote inquiry-based teaching and learning in science (Slotta & Linn, 2009). The Persistent Issues in History Network (http://dp.crlt.indiana.edu), directed by John Saye and Tom Brush, guides a community of teachers with a problem-based historical inquiry approach. This network includes multimedia databases of historical artifacts, videos of classrooms, and a selection of tools that teachers can use to scaffold historical inquiry and share resources and activities. Another valuable resource for creating knowledge-building communities is the Knowledge Forum (http://www.knowledgeforum.com/). The Knowledge Forum, designed by Carl Bereiter and Marlene Scardamalia, allows communities of users to create their own Knowledge Base, a database in which it can store notes, organize and connect ideas, provide critique, and "rise-above" previous thinking to develop new understandings. The site provides software designed to support these knowledge-building activities.

Summary

Determining appropriate uses of technology tools and resources in classrooms is always guided by philosophical and pedagogical orientations. Technology can serve important pedagogical and learning goals, be used to help students develop important social practices and subject matter understanding, and help students understand and participate in the world in important ways. In deciding what technology to use and how to effectively use it, social studies educators might ask if and to what extent the technology can help students ask questions (by exploring topics, developing background knowledge, etc.), locate good information sources, effectively analyze, interpret, and evaluate information, synthesize their work, and communicate findings with different audiences.

The tools we have thus far described in this chapter can help teachers and students move toward these goals. Yet, these tools are also limiting. The Web 1.0 resources (mostly static sites) require some time and effort for teachers to meaningfully integrate these resources into curriculum. These more separate, stand-alone resources also mostly lack the interactivity features and potential of Web 2.0. While Web 2.0 resources, such as wikis, blogs, and videocasts, offer opportunities for multiple traversals of subject matter, dialogue across difference, and building perspective (because students can be guided to engage with different claims and perspectives and representations of subject matter), there remains a paucity of resources that offer explicit criteria, standards, and approaches that guide more rigorous, systematic, academic, intellectual work with Web 2.0 resources. Moreover, as several recent books argue, technologies associated with Web 2.0 have been leading to practices that emphasize immediacy over deep engagement with information, promote belief over fact (Manjoo, 2008), encourage mediocrity (Keen, 2008), and substitute genuine expertise with ill-informed speculation (Carr, 2008). According to these critics, Web 2.0 platforms often promote the free exchange of misinformation and vacuous content, heightened sensationalism, a "hive" mentality, and "cyberbalkanization" (Sunstein, 2001).

While we are skeptical of the wide-sweeping implications of these claims (there is a diverse and vast array of practices on the Internet), we have dedicated much of the last decade to designing and developing a set of web-based tools to guide students and teachers to wrestle with these challenges, namely the insufficient interactivity of Web 1.0 resources and the need for more rigorous and systematic tools to guide intellectual work vis-à-vis Web 2.0 resources. Our work has led to the creation of the *Critical Web Reader*.

THE CRITICAL WEB READER

At Michigan State University, we worked on a technology, curriculum, and professional development project titled, Project TIME (*T*echnology *I*ntegrated into *M*eaningful Learning *E*xperiences). On this project, we helped develop a Meaningful Learning Toolbox (http://mltoolbox.org/about.asp) to support and scaffold students' inquiry practices. This toolbox included an internal e-mail system, a reflective journal, a tool that scaffolded students' work with websites, and a tool that enabled students to develop multimedia historical narratives to share their findings. After this project concluded, we noted that students especially needed guidance in critically evaluating web sources of information. Students typically struggled with evaluating the credibility of information, analyzing and evaluating claims and evidence, and adjudicating among competing or conflicting claims they found (Baildon & Damico, 2006; Damico & Baildon, 2007).

To more fully address this need, we designed and developed the *Critical Web Reader* (http://cwr.indiana.edu/), a set of web-based literacy and technology tools designed to guide teachers and students to engage strategically with web-based texts. Building from the work of Green (1988) and Durrant and Green (2001) and the three dimensions model of literacy– which integrates emphases on literacy, subject matter, and technology with three equally significant, interlocking dimensions: the *operational*, the *cultural*, and the *critical*—we set out to create a systematic yet flexible set of web-based tools to promote important inquiry and literacy practices and deep engagement with content. This set of tools takes any website, places it within a frame, and then provides "lenses" which include guiding questions, models, and suggestions that readers use as they engage with the website. A writing tool is also embedded within the frame where students record and save all their work with each website (i.e., their analyses, interpretations, and questions). With easy access to this work, teachers can assess their students' learning to inform their instruction.

The four primary lenses we developed include a *descriptive lens* to help readers determine the relevance and reliability of texts and links on a website; an *academic lens* to help readers examine claims and evidence on a site; a *critical lens* to help readers identify included and omitted perspectives on a site and evaluate how authors and web creators attempt to influence them (e.g., use of loaded words, provocative images, links); and a *reflexive lens* to help readers examine how their own beliefs, values, and experiences affect their reading. Table 3.1 provides a list of guiding questions for each of these four lenses.

These lenses scaffold a comprehensive reading of a web page and emerged from our work with a range of teachers and students in middle school and high school classrooms. The questions across the four primary lenses promote disciplinary reading (evaluating claims and evidence) and the type of critical self-reflection so crucial to a stance of *relational cosmopolitanism*. With the *Critical Web Reader*, students are guided in excavation practices– to dig into sources, to do the *intratextual* work that is necessary to analyze, interpret, and evaluate sources. The lenses guide students to pay close attention to source details (such as headings, topic sentences, authorial techniques, etc.) and to ground their interpretations in these source details. Students are also guided to evaluate the reliability of information by discerning fact from opinion, identify bias or ideological agendas, consider purposes, and examine authors' qualifications. Students also evaluate claims by looking carefully at evidence and the internal logic or structure

Table 3.1   Guiding Questions of Four *Critical Web Reader* Lenses

Lenses	Guiding questions

Descriptive	What do I first notice about this site?
	What useful information can I identify?
	   headings
	   topic sentences
	   images, photos, sound clips, videos
	   links
	   genres of writing
	
	What does this site tell me about the:
	   author
	   sponsor
	   intended audience

Academic	What do I already know about the topic?
	What claims does the author/creator make?
	What evidence is used to support these claims?
	   facts
	   statistics
	   examples
	   quotations
	   testimonials
	Are the claims and evidence convincing?

Critical	What perspectives are included in this site?
	What perspectives are omitted in this site?
	What does this site want me to think, believe, or do?
	What techniques does the author/creator use to influence me?
	   loaded words
	   use of images
	   use of links
	   other
	Are the techniques convincing? Explain.

Reflexive	What affects the way I read this site?
	   my beliefs, values, opinions
	   my emotions
	   my background, culture, experiences
	How might others read this site?
	   from different racial, ethnic, cultural perspectives
	   from different age and gender perspectives
	   from different local, regional, national, global perspectives

of arguments. The *Critical Web Reader* also promotes elevation practices, guiding students to do the *intertextual*, *contextual*, and *reflexive* sorts of work that is necessary to make meaning, such as situating information within the purposes of their inquiry, looking across source claims and their own prior knowledge to determine what claims they can reasonably make, and reflecting on their own positions and stances while reading.

We have also developed other lenses to guide students' work with websites. These lenses focus on philosophical or theoretical perspectives (e.g., feminist and black masculinities lenses) as well as lenses that target a particular genre of text (e.g., a video clip, a photo, a blog). The *Critical Web Reader* lenses have been used to guide inquiry work into a range of topics, many with an emphasis on complex, multifaceted topics, such as social class and poverty, Holocaust denial websites, child labor, immigration, ethnic identity distinctions in Taiwan, and English language learners in US classrooms.

In our current work we are situating the *Critical Web Reader* in a five-phase inquiry model that can be utilized in disciplinary, interdisciplinary, and transdisciplinary investigations using new media and technology. A primary goal of this current work is to guide students and teachers to grapple effectively with the epistemological challenges across these phases:

1. In Phase 1, "Launching the Inquiry," learners are prompted to access their prior knowledge relevant to the curricular content and/or their particular inquiry focus and identify and develop significant investigative questions (that are both central to subject matter themes and content *and* meaningful to them as learners).

2. In Phase 2, "Locating Relevant Sources," learners are guided to find and select appropriate resources for their investigations. They interrogate issues of authorship and perspective to locate reliable, useful, and credible information sources.

3. In Phase 3, "Working with Resources," learners evaluate resources (such as web pages, images, and video clips) through different lenses. Phase 3 emphasizes analytical, interpretive, and evaluative strategies, such as making evidence-based inferences with different types of texts and critically evaluating and adjudicating multiple (and oftentimes competing) claims and evidence.

4. In Phase 4, "Synthesizing Findings," learners compare and contrast information sources and synthesize what they learned or discovered while working with resources in Phase 3. In doing this work they systematically contextualize, corroborate, cross-reference, and compare and contrast information—contextual and intertextual work that is fundamental to inquiry investigations.

5. In Phase 5, "Communicating Ideas," learners create their own texts and share them to receive feedback from other students, teachers, or other audiences (e.g., community members, an organization, the broader public, etc.). In Phase 5, they learn to develop and share interpretive accounts of subject matter using discipline-based criteria. Depending on the performance or product that is the outcome of their inquiry investigations, assessment in this phase focuses on the depth of engagement in subject matter, clarity and effectiveness of expression, ability to communicate their thinking and new ideas to

others, and their use of different forms of communication (e.g., public speaking, use of technology and media, different genres and textual formats, etc.) to maintain the interest of their intended audience(s).

These five phases of inquiry can help students develop the 21st century skills increasingly identified by social studies and literacy educators as essential for participating in a digital global society.

CONCLUSION

Along with Gee, Hull, and Lankshear (1996) we argue that "the world has changed and the nature of learning and knowledge is changing along with it" (p. 1). As Gee (2007) notes, classrooms can be designed to support collaborative knowledge-building by allowing students to connect with each other and others outside of classrooms with various tools and technologies. Technology can be used strategically for the purposes of public reasoning and deliberation around important issues, to help students dialogue across difference and build perspective, and to support making connections with others investigating comparable social issues and problems. Technology tools can be strategically used to foster important 21st century skills and help students develop subject matter understanding through multiple traversals and representations of content. However, to do so requires that educators carefully consider how they might be used for these purposes. Grounded in inquiry-based education and new literacies perspectives, we see these guiding purposes as interrelated and mutually reinforcing.

The Internet, for example, provides opportunities for multiple and varied traversals of issues by allowing students to transact with different representations (web sources) of a particular issue, look across varied claims and representations to formulate their own claims, and then share their claims and engage with the claims of others. Web 2.0 formats for collaboration, content creation, and communication during the inquiry process can provide opportunities for students to share different inquiry questions about a particular issue, deliberate competing claims about the issue, and share their findings through interactive forms of critical peer review that challenge the claims and evidence they present. By engaging with diverse web-based information, students can build perspective in ways similar to what Dewey described: they can investigate a multifaceted problem (e.g., global climate change, the social impact of globalization, etc.), look at it from different angles (e.g., different disciplinary or theoretical perspectives), examine its various dimensions and depths, and pursue connections with other investigators to better address or solve the problem.

To fully reconceptualize the uses of technology to support social studies education in a global society we believe these ideas and approaches need to be implemented in the spirit of experimentation, innovation, and ongoing redesign and learning. The key ideas in this chapter constitute focal points for ongoing inquiries by teachers in their own contexts as they attempt to engage their students in inquiry-based learning with technology tools. In the next section of the book, Chapters 4–8, we consider examples of teachers using and modifying the *Critical Web Reader* tools to grapple with core epistemological challenges.

Part II

Exploring and Examining Challenges and Possibilities

Windows into Classrooms

4 Collaboratively Negotiating the Challenge of Locating Reliable, Readable, and Useful Sources

With Rindi Baildon

This chapter is about a fourth grade teacher, Rindi, and her students in an international school in Singapore wrestling with the challenge of locating reliable, readable, and useful sources about threats to tropical rainforests and their inhabitants. (Rindi initially used the term "trustworthy" because she thought her nine-year-old students could relate to the idea of trust, but she used trustworthy and reliable interchangeably.) As part of an interdisciplinary social studies and science unit, Rindi developed a research tool with her students to help them become more discerning in their use of information sources to investigate a complex, multifaceted problem. Helping students locate good information sources is increasingly challenging due to the accelerated growth of networked information, especially the Internet with its varied text structures and formats (Coiro, 2003). Determining which sources to select, which to trust, and which to avoid is essential in an age of information, especially when criteria for selecting sources of information seems to be in short supply (Alvermann, Swafford, & Montero, 2004).

As an upper elementary teacher, Rindi found herself repeatedly asking certain kinds of questions as students worked on research assignments. These questions typically encouraged students to consider the trustworthiness, readability, and usefulness of the sources of information they were using in their research. For example, she would often ask,

- *"How can you be sure that the information you found for your research topic is accurate? Do you trust that the information is correct?"*
- *"Is that website easy for you to read and understand by yourself? Can you retell it in your own words?"*
- *"Is that information helping you find answers to your research questions? Did you plan out questions about your topic to help you in the research process before you started searching for information?"*

Her students generally approached research projects with enthusiasm, yet most lacked effective strategies for evaluating sources or finding resources that were "just right" for them to use in their research. They typically didn't have a plan in mind as to what they were trying to find during their investigations. Most often her students were willing to use any source they could locate (from the library, Internet, home) that related to their topic, and they didn't carefully consider the reading level of the source. When taking notes, they often copied sentences or entire paragraphs they didn't fully comprehend. Pictures copied from sources were often used to fill up space and great care was especially obvious in the creative use of font and text color to make their work attractive.

The Web is increasingly used in student research and for even technologically savvy students the process of researching can often be summed up in one word: *Google*. For students, *Google* is a noun and a verb rolled into one. With Internet access, students type in a keyword, get a list of websites, open a few, copy and paste information into a word document, find a few pictures, and repeat the process. Then they move sections around, add color, fun font, and utilize Word-Art for the title. The Internet makes access to a great deal of information possible for students and allows them to become authors of information themselves (Kuiper, Volman, & Terwel, 2005). However, students typically don't question the reliability or accuracy of information and tend to make immediate decisions about information based on visual appearance and graphical elements, such as font sizes and styles. Students often lack systematic approaches for working with information sources.

CORE CHALLENGES OF LOCATING USEFUL AND CREDIBLE RESOURCES FOR STUDENTS AND TEACHERS

Finding credible, informative resources at appropriate reading levels is a challenge for both teachers and students. Teachers often try to manage this challenging and time-consuming process by finding resources for students or by sitting one-on-one with students to interpret and translate information into vocabulary they understand. Yet, trying to do this as each student pursues a different facet of a research topic is difficult. Rindi wanted to manage this challenge by helping students develop strategies for finding resources at their reading comprehension level, strategies for finding "student-friendly" material, and strategies for quickly checking to see that a source is trustworthy in the context of their research.

She believed that even her elementary age students could learn more systematic approaches. In fact, she believed it was especially important for young students to learn not only how to access information but also to learn strategies for critically evaluating information. "Do I trust this source? Can I understand this on my own? Can I use this source? Is this source what I am looking for?" These are questions she wanted her students to ask themselves repeatedly as they perused potential resources. Armed with effective strategies to guide their decision-making, she thought her students would be more likely to answer these kinds of questions in ways that helped them become more effective and efficient readers and researchers.

This chapter investigates what happened when Rindi and her fourth grade students (nine and ten year-old children) collaboratively developed a research resource guide for locating reliable, readable, and useful information sources during a research project on rain forests and their inhabitants. Guided by research that points to strategic readers being able to evaluate sources of information by applying certain criteria and guiding questions as consistent reading practices (Burke, 2002; Duke, 2004), we see Rindi work with her students to collaboratively develop criteria and a research tool with guiding questions to help them discern useful and credible resources.

In particular, Rindi guided students to think more critically and carefully about information by consistently modeling ways to think about information sources and engaging students in classroom dialogue about different ways to view information. Using a variety of activities, she gave students opportunities for multiple and varied traversals across information sources, giving them repeated practice with questioning the reliability, readability, and utility of information.

AN INTERDISCIPLINARY UNIT ON RAINFOREST DESTRUCTION

To examine what this looked like in Rindi's classroom, we first provide an overview of Rindi's instruction during the interdisciplinary unit on rainforests and then provide specific examples of Rindi's students wrestling with the challenge of identifying reliable, readable, and useful sources during the unit. The students in her class included ten boys and eleven girls, nine to ten years of age with diverse ethnicity (nine Caucasian, four Indian, two Filipinos, one Korean, five multiethnic). Her students were fluent English speakers with a reading comprehension range of third through sixth grade. This unit provides a good example of science and social studies working in tandem to help students develop scientific and social understandings about the destruction of rainforests and the consequences of environmental degradation in ecological as well as human terms. Students learn about key scientific features of rainforest ecosystems, such as canopy structures, the diversity and interdependence of species, and the adaptations of plants and animals. Students also learn about the geographic locations of rainforests around the world, indigenous peoples living in rainforests, rainforest resources and the ways humans have exploited rainforest environments for particular resources, and the impact of human activity, such as slash and burn farming, mining, and logging, on rainforest habitats. In this interdisciplinary unit, students are able to develop more integrated and comprehensive understandings of the causes and consequences of deforestation and the loss of habitats, species, and cultures in rainforest regions.

Rindi started the unit by having students investigate rainforest resources, locations, and environmental issues. For example, she taught the concept of adaptation to help students understand the adaptation of plants and animals in the canopy structure of rainforests and then built on students' understandings of this concept to explore the ways humans and human cultures have adapted to rainforest environments. During the unit, Rindi planned three opportunities for students to do research. They first researched where rainforests were located and information about the layers of rainforests. They then studied the flora and fauna of rainforests as well as rainforest resources used by humans. The third area of research was an investigation into indigenous peoples and their relationship to rainforests as well as the impact of human activity on rainforests. Rindi designed several research activities that required students to discuss and deliberate about information sources they wanted to use in their research. She started the unit by raising students' awareness of misinformation on the Web and the need to be selective and discriminating users of information. She also had the technology specialist in her school conduct a session on effective web search strategies and Internet safety. After talking to students about how to locate reliable scientific resources, Rindi had students find articles about rainforest layers. She then asked them to organize the articles they found according to whether the article said there were three, four, or five layers. Within groups, students usually had at least two to three information sources that supported each of these positions on rainforest layers. This activity was conducted to demonstrate how people, including scientific experts, have different ideas about rainforest layers and to teach students the importance of finding corroborating sources to make sure information is valid.

A similar activity required her students to find websites that identified rainforest resources (e.g., as medicines, food, etc.). In-class she had students put the names of resources on sticky notes to see which resources were corroborated by more than one website. If a resource was corroborated by other information sources students wrote "credible" on the pile of sticky notes that demonstrated that the resource was commonly found in different sources. She then had students develop categories (such as medicines, household products, foods, and building materials) to organize the resources and use Inspiration software to make connections between various types of resources and their uses. This activity reinforced the idea of corroborating and verifying information and provides an example of multiple traversals and opportunities to practice informational strategies.

Rindi also read aloud *The Lorax*, by Dr. Seuss (1971) as a prompt for discussing issues related to deforestation. Students then located statistical information in other texts on rainforest destruction. Since the class had discussed how rainforest destruction is occurring at ever-escalating rates, one of the criteria she and her students decided to use to evaluate information for this activity was currency (whether the information was up-to-date). These are just a few of the activities Rindi used to help students think more carefully and critically about information as they learned both science and social studies subject matter. In these brief examples, we see research activities designed to emphasize the importance of evaluating and corroborating information rather than accepting it at face value.

ADDRESSING THE CHALLENGE OF LOCATING RELIABLE, READABLE, AND USEFUL INFORMATION SOURCES

Because Rindi wanted to more fully explore the challenges students face in evaluating sources of information for reliability, readability, and usefulness and how she might better support students in doing this work, she decided to investigate these issues as a teacher researcher. To get a sense of what students knew about research, Rindi used a Likert scale to determine students' assessment of their own skills in doing research before and after the research project. She also had students respond to list of questions about a bogus website that she created. Rindi's construction of this site about the orangutan's social habits, diet, and an organization trying to help protect the orangutan was based on a fictitious website on the Pacific Northwest Tree Octopus used by Alan November (http://zapatopi.net/treeoctopus/). November has compiled several websites that can be used to engage students in validating information (see http://novemberlearning.com/resources/information-literacy-resources/iii-websites-to-validate/). This activity asked students to evaluate whether the website was useful to help them answer specific research questions. The students were unaware that Rindi had created the site.

When developing the website, Rindi purposely used text she considered beyond her students' reading levels, added fictitious information (over-exaggerated and silly information), and removed any form of authorship from the site. She also made sure this fictitious site did not answer the research questions posed in the scenario and then gave the site a believable URL: www.savetheorangutan. She also attached the phrase *googlepages* to the URL, which could have been a clue about the site's authenticity.

Rindi asked her students to evaluate the site as a source to find out about orangutans' social habits and diet, and efforts to protect the orangutan. She prompted them to record reasons for either using or not using the site and to provide as much detail as possible in their explanation. Rindi scored students' responses using a rubric. Rindi found from the Likert scale and bogus website activity that students were not aware of specific research strategies and the use of language referring to the trustworthiness, readability, and usefulness of a resource was not evident in students' responses when they evaluated the orangutan website the first time.

To gain a deeper understanding of students' research skills, Rindi asked her students to share the strategies they used when seeking resources for research assignments. She made a list on the overhead of their responses

to the question, "How would you go about researching the topic of orangutans?" that included the following:

- Search on Google, using a key word: "orangutan." Copy and paste
  the information found into a word document.
- Ask the librarian or teachers for good books or resources on
  orangutans.
- Go to the research room in the library where all of the books for the
  unit have already been pulled off of the general shelves and put in one
  place for fourth graders to use. Hunt for pictures on the cover and/or
  titles about orangutans.
- Take notes; copy as much information as you can.
- Rewrite it into a report, poster, or make a PowerPoint show using the
  information found. Add nice color, font, and pictures to make it look
  nice.

In this particular conversation with students, not one comment had to do
with finding trustworthy, readable, or useful information that followed
a research plan. Although website layout, font style, and use of graphics
are important design elements often selected to assist readers in certain
ways, students did not comment on how design features influence their
decisions when searching for or processing information. Rather, the focus
was on finding information quickly and copying it into an attractive fin-
ished product.

Based on what Rindi learned from the Likert scale, students' responses
about the bogus website, and the research strategies they shared in class
discussion, Rindi decided to address these issues with a series of activities
that addressed trustworthiness, readability, and utility.

Developing Criteria for Trustworthiness

To explore students' abilities to assess a source's trustworthiness, Rindi
presented a photo depicting a giant tsunami wave at its crest before crashing onto a heavily populated beachfront. (See: http://www.snopes.com/
photos/tsunami/tsunami2.asp#photo.) Rindi led an open-ended discussion
that began with the question, "What do you notice in this photo?" Students participated in a lengthy discussion of whether or not they trusted the
photo, with comments initially supporting the photo's trustworthiness at
face value to students questioning its accuracy at the end of the discussion.
Here is a progression of their comments:

- Wow . . . that's the tsunami that happened a couple of years ago in
  Thailand. So many people are going to be killed on that beach.
- Why aren't the people running away?
- I wonder where the photographer was standing to get that picture.

- That wave is higher than the tallest buildings . . . I didn't know the wave was that big . . . is that possible? Wait . . . my dad told me that the wave was about seven stories high . . . this wave is higher than the building, which looks like it's about 25 stories high.
- Where did you get this photo, Mrs. Baildon? I never saw any like that before.
- Something doesn't look right at the top of this picture . . . the wave looks like it is crashing way out in the ocean . . . I thought it sucked the water out before it could make that huge wave.

Here, we see the value of building perspective as students deliberate over a particular text. Rindi's students began the discussion with almost complete acceptance of the image as authentic and gradually raised questions about its believability. Several students referred to their prior knowledge (e.g., what parents had told them; other images they had seen) and began to question its authenticity. The discussion continued with many students questioning if the photo was actually "real" by the end of the discussion.

This discussion created a good opportunity for Rindi to ask, "Why do you think I'm showing you this photo?" She asked students to explain how they determined whether or not they could trust sources of information and guided them to relate these ideas to the research process in general. At this point Rindi and her students listed important ideas related to trustworthiness to keep in mind when looking at different sources of information:

- Is there an author/photographer identified with the source?
- Do I recognize the author/creator?
- Does the URL seem official or real?
- Have I found this same information in other books or websites?
- Does my gut feeling tell me that what I am reading/seeing is trustworthy?
- Does this information fit with what I might already know about this subject?

These questions, in turn, served as criteria and guiding questions that the students and Rindi generated together to help the children determine the trustworthiness of a source.

Developing Criteria to Determine Readability

The next set of activities focused on the concept of readability. Three different leveled texts about rainforests were presented to students: below grade-level (numerous photos, easy text to read, minimal amount of information); at grade-level (text supported with pictures, text easy to read, some challenging vocabulary that could be figured out in context); and above grade-level (small print, difficult vocabulary not easy to figure out in context, encyclopedia-style format, no charts or photos to support text). Looking at one piece of literature at a time, Rindi asked her students to discuss in small groups the readability of each resource.

During a guided discussion with her class, Rindi posed questions about how they determine if information is readable. For example, when she asked students if they would use texts they considered below their reading level, such as a *Ranger Rick* magazine, many students did not think such texts should be used. Rindi offered a different perspective, pointing out that *Ranger Rick* or even picture books might be good sources of information (as long as it could be validated) that they could use in their research. With the challenging, above grade-level *Encyclopedia Britannica* entry, Rindi asked students to discuss if it was at their reading level and whether it would be a good use of their time to try to use this information. She posed a range of similar questions to let students discuss how they might identify readable information sources and used the electronic interactive whiteboard to allow students to collectively read and discuss different web-based texts. As a result of this whole class discussion, the students and Rindi jointly constructed a list of questions that centered on readability when considering sources of information:

- Can I can read and understand this on my own?
- Can I understand most of the words and not lose meaning if I have to skip words?
- Is it a "just right" read for me?
- Is the layout easy enough to follow?
- Can I stop and retell what I have just read in my own words?
- Are there pictures or charts that help me understand the text better?

Developing Criteria for Usefulness

To explore the concept of usefulness, Rindi led the class through an activity focusing on the importance of making a research plan before searching for information sources. Since Rindi's students had knowledge and experience working through the writing process, she helped them understand how developing a research plan was directly related to the first stage of "brainstorming ideas" and "making a story plan" before embarking on a first draft in writing. Using a graphic organizer in the form of a web, the class brainstormed possible questions that would go along with the topic of rainforest layers. In groups they came up with the following guiding questions:

- What are the layers of the rainforest?
- What animal and plant life can you find in each layer?
- What are the physical differences of each layer?
- Can you find the same plants and animals in some of the layers?
- What would happen if one of the layers was missing?

These questions point to the need for content specific questions to guide students' determinations of usability. As Green (1988) notes, not only are literacy acts and events "*context* specific [they] also "entail a specific *content*" (p. 160). The students came to value that once a researcher has a plan, such as the need to gain the above information, these questions then become the researcher's focus when looking for information in various sources. Referring back to the three texts used in the readability activities, the class discussed which source(s) would help them answer these questions or which resource(s) would be *useful* in their quest for specific information. Based on this activity, Rindi and her students came up with the following questions to ask themselves as they searched resources for information that would help them with their research:

- Does this resource have what I am looking for?
- Does it follow my research plan?
- Do I need it?
- Is this worthwhile, or am I wasting my time on this resource?

Developing the "Research Resource Guide"

As a culminating activity and to be certain students were asking the "right questions" to make determinations of readability, trustworthiness, and usability, Rindi and her class synthesized the ideas they had developed in the previous activities into one "Research Resource Guide" that students agreed to use each and every time they considered using an information source.

At this point, students chose topics on the rainforest that they would spend the next two weeks researching individually using their newly created "Research Resource Guide" and numerous resources from the library, classroom, and computer labs. These information sources included websites and print resources, such as encyclopedia, magazines, and books.

Initially students utilized this guide sheet with frequent teacher reminders. Gradually the guide became an integral part of the research process, with students reading through the list more consistently as they considered an information source. By the end of the week, however, the sheets were tucked away, replaced by a research note-taking sheet with R-T-U (Readable-Trustworthy-Useful) headings to help students make decisions on their own about which resources to tap into. Students made use of this softer scaffolding by recording their ideas about readability, trustworthiness, and usability.

MANAGING THE CHALLENGE OF LOCATING RELIABLE, READABLE, AND USEFUL INFORMATION SOURCES

After the students completed their research projects, Rindi asked students to again review the bogus website she had created. When they reviewed

Research Resource Guide-Sheet

When deciding to use a resource for your research project, ask yourself the following questions:

Readable:

- Is this a "just right" resource for me?
- Can I understand the information on my own, or with a little help?
- Is it "kid-friendly?"

Trustworthy:

- Can I find an author or a publisher name?
- Do I recognize the resource? (URL, publisher, author, name, etc.)
- Is the information current? What is the © date?
- Can I find at least one other source with the same information?

Useful:

- Does this resource have what I am looking for?
- Does it follow my research plan?
- Do I need it?

Figure 4.1   Research Resource Guide.

the website this time, they had significantly different responses in their approaches to their research. Students were much more likely to analyze the website according to basic trustworthiness, readability, and usefulness criteria after using the "Research Resource Guide" during their research project on rainforests. Students' improved ability to determine the trustworthiness, readability, and usability of resources is evident in their written responses on the R-T-U note-taking sheet and in their reevaluation of the bogus website on orangutans. On both the R-T-U sheet and the bogus website evaluation, students made decisions by referring to notions of readability, usefulness, and trustworthiness.

Determining Trustworthiness

Determinations of reliability were evident when students conducted their research. During class discussions about their research, students were encouraged to verify facts by finding other sources that provided similar information. On their R-T-U sheets, students identified sources as trustworthy if they had "found the same info twice," confirmed the information was "up-to-date," or "trust[ed] the creator of the web site."

Examples of students' determinations of trustworthiness about the bogus website the second time included:

- "I cannot find where they got the information."
- "[T]his site is about 14 years old ... I would use newer information."
- "The address is really short; it's hard to be able to tell if it's a learning website, 'cause a lot of them that have "org" in them, and it also has "google pages" in the URL. All the websites I've found on Google don't have the word "google" in them at all ... Since the trustworthiness is kind of iffy, I'd have to find the information on another website."
- "I don't think [the site] is trustworthy because it does not tell you who wrote the website."

Students were surprised that they had been "fooled" the first time by the website Rindi created. This led to a class discussion about how anyone can put up a website and the importance of carefully considering whether information could be trusted.

Determining Readability

On the R-T-U sheets students also noted evidence of readability if they used the resource and often recorded that the source was "kid-friendly," "easy to read," or "has information I understand." At the beginning of their research, every student identified encyclopedias as good research resources because "they have lots of information." However, only three students listed encyclopedias as sources on their R-T-U sheets and students noted in discussion that encyclopedia entries weren't easy for them to understand. During the research project, Rindi saw few students using the encyclopedia.

Information sources at lower reading levels, such as *Zoobooks* magazines, were initially deemed by students not to be good resources, but in class discussion students acknowledged that lower-level reading materials could contain valuable information and help validate information from other sources.

For websites, students used a "five-finger test" they learned in-class. Generally, if students could read the site for a few minutes without coming across five comprehension problems, like difficult vocabulary, they considered it a readable source. Rindi also noticed that students commented on the layout of websites. Students noted websites looked "kid-friendly," "easy to read," or "easy to navigate." Students didn't ask for teacher help as often when using sources at a suitable reading level.

Students also provided reasons to reject some information sources, as the following sample of responses demonstrates:

- "[M]any of the words were too complicated to understand."
- "Sentences were too long and difficult to read."
- "I don't think it is kid friendly or readable because I can't read or understand the words."
- "I would rather find a trustworthy, readable, and useful website to find better information about orangutans. And if you were a kid and you used this website you'll be hanging on the dictionary like forever to find all the difficult words that you really don't understand."
- "I can't coax a meaning out, even using the context."

These comments indicate a range of decisions students made to reject sources based on vocabulary, sentence length, and degree of text difficulty.

Determining Usefulness

Students' research plans and guiding questions helped them make determinations of usefulness. Students quickly abandoned sources that didn't help them answer their questions. On their R-T-U sheets, some students commented, "this helps me answer my question[s]," "this tells me about . . . " and "this [source] gives me info I'm looking for."

Sample student responses referring to the usefulness of the fake website included:

- "[A]lthough it has tons of information it doesn't tell the orangutan's social habits, diet, or anything about an organization trying to protect them."
- "It doesn't have the info that I need. So it doesn't fit the U for usefulness or R-T-U (readable, trustworthy and useful)."

Summary

Rindi's observations and anecdotal records also indicate greater student independence in their research and the use of collaboratively developed strategies to determine trustworthiness, readability, and usefulness. It was interesting to note the progression of the use of the "Research Resource Guide." Initially students only used this guide sheet with frequent teacher reminders. Gradually this sheet became an integral part of the research process, with students reading through the list more consistently to consider resources. Eventually, students used the research note-taking sheet, with its simple reminder of R-T-U to help them make decisions on their own about which resources to use. Students were able to make use of this softer scaffolding to record their ideas because they had become more practiced in using the questions from the guide sheet.

Students' final research reports on rainforests provided further evidence of student learning. Not only were the reports consistently written in the students' own words, but the reports were on the whole well-organized and closely followed their research plans. Furthermore, a closer look at the resources students utilized provided a clear indication that they chose material more at their reading level, and in the case of citing website URLs, picked sites that were more familiar and "kid friendly."

CLASSROOMS AS SITES OF COLLECTIVE INQUIRY

In this chapter we see a teacher carefully planning and skillfully guiding her students in an interdisciplinary unit to investigate a complex multifaceted problem, the destruction of tropical rainforests. Rindi designed several research activities for multiple traversals into different facets of rainforest destruction from both science and social studies perspectives. She also paid particular attention to epistemological challenge two, addressing the problem of locating reliable and useful information sources. Multiple traversals of content included the use of key concepts, such as adaptation, that could be employed to study both rainforest habitats and human cultures, the use of literature to explore both the scientific and social dimensions of rainforest destruction, and several research activities that required them to learn more about rainforests and the consequences of human activity for rainforest habitats and human cultures.

The destruction of rainforests is both a social and environmental problem that cuts across national and disciplinary boundaries. For the unit, Rindi wanted students to understand important interrelationships between social studies and science subject matter— both subjects are necessary to more fully understand the issue of rainforest destruction because of the fundamental interrelationships humans have with their environment. She wanted students to understand how humans cause environmental destruction as well as the impact rainforest destruction is having on human societies. Interdisciplinary investigation allowed Rindi and her students to better understand these interrelationships as well as different facets of the problem.

Understanding complex human-nature interrelationships and the ecological crisis, of which rainforest destruction is but one manifestation, requires sifting through mounds of data, information and misinformation, and a range of claims and evidence. Our understandings and the solutions or actions we decide to take to address such multifaceted issues require that we manage the challenge of discerning useful and credible information so that informed action is possible. Rindi recognized this challenge as a fundamental challenge citizens face in the global society and designed lessons and activities that would help students develop and practice strategies to manage this challenge.

In each of the activities, we see Rindi and her students working as a collaborative knowledge-building community as they explored content and discussed and developed appropriate criteria for carefully thinking about information sources. Together, they used these criteria to develop a tool, the "Research Resource Guide" that could guide their work with information sources during their investigations. This collaborative work around the challenge of discerning useful and credible information helped build the strategic knowledge necessary for selecting sources of information (Duke, 2004; Leu & Kinzer, 2000) and parallels work done in disciplinary and interdisciplinary communities. In these collaborative knowledge-building communities, shared criteria are developed collectively through ongoing dialogue and deliberation and used to monitor and self-regulate decision-making processes during inquiry (Lamont, 2009).

Learning to ask questions repeatedly and deliberately about information (Burke, 2002) and developing criteria through dialogue and deliberation to guide decision-making processes are not only important literacy and inquiry strategies, they are important forms of public reasoning. By facilitating ongoing class discussion about the reliability, readability, and utility of information sources, Rindi was helping students engage in public deliberation about a significant epistemological challenge. Her students were also learning to collectively develop shared standards and procedures for their work. In this sense, we see Rindi and her students enacting practices of *relational cosmopolitanism*. She and her students were participating in a "community of reason" (Nussbaum, 1997) to collaboratively develop criteria and standards to guide their work together. The criteria and tool ("Research Resource Guide") that she and her students developed became focal points for public reasoning in her classroom and as students considered different sources of information encountered in their investigations. Rindi's questioning sought to connect with students' prior knowledge and experiences and she saw her students' diversity as an asset for building perspective about the reliability, readability, and utility of information. Through activities that required dialogue and deliberation about information sources and subject matter, students explored the problems of rainforest destruction and discerning useful and credible information sources critically, variously, and publicly (Doll, 1993).

The urgent problem of protecting the Earth is one of the most important tasks facing global citizens (Noddings, 2005). It requires students and teachers to develop important connections to subject matter and each other in ways that foster care and concern for the planet. Engaging students in important conversations and shared inquiries to develop understandings about problems related to the survival of species on the Earth is a vital first step toward developing shared understandings and commitments about a global problem that requires collective action.

There is a need for continuing dialogue with students of every age about the appropriateness of sources, making good information choices, and making sense of information as they engage in the research process. All students benefit from rich conversations about informational texts and opportunities for input into developing key criteria and guiding questions and even the development and use of literacy tools, such as the research guide. It is through teachers planning for and guiding such questioning, dialogue, and deliberation in classroom communities of practice that they not only learn to become better readers and researchers but learn a method of intelligence that can help them become effective citizens in new global landscapes.

5 Examining the Claims and Credibility of a Complicated Multimodal Web-based Text

This chapter examines how a group of Mark's ninth grade students grappled with our third epistemological challenge– evaluating resources, especially the credibility, claims, and evidence of multimodal texts. In particular, we examine the challenges students had in evaluating the claims and credibility of a controversial Internet video, *Loose Change 9/11*, a well-documented and comprehensive multimedia account that argues the "real story" of September 11, 2001 was covered up by the United States government. Evaluating claims and determining the credibility of multimodal texts, especially on/within the Internet with its "vast network of relations of credibility" (Burbules & Callister, 2000) and ever-expanding reach and impact across the globe, is particularly challenging because these texts mix images, music, graphic arts, video, and print to make sophisticated claims supported by various forms or types of evidence. The challenges are compounded when the text deals with a complicated sociopolitical event.

We begin this chapter describing some of the challenges with evaluating claims and discerning credibility in the Internet age. We then consider a core *elevation practice*, taking into account the broader contexts of production and reception of *Loose Change 9/11* as a multimodal text. We then step into the high school classroom to highlight the range of *excavation* and *elevation* practices students mobilized to "read" this video and the challenges they experienced evaluating the video as a multimodal text.

CHALLENGES OF DETERMINING THE CLAIMS AND CREDIBILITY OF INTERNET SOURCES

Discerning the credibility of information sources requires being able to critically analyze when, where, why, and how texts were produced, whether claims are logical and supported with valid evidence, and author(s) qualifications and reliability in terms of the claims being made. It requires corroborating information by checking into facts, comparing different accounts, and further investigating inconsistencies or discrepancies between differing accounts (Baildon & Damico, 2006). This is challenging work for adults as well as young people.

We believe this work is even more challenging in the complex ecology of networked information because information, ideas, and texts can be linked to other information, ideas, and texts in multiple ways (Burbules & Callister, 2000). Coiro and Dobler (2007) argue that Internet texts offer an overwhelming array of possibilities for intertextual connections and "are often intermingled with hidden social, economic, and political agendas" (p. 42). Because of the relative ease of creating and disseminating digital texts on the Web, the lack of a vetting process for many of these postings, and the fact that the authorship of Internet texts as well as authors' credentials are sometimes hard to determine, it is difficult to source and contextualize texts by examining authors' purposes, biases, and perspectives or their social, cultural, and political positions.

Adding to this complexity are digital multimodal texts which possess combinations of linguistic, gestural, aural, visual, and spatial modes through a mix of images, music and other sounds, graphic art, video, and print. The modes and multiple texts in any one multimodal text dynamically interact within the text to produce complex claims, and they can reference other information and texts in a multitude of ways to further complicate the assessment of claims and credibility.

Moreover, each of the types of texts used in the construction of a multimodal text may connect to students' prior knowledge and experiences in different ways and require students to draw on a range of symbolic resources and strategies. The multiple texts used may need to be analyzed individually as well as considered together to determine their effects and credibility. In making "modality judgments" (Hodge & Kress, 1988), people draw on their knowledge of contexts, uses of media, textual representations, and modes of communication to evaluate the plausibility of claims made in a specific text.

THE IMPORTANCE OF ELEVATION: UNDERSTANDING THE CONTEXTS OF PRODUCTION AND RECEPTION OF LOOSE CHANGE

Identifying and evaluating claims and assessing the credibility of web sources of information, then, requires having enough background knowledge to contextualize information and authorship and being able to read intertextually across assorted texts and modalities to corroborate claims and evidence. These are core *elevation practices*. Understanding texts (and the past) depends on the active process of weaving together or connecting things into meaningful patterns. This process of contextualization involves understanding temporal and spatial contexts as well the *Zeitgeist*, or climate of opinion in a certain time and place, and considering the ways they shape both the production and reception of specific texts (Wineburg, 2001).

Similarly, Fairclough (1989) argues that texts, social practices, and contexts are bound up in ideology, or the "common sense assumptions" that are implicit in the conventions that govern people's interactions (often with people not consciously aware of these conventions). Thus, to understand any text and, more specifically, to investigate the ways readers make meaning of the multimodal text, *Loose Change 9/11*, it is essential to consider some of the social, historical, and political contexts and discourses that shaped both its production and reception.

The website for *Loose Change 9/11*, http://www.loosechange911.com/, highlights some contexts the authors of the online video use to frame the video's production and reception:

> [This] independent documentary has grown from a cult following to a grassroots organism that can no longer be contained. The central premise of *Loose Change* is that the United States Government was, at the very least, criminally negligent in allowing the attacks of September 11th, 2001 to occur. However, when one looks deeper into the evidence, one might come to the startling conclusion that our own government might have been directly responsible for the attacks themselves. *Loose Change* merely scratches the surface of information that points to a massive government cover-up regarding 9/11. We highly encourage you to take it upon yourself to research the events of 9/11 for yourself and come to your own conclusions. *Loose Change* is currently in two editions, with a third being developed for American theaters, intended to be released in 2007.

The video, first posted on the Web in April 2005, is one hour and 22 minutes long, written, directed, and narrated by Dylan Avery, produced by Korey Rowe, and based on research by Jason Bermas. All three are from Oneonta, New York, in their early 20's, and produced the video for $6,000 using a laptop computer (Sales, 2006). With its low production costs and relative ease of its distribution, *Loose Change 9/11* is clearly a product of a decentralized "networked information economy" rather than the industrial economy with its more rigid controls of the means of production and distribution (Benkler, 2006).

The movie consists of Avery narrating over still photographs, news footage, computer-generated simulations, diagrams, models, and other sources relating to 9/11, with an underscore of hip-hop and urban style audio tracks. The film includes considerable video content from CNN, NBC, and FOX News as well as a number of interviews with eyewitnesses and "experts." A range of historical, scientific, mathematical, and documentary evidence is marshaled to support the main claims of the film, which basically consist of the following assertions: 1. Individuals within the US government or with strong links to government officials (i.e., neocons, members of The Project for the New American Century) knew of the impending attacks and did nothing to stop them since they would serve as a catalyst for military buildup and imperial expansion; 2. The collapse of the World Trade Center buildings was not due to the airplane crashes but was the result of explosives planted in the building; 3. A commercial airliner did not crash into the Pentagon; 4. The public has been misled about what really happened to the plane that crashed in rural Pennsylvania; and 5. The US government has misled, misinformed, and kept information from the American public about 9/11.

Effectively combining multiple modalities, the creators string together a range of claims and evidence to present a compelling narrative that challenges viewers to question what they know about 9/11, specifically about government and media accounts of what transpired on 9/11. As Avery noted in a *Vanity Fair* interview, "You have to be a skeptic . . . You can't believe anything someone tells you just because they told you to. Especially your government, and especially your media—the two institutions that are put there to control you. And you're going to tell me you're going to take their word for everything? I don't think so" (Sales, 2006).

The 911 Truth Movement and *Loose Change* as a Conspiracy Theory Text

Loose Change 9/11 has become an integral part the 911 Truth Movement, which consists of a number of websites (e.g., http://www.911truth.org/; http://www.911truthmovement.org/), books (e.g., *The New Pearl Harbor; 911 The Big Lie*), and films (e.g., *9/11: Press for Truth*) that challenge mainstream accounts of the attacks. It has generated a great deal of response in the alternative press (e.g., www.alternet.org), spawned a group of people calling themselves "Scholars for 9/11 Truth," and led to the peer-reviewed online *Journal of 911 Studies* (http://www.journalof911studies.com/). Various people in the movement usually point to evidence that neoconservatives since Reagan have had grand imperial designs, have willfully misled, misinformed, and lied to the American public by skillfully using the media and effective public relations tactics, and point to the body of evidence that should have warned the intelligence community and the Bush administration of the attacks. As the 911Truth.Org site notes, the mission of the movement is "to expose the official lies and cover-up surrounding the events of September 11th, 2001 in a way that inspires the people to overcome denial and understand the truth; namely, that elements within the US government and covert policy apparatus must have orchestrated or participated in the execution of the attacks for these to have happened in the way that they did" (http://www.911truth.org).

Because *Loose Change 9/11,* along with other texts of the 911 Truth Movement, aims to illumine the ways the United States government "conspired" against the American people, it can be viewed as a conspiracy theory text, defined by Allen (2006) as "hypotheses [that] often consist of a vast pile of circumstantial evidence shaped into a seemingly coherent whole with the strong glue of faith" (n.p.). Conspiracy theories produce "heroic strivings for evidence to prove that the unbelievable is the only thing that can be believed" (Hofstadter, 1964, n.p.), thus, even if a reader is able to "debunk one or even many allegations . . . the pile still stands, impressive in its bulk and ideological coherence" (n.p). Conspiracy theories remain alluring, as Allen (2006) describes:

> There is something comforting about a world where someone is in charge– either for good (think gods) or evil (think Bush insiders plotting 9/11). Many people prefer to believe a Procrustean conspiracy rather than accept the alternative: Life can be random, viciously unjust, and meaningless; tragedy and joy alike flow from complex combinations of good and bad intentions, careful plotting, random happenstance and bumbling incompetence. (n.p)

Americans seem particularly invested in conspiracy theories. There is a long American tradition of expressing popular discontent as sinister conspiracies (Hofstadter, 1964). Regarding the events of 9/11, over 40% of Americans now think there was a government cover-up (Zogby News, http://www.zogby.com/search/ReadNews.dbm?ID=855). The public's willingness to believe in 9/11 conspiracies has even been spoofed in a *South Park* episode (Stone & Parker, 2006) in which Kyle proves that the 9/11 conspiracy theories are actually the result of a government conspiracy to create a conspiracy because they want people to think the government is in control of everything. A whole industry around 9/11 conspiracy theories seems to have developed since 9/11, leading President George Bush to note in a speech to the General Assembly of the United Nations, "Let us never tolerate outrageous conspiracy theories concerning the attacks of September 11" (Sales, 2006). It has also generated efforts to identify erroneous evidence and faulty claims and generally debunk 9/11 conspiracy theories (e.g., the book, *Debunking 9/11 Myths*). Specific sites to debunk *Loose Change* provide point-by-point critiques (e.g., www.911research.wtc7.net; http://screwloosechange.blogspot.com/).

Understanding *Loose Change* as a conspiracy theory text is an *elevation practice*. Attention to conspiracy theory aligns with the need to investigate the cultural mediation of information, especially new media accounts (Nixon, 2003). A consideration of a text's production and reception helps to identify certain social forces and systems of ideas that shape dominant narratives and ways of making meaning that have currency in the larger society. Because conspiracy theory can be understood as a particular genre, discourse, or style evident in *Loose Change 9/11*, it is important to situate this text in broader social contexts.

SETTING THE STAGE FOR READING LOOSE CHANGE 9/11 IN A CLASSROOM

The 32 students who viewed and responded to *Loose Change 9/11* were members of two of Mark's ninth grade Humanities (combined social studies and language arts) classes in an international school in Taiwan with a predominately Asian-American student population of 2,200 K–12 students. There is a strong college preparatory focus at the school with the expectation that students will do well on Advanced Placement (AP), International Baccalaureate (IB), and SAT tests and gain admittance to top universities in the United States and other places around the world.

The Asian Studies curriculum that makes up the ninth grade Humanities program is an interdisciplinary curriculum comprised of five units of study: Geography and Identity; Beliefs and Values; Conflict and Change; Contemporary Asian Challenges; and an experiential learning unit based on trips to nearby Asian countries. Each unit is designed using the Understanding by Design framework (Wiggins & McTighe, 1998) and throughout the curriculum there is an emphasis on students identifying and evaluating claims and evidence in a range of texts (e.g., websites, primary sources, literature, visual texts, etc.) as well as having students make their own claims (in writing and other textual formats) supported with evidence, sound reasoning, and elaboration.

The Humanities curriculum allowed Mark to engage students in a range of classroom activities that focused on collaborative meaning-making with texts and subject matter. During the Geography and Identity unit, for example, students were encouraged to become anthropologists and social researchers to observe and write about different aspects of daily life in the surrounding community. Based on the theme, "Old World meets New Economy," students visited local spaces to record, through writing and digital photography, the sights, sounds, and smells of a traditional and modern social spaces. Students compared and contrasted a traditional Chinese medicine shop and a modern pharmacy, a park where people practiced Tai Chi and a modern gym like California Fitness, or a traditional tea shop and a Starbucks. Working in pairs, they compiled their writings and photographs into a web page that portrayed how these two places represented the traditional and modern ways of life in the community.

During the Beliefs and Values unit, students analyzed and interpreted different religious symbols and icons for Taoism, Buddhism, Hinduism, and Islam. After studying the histories, beliefs and values, and religious practices of these religions, they then worked in groups to create movies by combining narration with representative music and images to highlight core beliefs and values of their assigned religion.

In the Contemporary Asian Challenges unit or "research unit," students were taught an array of inquiry skills and strategies to investigate a range of complex issues in Asia. Topics typically focused on environmental issues, human rights concerns, regional conflicts and war, economic issues, such as poverty, and social issues, such as child labor and prostitution. Students were allowed to look at these issues across different Asian nations or within a particular nation. Working either individually, as partners, or in collaborative research teams, students conducted research on their selected topics using web and print resources and students had choices about investigative questions they wanted to pursue, the types of information sources they would utilize, and the ways they would share their findings. The Humanities teaching team wanted to honor students' choices and believed their active participation in the planning and development of their investigations would provide greater ownership and engagement in their learning. Some of the choices students made to share their findings included an NGO mailer highlighting the particular issue, an interpretive dance performance (that used mixed media to portray the SARS crisis in one Asian society), websites, magazine formats, artwork, and video. For the unit, the Humanities team prepared an inquiry guide to help students develop their investigative questions, locate good information sources, and utilize good research strategies. The teachers used and modified the *Critical Web Reader* (*CWR*) lenses to guide students as they worked with the information sources they located. The "Academic" lens guided them to draw upon prior knowledge and to examine claims and evidence in a source, the "Critical" lens scaffolded students in evaluating how authors attempted to influence them, and a synthesizing lens asked them to look across the various claims they had found to develop their own claims.

In sum, the curriculum and the pedagogy Mark enacted in his classroom valued inquiry-based learning, the deep analysis of issues and a range of texts, exploring multiple perspectives, and the collaborative sense making and production of knowledge in a community of learning. Students were well-practiced in critically analyzing and evaluating a range of texts, such as literature (e.g., *The Good Earth* by Pearl Buck), religious symbols and icons, local sites (spaces as texts), and websites for their research. Systematic approaches for deliberating and discussing certain texts, questions, and issues were used throughout the school year in a range of learning activities, such as seminars, simulations, and debates as well as opportunities for students to create products and performances of learning.

The ninth grade students viewed *Loose Change 9/11* on the last regularly scheduled class of the 2005–2006 school year. Mark was initially reluctant to view *Loose Change 9/11* after first finding out about it from his fifteen-year-old son. Mark was aware of some of the conspiracy theories circulating about 9/11 and usually quickly dismissed them. It wasn't until he received the following e-mail from one of his students that he finally decided to view the video: "hey doctor b. look what i found on google video! http://video.google.com/videoplay?docid=-8260059923762628848. I think it's pretty convincing!" Because the video did seem to make convincing claims and raised issues of credibility in the age of video, photo, and information doctoring, manipulation, and spin, conspiracy plots, fear and distrust, information and data overload, skepticism toward truth claims, and the willingness of people to believe almost anything, Mark decided to share the video with his students to see how they made sense of it and specifically how they would determine whether it was credible or not. Mark identified *Loose Change 9/11* as a "teachable text" (Schweber, 2010) that offered an opportunity for a seminar discussion in which participants plumb for meaning (Parker, 2006), in this case through an investigation of claims and credibility of a complicated text.

Using the Understanding by Design framework (Wiggins & McTighe, 1998), Mark identified two "desired results" or "enduring understandings" that guided his pedagogical approach with the video: 1. Evaluating claims (and evidence) and credibility with multimodal texts, such as *Loose Change 9/11*, requires careful and critical analysis of specific components of the video as well as how these component parts are combined to create meaning; and 2. This careful and critical analysis is best done in a community of inquiry where different perspectives and meanings can be shared and developed.

These desired results led Mark to develop four "essential questions" to guide the classroom activity with the video:

- What is believable about this text?
- What isn't?
- How do you know?
- What might make the text more or less believable?

Mark framed the in-class viewing of the video by noting that his son and another student had brought the video to his attention, that he found it challenging to analyze for a number of reasons, and that he wanted to see how they might make sense of it. He shared the four questions with his class as a handout with a place for students to record their thoughts and told students that after watching the video they would have time to write out their responses to the questions as preparation for class discussion. During the class discussion, Mark provided students an open forum to share their views about the video. Because the curriculum and Mark's classroom practice had provided repeated opportunities for collective meaning-making with a range of texts as well as opportunities to discuss various social studies issues through simulations, seminars, and other learning experiences, students were able to sustain a rather lively discussion about the video with very little prompting from Mark.

Wanting to better understand students' reasoning about the video, Mark collected evidence that included his field notes (a "running record" of what transpired during the class discussion as well as his reflections during and after the class), an audio and video tape of the class discussion with parts transcribed, and students' written responses to the four questions noted above. These pedagogical goals led to a primary research question: How do students think about and evaluate credibility in this multimodal text (*Loose Change 9/11*)?

STUDENTS DETERMINE CREDIBILITY
IN LOOSE CHANGE 9/11

Looking closely at the classroom discussion, students' written responses to the questions posed, and Mark's notes surfaced three sets of intersecting challenges that the students experienced with *Loose Change 9/11*: 1. Accessing prior knowledge *and* identifying gaps in their own understandings; 2. Determining the reliability and strength of evidence *and* acknowledging being "overwhelmed" with the information; and 3. Considering internal and external credibility. Cutting across these issues was a key finding—the significant role images played in students' determinations of credibility.

Accessing Prior Knowledge and Identifying Gaps

When Mark asked his students to explain, "How do you know (the video is believable or not)?" students referred to their prior knowledge by noting the general climate of distrust surrounding the Bush administration, a distrust that many students shared. They also discussed how they had seen "similar video clips on the news" and that they had "similar thoughts" about what had happened during the 9/11 attacks. In general, a majority of students felt that many aspects of the film "fit" with what they already knew or what they had heard about 9/11.

Others noted that although much of the evidence used in the movie is available to the public, their own lack of knowledge was a factor that interfered in deciding whether or not the video was believable. One student said she didn't understand the references made at the beginning of the movie to Cuba (the proposed plan during the Cuban Missile Crisis in 1962 to stage fake terrorist attacks as a pretext for invading Cuba). Another student stated, "this clip seems very believable, maybe because of our lack of knowledge . . . it is easier to believe." Students also noted that although much of the scientific and historical material presented in the film gave the video an air of authority, it was information they were unable to adequately assess and this interfered with their ability to determine the credibility of information in the video. Some students also noted a lack of background knowledge that would enable them to detect counterfeit documents and artifacts used to support assertions in the movie and resolve conflicting interpretations of evidence, such as those presented by the United States government and the maker of the video.

Determining Reliability of Evidence and Acknowledging Being Overwhelmed

In response to the question "What is believable about this text?" Mark's students referred to the different types of evidence they encountered. Most students noted the variety of sources used to support assertions, such as video clips, news articles, photos, quotes, and three-dimensional models, which led them to conclude that these multimodal forms provided "strong" evidence and good detail and description that made claims believable. Some students specified certain multimodal qualities such as the narrator's tone and "firm voice," interviews with experts, and detailed visual models and explanations using scientific evidence or "scientific proof." The sheer amount of evidence also shaped discernments of credibility. The cumulative effect of these multiple representations and high quantity of information ("the heroic striving for evidence" suggested by Hofstadter) led to favorable assessments of credibility from students.

Students did question the reliability of specific types of evidence, such as the eyewitness accounts and bystander testimony used throughout the video. One student noted, "people saw different things that hit the Pentagon. Some said it was a helicopter, small jet, an airplane. It is hard to believe what it actually was" while others commented, "the people that were there and saw it said different things," there "were too many different views," and "eyewitness reports could be very wrong." During the discussion, one student pointed out that "during panicky times, your memory isn't reliable." Students seemed to discredit eyewitness testimony because they produced differing accounts, including reports that could be inaccurate.

While students deemed much of the evidence used to support the authors' assertions to be "strong," many students also expressed feeling "overwhelmed" by the "tons of information" used in the video. Because the genres, claims, and types of evidence overlapped and intersected in myriad ways, yielding a somewhat disorienting cumulative effect, it was challenging to read and evaluate the video. Students spoke specifically about grappling with the multitude of images of print documents, video footage, animation, interviews, photo images, reconstructions, sound effects, charts and graphs, and mathematical equations—all used as evidence for assertions.

Internal and External Credibility

Students struggled in assessing internal and external aspects of credibility. They tried to determine the credibility of evidence used within the video to support claims and evaluate the video's internal logic (whether linear or spatial). Most students acknowledged how persuasive the video was, yet several problematized how many of the news articles and documents presented as evidence were other web sources of information (i.e., how the Web works as a "self-sustaining reference system" (Burbules, 2001)); these students believed this made the claims and evidence less credible. In other words, some students deemed the intertextual references provided within the video and on the website to be insufficient for helping them evaluate information in the video. While there were some students who raised these kinds of concerns about internal credibility, most students believed the cumulative effect of the multiple representations supported the internal consistency of the video. Generally, most students thought the video was well-produced and effectively combined different modalities to create a compelling narrative.

In terms of external criteria for assessing credibility, students considered issues of authorship to evaluate the video. Students wanted to know about the experiences or qualifications of the creators of the video. One student commented, "These guys are like, what, students? And they sure bent over backwards to find all this info and they sure knew what they were looking for." Other comments from students included: "we don't know if the creator is credible," "the creator may only show one side of the story," "there are gaps he leaves unfilled," and "I have no idea who the narrator is (I need background information)." Another student noted, "The author makes claims and he sounds like some sort of expert even though he most likely isn't. A lot of his claims about the crash into the Pentagon could be bad physics." Others noted that the creators were obviously biased. A concern that the movie was not released in theaters also surfaced. One student commented, "It's just a Google video" while another thought the video would be more believable if it "was published."

Students' knowledge of the larger contexts surrounding 9/11 also served as evaluative criteria for many claims and evidence in the video. Most students were already familiar with many basic claims made in the movie—that the US government covered up certain facts about what happened, that the Bush administration had information about the impending attacks, that the World Trade Center towers were brought down by controlled demolition explosions, and that military buildup and the war on terror have benefited some Americans financially and politically. However, students also referred to what was absent—counter arguments, contradictory evidence, and other theories and claims about what happened. The lack of alternative intertextual referents remained a concern as several students indicated that they wanted to see more perspectives or hear different stories about what happened. They wanted to know more about other theories and claims made about the 9/11 attacks. For example, during the class discussion, one student noted that claims weren't consistent with what he had seen on the Discovery Channel about the collapse of the buildings. He also added that people are often too willing to accept conspiracy theories when they don't understand something. To support his point he cited examples of other conspiracy theories, such as the moon landings and the story that alternative energy source cars have been blocked by the auto and oil industries.

Power of the Visual

Students generally placed their greatest trust in images, such as photos, diagrams, models, and video clips. In terms of reliability, visual representations had greater currency than explanations (e.g., from eyewitness accounts or interviews) or print materials that were presented as evidence. One student noted, "The pictures proving the evidence makes it very believable," while another added, "diagrams make it believable." Referring to the video and photo clips used in the movie, one student noted, "The clips have genuine traits that when you see it you know it is real." Another added that visual comparisons made the video believable: "e.g., this is what a normal plane crash should look like, this is what the scene at the Pentagon looked like" while another student argued that "more pictures from 'different' angles" would support some claims and make the video more believable.

Like eyewitness accounts, video and photo representations claim a direct connection to events. However, students didn't question whether images had been taken out of context and rearranged in new combinations to produce "reality" (Lasch, 1984). Several students wanted corroborating evidence or explanation to support eyewitness accounts but seldom challenged visual evidence. This supports Kress' (2003) notions about print being supplanted by images in the new media age and the corresponding need for greater attention to issues of visual literacy as a core component of multimodal literacy education.

EXCAVATION, ELEVATION, AND THE NEED FOR DIALECTICAL TACKING

Overall, we believe students in this ninth grade classroom did some important work in evaluating the credibility of *Loose Change 9/11*. However, multimodal texts like *Loose Change 9/11* complicate discernments of credibility in two ways: 1. There is a dynamic intertextuality among the different modes and texts within the video; and 2. There is intertextuality between the video as a whole and other texts and discourses (existing outside of the video text). The metaphors of excavation, elevation, and dialectical tacking are useful for thinking about ways to manage these challenges.

Excavation Practices

To more effectively analyze the dynamic intertextuality of different modes and texts within a video, students may first have to critically analyze and evaluate information provided by individual modes and texts. Many students questioned the reliability of specific types of evidence used in the video, such as the eyewitness accounts and bystander testimony, but struggled to evaluate all of the many claims and evidence within the video. Since a point-by-point analysis of each mode and specific claims and evidence is difficult while viewing video (without pausing and reviewing it), this led them to make more general determinations of "fit." Focusing more specifically on excavation work with the video might have helped students pay close attention to specific textual details (such as reading a transcript of some of the interviews or listening to the sound track) in order to ground their evaluation of claims in specific textual details. For example, a lesson could have identified two or three specific claims used in the video and focused on discerning fact from opinion, identifying bias or ideological agendas, and examining more closely authors' qualifications to make such claims. Discussion might have also focused on identifying specific techniques (such as loaded words, use of provocative images or diagrams, links to highly reputable websites, etc.) that the authors/creators used in the video.

These excavation practices are similar to strategies used in close or "deep" reading, strategies that are especially necessary in a digital culture (Wolf & Barzillai, 2009). Academic disciplines provide a range of tools that can help students do this analytical, interpretive, and evaluative work with texts. Historians, for example, often evaluate, analyze, and interpret a range of primary sources, such as political cartoons, oral accounts, interviews, diaries/journals, images, sound recordings, and film. The analytical and interpretive strategies they use with different texts can be employed to support the excavation of texts or claims and evidence within multimodal texts.

Elevation Practices

Students wanted to know about the qualifications of the creators of the video and also referred to what was absent—counter arguments, contradictory evidence, and other theories and claims about what happened on 9/11. Elevation practices include corroborating sources of information by comparing and contrasting different texts, looking for similarities and differences, identifying gaps, and considering what other information is necessary to cross-check sources of information.

Elevation also involves considering the broader contexts of textual production and reception. This requires that students question when, where, and why a text was produced and what else was happening within the immediate and broader contexts of the text's production. For example, to fully make sense of the video students should understand that all texts, including photographs and video clips, are authored—created by particular people for specific reasons. In an age where image doctoring ("photoshopping") is part and parcel of our communication, the prevailing trust in visual representations needs to be critically examined.

Although Mark's students tended to trust visuals, such as photos, diagrams, models, and video clips, there is some evidence of the ninth graders in this classroom engaged in other important elevation practices. They evaluated the credibility of *Loose Change 9/11* by drawing on their own prior knowledge and stances, noting their familiarity with certain information, images, news clips, and theories, and by situating their responses within larger social contexts, such as the general climate of distrust of the Bush administration. What is less clear is the depth of the students' understandings about *Loose Change 9/11*. In our own recursive readings of this sophisticated multimodal text, we find our own understandings enriched when we investigate more closely what specifically is shaping our discernments of credibility with the video. We know our thinking is shaped by the prevalence of conspiracy theories, the widespread distrust of the US government (especially the Bush administration), the difficulties of discerning "truth" and the postmodern incredulity of truth claims, the challenges of making sense of the overwhelming amount of information we have access to in an "information society," the widespread use of "spin" and propaganda techniques, and so on. We are aware of how these factor into how we make sense of this text. We also know that, as with all texts, we must remain ever-vigilant about our own reflexivity as readers—to consider how a text resonates with us, how it activates certain frames, mental schema, and emotions, and how it aligns with or disturbs our own theories, political perspectives, or ways of seeing and being in the world. And for us this is an ongoing challenge with *Loose Change 9/11* as additional versions of the video are released (*Loose Change 911: An American Coup* was released in September 2009). Online videos as multimodal texts are often not frozen in time; these texts can be dynamic, changing as new versions are produced and distributed, calling for dynamic literacy practices to continually situate the productions (including revisions) and receptions in changing contexts, in relationship to other texts and new information, and in terms of one's own beliefs and positions.

Dialectical Tacking

Since claims and evidence are represented in multiple ways, readers/viewers have to move recursively in "a potentially endless process [in which] reviewing and rereading will produce ever-new insights as we construct new connections and make modifications of our previous interpretations" (Sipe, 1998, p. 106). This entails an ability to think laterally across associations and modalities as a way to cultivate "critical understandings of the *relations* among ideas, their sources and histories, intertextual referents and consequences" (Luke, 2003, p. 401). In other words, the ability to corroborate claims and evidence depends upon a capacity to skillfully consider and discern "connection codes" across texts and contexts (Luke, 2003).

Dialectically tacking between excavation and elevation requires recursively and reflexively moving between the analytical processes of digging into texts while stepping back to consider broader contexts that shape textual production, reception, and meaning. It also means inviting multiple perspectives and diverse viewpoints, using our imaginations to try to understand difference, and stepping back and observing our own meaning-making to assess our understanding.

Dialectical tacking and reader reflexivity, though not central to the ways Mark and his ninth graders transacted with *Loose Change 9/11*, advances conversations about discerning the credibility of multimodal texts. It points to the need for greater attention given to the "epistemology of text" (Wineburg, 2001) and the epistemological dimensions of literacy and inquiry practices with multimodal texts—meaning that educators should ask what it means to know and *how* knowing takes place, instead of just asking *what* students know (Delandshire, 2002). Educators need to not only engage students in conversations about how a text like *Loose Change 9/11* was constructed, the quality of the information presented and the broader contexts that help us understand the video and its claims and use of evidence must be considered. There is also a need for continuing dialogue with students about the range of beliefs, experiences, and prior knowledge they and we bring to the video and how these lead us down similar and possibly divergent pathways of meaning-making. This is an ethical commitment that can help us be mindful of the danger that:

> [O]ne will simply choose to accept information that plausibly confirms one's prior beliefs or what one wishes were true. None of us can be entirely immune to this weakness but, to the extent that credibility judgments are recognized as having an ethical element, the consequences of doing so, for ourselves and for others, can at least be brought to the surface. (Burbules, 2001, p. 452)

After this experience with Mark's students, our approach to more directly attend to the "epistemology of text" was to create two *Critical Web Reader* lenses specifically for a text like *Loose Change 9/11* (Baildon & Damico, in press). The first lens focuses on *textual critique* and includes these questions:

- When, where, and why was the video produced?
- What does the creator of the video want me to think, believe or do?
- What techniques (e.g., use of load terms, emotive images, combinations of different modes and texts, etc.) does the creator use to influence me? Are they convincing? In what ways?
- How might immediate and broader (e.g., local, national, global, historical, social, cultural, economic) contexts have shaped the video's production?

The second lens focuses *reader reflexivity* with these guiding questions:

- What prior knowledge, personal experiences, and other texts help me make sense of the video?
- What additional thoughts or questions do I have about the video? What additional information is necessary to understand the video?
- What affects the way I read this video (e.g., prior experiences and learning; my values, opinions, emotions; my background and culture)?

- How might people from different backgrounds and with different experiences read this video (e.g., from different ethnic, cultural, national, age, gender perspectives)?

These two lenses promote *relational cosmopolitanism* by encouraging readers to work critically with the text in several essential ways. The questions guide readers to consider the contexts and purposes of the text's production, investigate the authoring and design decisions embedded in the text, evaluate what they as readers bring to the text, such as background knowledge and experiences, and consider how people with different backgrounds, beliefs, and values might read the text. As with the primary *Critical Web Reader* lenses, these additional lenses work best when used to cultivate dialogue in a "community of reason" (Nussbaum, 1997), where the participants in the community can jointly grapple with the challenges of making sense of complicated text like *Loose Change 9/11*. These "participatory events" (Dimitriadis & McCarthy, 2001) can involve readers of all ages in collaborative and critical investigations about core issues, such as credibility. For social studies and literacy educators, these investigations are also fundamentally about what it means to live and participate in a society increasingly shaped and mediated by Internet texts and technologies.

6 The Challenge of Synthesizing Web-based Information in an Inquiry-based Social Studies Classroom

Synthesizing findings in the inquiry process involves a host of complex challenges for students and their teachers. From conducting effective searches to skillfully reading as well as composing web-based texts, readers need to navigate the dynamic and sophisticated "ill-structured domain" (Spiro, Collins, Thota, & Feltovich, 2003) of the World Wide Web. It requires that students be able to look across multiple claims, consider different perspectives, decide what is significant, and synthesize a range of information sources in a coherent fashion. This challenge is intensified with web-based inquiry because readers need to make difficult informational decisions in the vast ecology of networked information. These decisions include determining what information is needed based on one's purposes, what information to pay attention to while searching, judging which information is credible and useful, evaluating and weighing oftentimes competing claims and evidence, and putting information together in ways that will make sense to oneself and others.

This chapter considers this challenge with an examination of the ways three ninth grade students engaged with websites in an inquiry oriented Humanities (social studies and English) curriculum focusing on "Contemporary Challenges in Asia." The ways students responded to this challenge depended on several complicated and interrelated factors: their purposes for reading; their inquiry questions; their own beliefs and previous knowledge about a topic; and their receptivity to modifying their views. Since these factors interact dynamically in the context of inquiry-based learning, each is difficult to evaluate separately and this poses special challenges to teachers and researchers.

With case studies of three readers, this chapter grapples with these challenges and considers implications for conceptualizing and guiding literacy and inquiry practices with students. Specifically, we examine what factors shape the inquiry and literacy practices necessary for synthesizing web-based information during inquiry investigations and how students might be better supported in doing this work.

SYNTHESIZING INFORMATION IN SOCIAL STUDIES

There is a growing body of research that suggests it is through the careful and critical reading of multiple texts that students develop subject matter understanding. This research shows that when students engage in source evaluation with multiple information sources they gain more conceptual knowledge (Sanchez, Wiley, & Goldman, 2006) and learn more subject matter content than from reading textbooks (Nokes, Dole, & Hacker, 2007). There is also research that suggests learning outcomes improve when students are required to focus on explanations and information integration across multiple sources during inquiry tasks (Wiley & Voss, 1999). Thus, explanation-based syntheses with multiple texts in inquiry-based learning environments can support subject matter understanding.

However, a reader's ability and willingness to critically evaluate and then synthesize claims and perspectives during inquiry-based reading in classrooms often depends on several complicated and interrelated factors or "multiple contingencies" (Roth & Duit, 2003). In their study of literacy practices in a physics classroom, Roth and Duit demonstrate how students' prior knowledge, the types of representations and texts they encounter, the tools and artifacts they utilize, and the contexts in which they read interact in dynamic ways to give an "emergent character" to the literacy and inquiry practices students draw upon and develop. Roth and Duit go on to argue that researchers and teachers must consider the interplay of these factors because there is wide variation in the ways students read and inquire into texts.

Leander and Rowe (2006) make a similar case in their discussion of "literacy in use." They argue that adaptability, flexibility, and innovation characterize literacy in use: "literacy in use necessarily involves students generating new ways of connecting texts, modalities, and performed identities" (p. 432). This chapter zooms in on the synthesizing work of three students as "literacy in use" during an inquiry-based unit. We attend particularly to the ways these students evaluated claims and evidence, made connections between their purposes and stances with the texts they read, and their need to formulate and share their own claims and findings.

LITERACY AND INQUIRY TOOLS TO
GUIDE WEB-BASED INQUIRY

In work comparing novice (students) and expert readers (historians) of historical texts, Wineburg (2001) found that what distinguishes experts' sense-making is their ability and "knowledge of how to establish warrant and determine the validity of competing truth claims" through the skillful use of three key heuristics: sourcing (considering issues of authorship);

corroboration (systematically cross-referencing and comparing sources); and contextualization (situating sources in spatial and temporal contexts). Because this sophisticated intellectual work is "unnatural" (Wineburg, 2001) and novice readers often struggle with employing these three heuristics, our work has centered on creating and implementing web-based tools to guide this work with Internet texts. These literacy and inquiry tools help readers consider different perspectives, critically evaluate multiple claims, develop contextualized interpretations, and share their own claims in ways that are meaningful to them (Damico, Baildon, & Campano, 2005).

This chapter explores the use of a modified version of the *Critical Web Reader (CWR)* lenses to guide students' work with web-based information sources. We focus mainly on how students worked to synthesize their findings during an inquiry unit, but demonstrate how synthesis is interdependent with a range of factors that are central to inquiry-based learning. Similar to the previous chapter, the chapter focuses on Mark's social studies classroom with ninth grade students in an international school in Taiwan. In this setting, Mark worked closely with the Humanities team of English and Social Studies teachers to create an inquiry-based unit called "Contemporary Challenges in Asia." This collaborative work included modifying *Critical Web Reader* lenses to guide students through an inquiry process in which the students developed investigative questions, collected, analyzed, and synthesized sources of information, and created a final project (i.e., a written essay and another type of text) to represent and communicate their findings. During the six week Humanities unit, students, working either individually, as partners, or in small groups, were guided to investigate a range of complex, multifaced issues, such as child prostitution in Thailand, sweatshop labor in Indonesia, Japanese whaling, the SARS epidemic in Taiwan, infanticide in India, the endangered species trade throughout Asia, separatist movements in Nepal and the Philippines, and drug trafficking in the Golden Triangle.

When the team began planning the unit, Mark suggested that they consider using the *Critical Web Reader* to guide student inquiry. Team members were generally intrigued about the potential of the tool to support student inquiry; some were excited to try it while others were more reserved about its potential use because they thought it might distract students from the subject matter focus in the unit, which in previous years was to learn about the causes and effects of problems in contemporary Asia. The *Critical Web Reader* could (and did) shift the primary teaching and learning goal from the acquisition of content (causes and effects) to a critical examination of claims and evidence related to problems in contemporary Asia (Baildon & Damico, 2008).

After much discussion about how students read sources of information and make use of information during the research process, the team decided they would modify the tool to meet the learning outcomes for the unit. For example, the first *CWR* lens (renamed *CWR-Lens I* by the team) was redesigned to have students record their research question(s) and an explanation of what they wanted to learn and do with their findings. It also required students to scan websites to briefly describe information on the site and explain why it was relevant to their research purpose. The first lens also asked students questions about author qualifications, purposes, and intended audiences to determine how credible or trustworthy a source was.

The second lens (named *CWR-Lens II*) required students to critically analyze and evaluate claims and evidence in sources. They were prompted to consider the validity of the source's claims by analyzing evidence used to support the claims. This lens also asked students to make connections between their research purpose, their background knowledge, and source information by asking students what personal experiences, prior learning, or other readings helped them understand the source.

The team redesigned the third lens (*CWR-Lens III*) to help students synthesize sources of information. This lens asked students to consider how they might use the source (e.g., summarize key points, paraphrase part of text, use direct quotes, images, charts, graphs, or statistics, etc.) and then had students summarize what they knew about their topic based on their research and the key claims and evidence they had found that would best help them answer their research question(s). This tool also asked students to "look across claims and evidence" and consider what claims they found "most interesting, intriguing, compelling, valid or convincing, significant, etc." and it provided a space for students to reflect on their learning about their topic.

After students were introduced to an inquiry process consisting of five steps (explore and develop investigative questions; gather and evaluate information; analyze and interpret the information; synthesize findings; and communicate new understandings) and provided direct instruction for each of the steps, Mark and his colleagues introduced students to the modified *Critical Web Reader* tools. For several class periods, students worked in the school's computer labs conducting their research using the modified tools. To guide students in each phase of the inquiry process, the Humanities team outlined the following steps:

1. Phase 1: Explore and develop inquiry questions:

   - Choose a topic that is interesting to you and related to an ongoing, current issue in Asia.
   - Do preliminary reading/research to better understand the issue.
   - Using criteria for good inquiry questions, develop an overarching question about your topic that will guide your research.

2. Phase 2: Gather and evaluate information:

   - Continue to research using the Internet to find five to seven *really good* sources.

- Evaluate each source's credibility and utility in the context of your topic.

3. Phase 3: Analyze and interpret information:

- Identify and evaluate claims and evidence to gather deeper meaning and understanding from three to five of your chosen sources.
- Practice writing an annotated list of works consulted.

4. Phase 4: Synthesize findings:

- Consider how you might use each source (e.g., summarize key points, paraphrase part of text, use direct quotes, images, charts, graphs, or statistics, etc.).
- Complete Preliminary Self-assessment of "What I Have and Know So Far" to identify your sources' claims and perspectives and your own opinion about some of these claims ("What claims do you find most common? Most interesting? Most contradictory? Most creative? Most reasonable? Most flawed? Most intriguing? Most far-fetched? Most unusual? etc.").
- Determine how to organize your in-class essay (e.g., "cause-effect-solutions; describing two different sides of the issue; comparing the economic, political, or social issues involved, etc.").

5. Phase 5: Communicate new understandings:

- Write an in-class essay demonstrating your analytical, interpretive, and synthesis skills.
- Develop a product or performance to share your learning (e.g., an NGO mailer highlighting a particular issue, research paper, website, a magazine, artwork, a video, etc.).
- Produce a commentary which explains how the research you did is reflected in your final product or performance.

To help students synthesize their findings, students were required to complete an "Annotated List of Works Consulted" in which they provided a summary of at least five website sources and "an assessment of each source (its relevance, usefulness, credibility, and/or bias)" used in their research. To help them write their in-class essays, the Humanities teachers had them complete a preliminary self-assessment activity that required them to look across the claims and evidence they had found. Students then completed a pre-writing activity that asked them to write a summary of what they knew about their topic and to identify three claims they wanted to develop in their essay. Based on this writing activity, students shared their findings in small groups for feedback. The final activity before writing their in-class essay was writing an outline to help them organize their findings and the claims, commentary, and conclusions they would make in their essay.

The Humanities team developed an inquiry guide with resources for students to use in each phase of the inquiry process. These resources included description of the inquiry model and each phase, tips and guides for each phase, *Critical Web Reader* guides and models of completed *Critical Web Reader* guides (that were used during class instruction), and rubrics that would be used for evaluating student work during the unit.

CASE STUDIES OF STUDENTS' INQUIRY AND LITERACY PRACTICES

In this chapter we zoom in on the work of three students—Stan, Annie, and Pierre—to better understand the specific literacy and inquiry practices they used to synthesize their findings. These three students provided a rough range of students' performance levels. Stan and Annie were high performing students while Pierre was one of the lowest performing students in the Humanities classes. The three students also differed in their goals and purposes for reading, which supported our goal to identify and explore what these differences might mean. Two of these students (Stan and Pierre) also addressed a similar topic (intellectual property rights), which offered us an opportunity for a potential comparative analysis of these two readers' work.

Stan

Stan is a citizen of the Netherlands, a bright and very conscientious student, highly proficient in the use of technology (as evidenced by movies and websites he produced in-class), and always very eager to participate in class activities and discussions. For his inquiry project, Stan posed the questions: "What are the causes and effects of infringement/duplication/piracy of intellectual property rights (IPR) in China? What are the fundamentals of piracy and why does it occur?" He initially planned to communicate his findings as a movie, 3D animation, or slideshow presentation, but he ended up creating teacher and student resource booklets on piracy in China with an accompanying video on a CD-ROM.

Stan identified himself as a "downloader." As he noted when identifying his prior knowledge about his topic:

> I have had a great deal of experience with piracy just because it is such a common practice in our standard lives today. As well as taking part in piracy (downloading music/software/movies, etc.), I have also been around hundreds of others who are just as bad a pirate as I am. As well as actually participating in piracy myself, I have also read and heard about it from multiple sources.

Stan began his inquiry with a clear purpose in mind: as a downloader and a "pirate," he wanted to find web sources to support his pro-piracy argument. Since he had already decided the position he wanted to take in his research, Stan primarily sought new information that would support the main claims he wanted to make about piracy. And throughout his work Stan maintained an a priori skepticism to any claims and evidence that conflicted with his view about piracy. This was especially evident with his analyses of the claims and evidence he found. For example, he was dubious of what he considered "the United States' positions" on piracy because these perspectives countered or challenged his own views. Stan, instead, sought out sites he deemed reputable, such as the Creative Commons site (http://www.creativecommons.org), which discussed the benefits of file-sharing. In his evaluation of the Creative Commons site Stan described it as an "interesting and . . . completely modern approach to copyright in the information age," differentiating it from other sites he read, such as the Motion Picture Association of America (http://www.mpaa.org/home.htm) and the Business Software Alliance site (http://www.bsa.org/usa/antipiracy), which supported anti-piracy measures. Stan saw Creative Commons as providing a reasonable solution, to some extent a middle ground, between the idea of total control in which "all rights are reserved" and total anarchy in which there are no intellectual property rights.

During the synthesizing phase, Stan focused on whether something "fit" with his own views, and he pointed out that he thought the *Critical Web Reader* tools were tedious, possibly, in part, because he already knew which arguments he wanted to develop in his paper. He analyzed and evaluated websites with the clear purpose of finding information he could use to support and strengthen pre-formulated ideas about IPR in China. He was not willing to critically interrogate or even consider sources that did not fit with his expressed "cause" of developing a pro-piracy position in his research.

Annie

Annie is a highly motivated and conscientious Taiwanese-American student who participated actively in class discussions and often engaged in debate and disagreement with other students (and with Stan, in particular). Her research question was "Should Taiwan declare its independence?" When Annie explained her research purpose, she said she chose this question to further understand this "modern" and "controversial" issue and also because her family had long supported Taiwanese independence from China. Through her research she hoped to "come to a conclusion whether it is a wise decision for Taiwan to declare its independence." It bears noting that Annie's question is highly complicated for several reasons. She sees herself as Taiwanese and American with Chinese heritage and cultural background. Also, while Taiwan is a democracy and a key trade partner with the US, it has recently developed close economic ties with China.

Moreover, if Taiwan were to declare independence, China has threatened military action, which would certainly provoke a strong response from the United States.

Of all the students in this study, Annie referred most often to her own position as a reader. For example, she noted that "I am Taiwanese and I admit that I am somewhat of a secessionist and therefore it is easy for me to side with . . . claims that the increased hostilities between China and Taiwan is China's fault." When reading information from a site developed by the Global Security Organization (http://www.globalsecurity.org/wmd/libaray/news/taiwan/2004/taiwan-040219-cna04.htm), for example, Anne noted: "since my family and I are supporters of President Chen [of Taiwan], I find it easy for me to believe his claims and agree that what he says is correct."

Although Annie referred several times to her family's position on this issue and her own biases, she seemed genuinely open to considering sites with competing claims about Taiwan's independence as well as information that surprised or contradicted what she knew about the topic. For example, after finding an article by Richard C. Bush, III, a Senior Fellow and Director of the Center for Northeast Asian Policy Studies and learning about the US policy of "strategic ambiguity," Annie was surprised by his claim that "the United States being unclear on its stand in this issue actually increases the safety of Taiwan." Annie was also surprised when she read the web page entitled, "Taiwan's International Legal Position" (http://www.taiwanadvice.com/ustaiwan/) which included the claim: "Taiwan is still an unincorporated territory of the United States Military Government." Annie believed this was a well-supported claim because "the author supports his claims by taking apart laws, amendments, and treaties in the past that don't specify to whom Taiwan is rewarded." Specifically, she noted that the article referred to the terms of the San Francisco Peace Treaty after WWII when Japan renounced its rights to Formosa (Taiwan) and the United States had to acquire it as an unincorporated territory because the treaty didn't specify to whom it should be transferred.

As she synthesized her findings and prepared to write the in-class essay, Annie noted: "many claims on this issue could be biased because this whole issue started with the ambiguity of the law/treaty when Japan gave Formosa up." She said her research helped her "know a lot of different points of view of why Taiwan should or should not be independent." She also concluded "that Taiwan should not declare its independence" as she settled on her main claim: "Despite being Taiwanese and wishing most of my life that Taiwan [should be] free, it is a bad decision. Taiwan should not declare independence to risk attack." Annie concluded her essay by saying, "If Taiwan is, in fact (de facto), independent it is a good status quo. Taiwanese citizens will always be Taiwanese citizens regardless of the title of the country. In conclusion, Taiwan should not declare its independence."

During her inquiry we see Annie drawing on her prior knowledge and stance on the issue of Taiwanese independence and willing to consider new perspectives and claims, such as the concept of "strategic ambiguity" and the notion that Taiwan was an unincorporated territory of the United States after World War II. As part of her synthesizing work she also moved from a secessionist stance (i.e., a clear separation between Taiwan and China) to a more interdependent stance as reflected in her essay.

Pierre

Pierre is a French-German student who uses English as a third language. He can be described as a low-level reader yet a bright, underachieving (C/C-) student. He is a very enthusiastic technology user (which was a concern to his parents, who believed Pierre was spending too much of his time computer programming and playing computer games). Pierre's initial inquiry question was "What are IPR (intellectual property rights) and why are they important? What can Taiwan do to enforce IPR? What can you do?" However, these changed quickly during his investigation to "Are intellectual property rights (IPR) the best for Taiwan and does Taiwan currently enforce them well?" He initially wrote that he was interested in this question because Taiwan is "being accused of not respecting/enforcing IPR." During his research, he noted that he wanted to learn more about IPR because, "I download things myself although I know it's not legal. I also heard that Taiwan is being accused of not enforcing IPR enough. I want to find out whether this is true."

Pierre started with websites that he considered more "neutral" and which provided basic information or background knowledge. In his initial scanning to locate sources related to his topic, Pierre first read the Government Information Office of Taiwan website (www.gio.gov.tw) and determined that it contained "good information about IPR in Taiwan" which helped him understand "how Taiwan already enforces IPR." Although he believed it to be a credible source, he stated that "the Taiwanese government tried to look good in front of other countries and the goals of this site might also be to convince readers that IPR is important to Taiwan." Pierre then moved to sites that provided more sophisticated information and that more clearly represented certain interests and agendas. For example, he determined that although information from the Motion Pictures Association of America (MPAA) site (www.mpaa.org) "is supposed to be neutral," the obvious "goal of MPAA is to defend the movie makers and to fight piracy all over the world." In his analysis of this site, Pierre recognized the site did not represent the views of people who download movies illegally. Pierre also questioned another website, which presented a clear position on IPR: the Chaos Computer Club (www.ccc.de/campaigns/boycott-musicindustry), a site written in English and German (with only a small part of its content and links in English). In his summary of this site, Pierre believed the main claim on this site was valid ("the music industry is spreading false information to shy off people from downloading . . . and that individuals' freedom is sacrificed for the music industry and market stability") and supported by evidence (links to authoritative sites), but he also acknowledged the one-sided quality of this perspective.

There is also evidence of Pierre rethinking his stance and position on IPR. In the early stages of the project, he noted: "I download and use copyrighted software using file sharing programs myself. I do know and have heard about people saying that it is illegal and results in a huge loss of money and jobs of the original creators. However, I am not willing (and can't) spend money to buy all my movies, software and games legally, since I can get it easier and cheaper by downloading it or copying disks . . . Since I'm not the one who creates music, I am just interested in getting products as cheaply as possible." Yet, in response to the question, "How do my own beliefs/values/perspectives shape or influence my reading of this site?" he described how his research compelled him to "question whether it actually is morally wrong to download copyrighted material. I didn't even think about this before researching."

Across Pierre's work, we see increasing sophistication in the information he recorded, the evaluation of the claims he encountered, and with his own stance and position about IPR. As he synthesized his findings, he provided basic information about IPR, explained why it's an important issue ("it allows individuals or companies to profit from an idea and protects [others] from using it making more money"), described problems with IPR ("it is almost impossible to enforce"), described Taiwan's interests ("trade agreements with the US and other countries"), and concluded with his own opinion. Pierre wrote that he believed IPR mainly benefits "big companies" and that a compromise could be worked out in which people would be allowed to download. He argued: "the price of MP3 players, CD burners, internet connections, and other means of reproducing material could be raised. The money could then go back to the original creators." Pierre presented a thorough and well-researched paper that offered an informed solution to a complex problem.

A CLAIMS CONTINUUM AND RECEPTIVITY CONTINUUM

To better understand how students synthesize information during inquiry investigations, we developed an analytical table to chart the work of Stan, Annie, and Pierre across each phase of the inquiry process.

Analysis across the three students yields an account of "literacy in use" and provides evidence that several interrelated factors shaped the ways these students read, evaluated, and used web sources of information in their investigations. Several factors shaped the ways students synthesized their findings during the inquiry process. In particular, each student started from different stances toward their topics and identified certain interests and purposes in their work, and these factors shaped the ways they engaged with the web texts they used, how they evaluated claims and evidence, and their receptivity toward adopting different perspectives about their inquiry topics.

Table 6.1　Three Students' Inquiry Approaches

Name	Performance Level	Purpose for Reading/Inquiry	Inquiry Question(s)	Evaluating Claims
Stan	High	*Support his "cause"* that IPR rules should be re-considered); was a high tech user interested in tech-related issues.	"What are causes & effects of piracy of intellectual property rights (IPR) in China? What are the fundamentals of piracy and why does it occur?"	*Low-Intermediate* -Drew on prior knowledge & stance. -Dismissed certain claims ("US claims"). -Acknowledged competing claims, but dismissed them to support claim he wanted to make
Annie	High	*Understand* a highly personal & controversial issue that is meaningful to her & family.	"Should Taiwan declare its independence?"	*Intermediate-Advanced* -Acknowledged multiple & competing claims. -Expressed some reservations about claims based on authorship. -Noted potential bias of her own views.
Pierre	Low	*Get basic info and key perspectives* about IPR in Taiwan & different perspectives about what can be done to deal with IPR issues.	"Are intellectual property rights (IPR) the best for Taiwan and does Taiwan currently enforce them well?"	*Intermediate* -Considered some sources "neutral," -Considered two main claims & stances on IPR. -Tried to present balanced view but acknowledged own interests and values.

Continued

Table 6.1   Continued

Name	Performance Level	Examining own beliefs	Type of Reader/ Inquirer	Receptivity to changing views
Stan	High	*Some reflexivity* Acknowledged IPR interests & positions but didn't critically reflect on these or shift his thinking. Referred to & used own positions as reason for pursuing claims he wanted to make.	*Instrumental –* wanted to support his "cause." Read to add "weight" to or build up argument he wanted to make.	*Low –* steadfast in views about IPR & piracy.
Annie	High	*Significant reflexivity* Acknowledged her own position and how it may shape her use & evaluation of certain sources. Used initial beliefs as reason for pursuing research.	*Self- Reflexive –* continually took into account own stance, prior knowledge & position on issue but was willing to be flexible & change position.	*High –* willing to consider new claims & incorporate them into her thinking about the issue; changed stance on issue.
Pierre	Low	*Some reflexivity* Acknowledged he is a downloader and his own position and interests. Tried to present a balanced view in in-class research essay.	*Adaptive –* Started by wanting basic background info and facts; wanted to consider main viewpoints, present balanced view, and offer his ideas about IPR. Moved from basic to broader views.	*Moderate –* Identified his position, but seemed to genuinely want to better understand issue; presented balanced view and reconsidered own views and position.

To explain some of the variability across these three students we also developed two continua: a claims continuum and a receptivity continuum. These continua help us understand some of the factors that shaped student work as they synthesized their findings. These continua can also guide practitioners invested in identifying the web inquiry practices and needs of their students.

A "claims continuum" (Baildon & Damico, 2006) offers a way to situate students' level of facility with evaluating and synthesizing claims and evidence. How readers evaluate claims and evidence, to a large degree, will determine which claims they will use or build upon to synthesize as findings. Readers with a *beginning* understanding of claims and evidence tend to: accept claims as true without considering other possible claims that could be made about the topic; believe in one interpretation as "factual"; view reading and inquiry as getting the facts about something; and do not evaluate how one's own prior knowledge shapes the assessing of claims. They tend to adopt claims they find rather than synthesize across claims. Readers with an *intermediate* understanding of claims and evidence identify claims and counterclaims and consider supporting evidence for each; understand that there can be different views and perspectives about the topic; acknowledge different claims, but may not evaluate the different claims or address why different claims exist; view reading and inquiry as consisting of differing accounts and perspectives of topics/issues; and consider their own prior knowledge and beliefs to assess claims. Readers with an intermediate understanding of claims tend to acknowledge different claims but may be unable to effectively evaluate and synthesize them in a coherent way. Readers with an *advanced* understanding are aware that multiple claims can be made and that claims must be rigorously tested according to certain disciplinary procedures and standards; make sure claims are logical and supported with valid evidence; debate competing interpretations and even question the veracity of widely accepted facts; corroborate claims, critically compare and contrast differing accounts, or further investigate inconsistencies between differing accounts; and reflect critically on their own prior knowledge, beliefs, and values as they assess claims and evidence. Readers with an advanced understanding of claims are able to evaluate disparate claims and weave them together in a coherent and meaningful way to develop their own claims.

We see Stan's work as demonstrating a *low* to *intermediate* understanding of claims and evidence. He acknowledged competing claims, but largely ignored them when synthesizing findings because he was primarily concerned with supporting claims he wanted to make from the start of his inquiry. He was able to draw on prior knowledge and identify his stance on IPR and made intertextual references, but quickly dismissed certain claims (e.g., "US positions") that conflicted with his "cause" rather than seriously consider their merit or critically evaluate them. Pierre can be seen as demonstrating an *intermediate* understanding of claims. He viewed some sources as "neutral," as presenting basic facts and information, and did not necessarily acknowledge the claims these sources made. He considered main claims and stances on IPR, acknowledged their perspectives and bias, but did not fully evaluate the different claims or address why different claims exist. Annie represents a moving between an *intermediate* and an *advanced* understanding of claims and evidence. Annie acknowledged multiple and competing claims, wove them into her work, identified and evaluated claims based on supporting evidence, and expressed some reservations about claims based on authorship, potential bias, and her own views.

In terms of synthesizing their findings, each student took a different approach based on their orientation to claims and evidence. Stan only synthesized information that supported the claims he wanted to make from the start of his inquiry. Pierre synthesized basic information that was necessary for him to better understand the range of claims he found but treated the different claims and perspectives about IPR as separate and didn't fully address the different positions or develop an integrated position that made use of the different claims he encountered. Annie was most fully able to synthesize the different claims she found while acknowledging the limitations of some of the claims in her work.

Types of Readers and their Receptivity to Changing Views

The ways the students approached their investigations and web sources of information depended on their purposes, their orientations or inclinations toward certain texts and sources of information, and their stances toward their own views and the perspectives and claims of others. Each of these factors shaped how they synthesized their findings. This led us to consider possible characteristics for each student as well as evaluate each student's receptivity to modifying her or his views.

We see Stan as an *instrumental* reader with low receptivity to changing his views in his stance toward new information and claims and evidence. During his research, Stan repeatedly focused on whether something "fit" with his own views, analyzing and evaluating websites with the clear purpose of finding information he could use to support and strengthen pre-formulated ideas about IPR in China. We consider Pierre an *adaptive* reader with moderate receptivity to changing his views. He initially wanted to learn more about the basic issues related to IPR and then sought different positions on IPR so that he could better define his own position. Pierre, mentioning his own interests in downloading and using copyrighted software, acknowledged that his research made him begin questioning moral issues related to IPR and he tried to provide an informed, balanced view of IPR by suggesting a compromise position. Annie can be characterized as a *self-reflexive* reader who was continually aware of her stance on the issue of Taiwan's independence and how her preconceptions interacted with the different sources she encountered in her research. She had high receptivity to changing her views and actually modified her position on Taiwan's independence because she was willing to consider new perspectives and ideas. She initially identified herself as a "secessionist" and noted that her family had "always been a supporter of the independence of Taiwan." However, as a result of her research, she ended up supporting the status quo in Taiwan by arguing that de facto independence was better than Taiwan declaring independence and risking attack from China.

While Table 6.1 highlights some of the ways these three students read, evaluated, and used web sources of information during an inquiry-based unit, it bears noting that Table 6.1 is framed by an understanding that these inter-related factors of web reading—such as, purposes for reading, inquiry questions, one's own beliefs and previous knowledge about a topic, and receptivity to modifying one's views—are not static. In this context where Stan, Annie, and Pierre and their classmates were given some autonomy to make choices (about topics, questions to pursue, sources to investigate, arguments to make, etc.), the literacy and inquiry practices (like all cultural practices) were varied and dynamic as they proceeded through their investigations. For example, their purposes for reading and inquiry questions changed (in subtle and more significant ways) and they were invited to reconsider their previous knowledge in light of what they were learning about their topics. A similar logic frames the descriptors for these three readers—*instrumental, self-reflexive,* and *adaptive.* Consider Stan, for example. While we used the description *instrumental* reader for Stan and concluded that he demonstrated a low to intermediate understanding of claims during this project, he was a highly proficient and critical reader, perhaps the most nimble reader in the class (especially of web-based texts), and quite capable of evaluating and adjudicating among competing claims and evidence. Yet, his inquiry emphasis and approach to synthesizing findings for this project were guided by his desire to develop a strong case to support his position as a cyber pirate, which resulted in his dismissal rather than careful evaluation of competing claims and evidence. Thus, it would be misleading and inaccurate to universalize from this one project to conclude that Stan is *in general* an instrumental reader. Because different motivations and purposes engender different types of reading as well as positions readers are likely to assume along claims and reflexivity continua, it is more appropriate to see Stan in this situation as a reader and writer with "activity" or "project specific" instrumental goals. Knowing Stan, we also believe that he was well-aware of how he was positioning himself (or how he might be positioned—even somewhat unfavorably) in terms of claims and receptivity continua, yet remained committed to gathering the data he needed to compose the argument he wanted to make. This type of meta-level awareness seems especially important because it suggests that although Stan could be categorized as "low-intermediate" and "low" along claims and receptivity continua and deemed an instrumental reader who demonstrated only some reflexivity in examining his beliefs on this project, this could have been (and likely was) a conscious choice based on an awareness of other possible paths he could have pursued on a project like this.

CONCLUSION

What emerges from taking a close look at three students' work during this inquiry-based curriculum unit is a conception of inquiry and reading as highly dynamic and fluid activities in which a number of factors converge to shape the ways readers transact with texts and synthesize their findings. Considering the three readers' "literacy in use," where change, diversity, and innovation prevail over stability, repetition, and structure (Leander & Rowe, 2006), we see how each student started from different vantage points and used literacy and social studies tools (modified version of the *Critical Web Reader*) to engage a range of texts, evaluate different perspectives and claims, build more layered understandings of their topics, and consider the claims they wanted to make and share with others. Implications of this work point to the need for further conceptualization of the relationships between literacy and inquiry practices. Such conceptualizations must be sensitive to the contexts and factors that shape the inquiry and literacy practices students demonstrate in classrooms, especially in terms of specific subject matter such as social studies, as well as the extent to which certain tools, such as the *Critical Web Reader,* can support increasingly sophisticated and nuanced web reading. To understand students' literacy and inquiry practices and to better support and scaffold key inquiry and literacy practices, such as synthesizing information, it is important to consider students' purposes for reading, the inquiry questions and beliefs about their topics that guide their investigations, and their ability and willingness to consider multiple and competing perspectives and claims.

More needs to be understood about the specific challenges students face as they engage in inquiry, such as the challenge of synthesizing findings. For example, we need to consider the trade offs of allowing Stan to ask questions determined by a position he already holds and that results in him pursuing limited traversals of the terrain related to IPR. He's learning to take a stand for a cause he believes in yet is unwilling to fully consider different perspectives or dialogue with different viewpoints that might challenge his position. His position of advocacy is supported at the expense of his reflexivity, open-mindedness, and his ability to build perspective. Pierre starts in a different place and needs to take his own traversals across the terrain of IPR. He starts with a need for basic information that can help him better understand the issue he is investigating, moves to build perspective, but doesn't fully integrate these perspectives to synthesize his findings. He may require more time and practice to fully integrate his findings in ways that are more coherent and cohesive.

The "synthesizing mind" (Gardner, 2006) is absolutely vital in a global society of transnational flows of information, ideas, and perspectives. It includes being able to take information from disparate and diverse sources, putting it together in novel and productive ways, and being able to use a range of synthesizing tools, such as narratives, taxonomies, metaphors, themes, and theories. Gardner (2006) refers to this as a "searchlight intelligence" that is "always scanning the environment" to make connections (and identify differences) across various informational horizons (p. 66). It involves being able to compare and contrast, integrate ideas, and draw conclusions, and it is essential for developing understanding. These are what we have referred to as elevation practices.

Greeno and van de Sande (2007) view conceptual understanding and growth as achievements in discourse practices that include "explicit methods of presenting, discussing, and using concepts and conceptions, evaluating alternative conceptual understandings, and fostering and evaluating members' progress in their knowing and understanding concepts and conceptions in the community's domain" (p. 10). Guiding students to develop their own explanations and findings by looking across different claims, helping them make connections between disparate claims and information, scaffolding strategies for comparing and contrasting accounts, and developing tools and heuristics that can support their organizing and integrating ideas to make their own original claims supported by evidence are important practices in inquiry-based classrooms.

From this perspective, we can see Stan, Annie, and Pierre acting with varying degrees of achievement. Each student was able to select, adapt, and apply critical judgment about "the appropriateness, utility, relevance, and meaning of alternative understandings, strategies, concepts and methods" to better understand their problem and make a positive contribution to the community of learning through their final product or performance (Greeno & van de Sande, 2007, p. 12). They were guided to read sources carefully and critically and then synthesize information from sources in the context of investigating complex issues, to engage with information strategically, negotiate meaning by considering a range of claims and perspectives, and learn practices that allow them greater participation in meaning-making activities. These practices support knowledge-building.

Investigating complex, multifaceted issues, such as those selected by the students during the unit, and providing opportunities for them to consider different claims and perspectives, and then develop their own claims and findings, provides one example of students taking multiple and varied traversals across a problem space, dialoguing across difference (by considering different claims and perspectives), and building perspective. Gardner (2006), for example, argues that "multiperspectivalism," which "recognizes that different analytic perspectives can contribute to the elucidation of an issue or problem" (p. 71) is critical for this work because different perspectives require negotiation (dialogue across difference) and integration to more fully understand the object of study. It involves participating in discourses in ways that allow one to engage with different perspectives, negotiate meaning, and construct one's own explanations. Students need guidance and practice in doing this challenging work.

Closely examining this work also helps us recognize synthesizing as a practice of *relational cosmopolitanism*. Being able to look across multiple claims, consider different perspectives, and dialogue across difference, and the kinds of negotiation this requires, are vital in an age of intensifying transnational flows and complexity. *Relational cosmopolitanism* also involves critical self-reflection, and when we apply this lens to the work of Stan, Annie, and Pierre, we realize more might have been done to encourage these students to fully consider their own relationships to the issues they investigated in ways that involved critical questioning of their own positions. For example, encouraging Stan and Pierre to consider different perspectives and the political and ethical implications of their positions could have guided them to more fully "enter into the give-and-take of critical arguments about ethical and political choices" (Nussbaum, 1997, p. 62). Mark, for instance, could have structured opportunities for them to engage arguments about how social and economic class disparities can influence how "pirates" are viewed and whether or not their actions are criminalized. Stan, an economically and educationally privileged adolescent, engages in piracy practices that invoke a certain degree of glamour and suggest someone being invested in "fighting the good fight," in this case, a fight against corporate power. And, for the most part, mainstream society would not criminalize someone like Stan. However, there are also pirates from economically and educationally disadvantaged backgrounds whose piracy practices (e.g., in their local communities rather than across the world vis-à-vis the Internet) would much more likely be criminalized. In terms of *relational cosmopolitanism*, then, synthesizing requires that people see their own beliefs and values in relation to others' beliefs and values so that new understandings can emerge. Teachers can guide students to engage the "tension between values that do not go together" as one of the "chores of complexity" which, in turn, helps build "a foundation for the development of intellectual judgment" (Wieseltier, 2010, pp. 41–42). Through this type of dialectical exchange socially transformative syntheses and individual growth are possible.

SUMMARY OF CHAPTERS 4, 5, AND 6

In Chapters 4, 5, and 6, we came to understand the ways groups of students—a class of fourth graders in Singapore and two groups of ninth graders in Taiwan—grappled with core epistemological challenges: the challenge of discerning credible and useful resources in Chapter 4, the challenges of evaluating claims and evidence and discerning the credibility of a complicated multimodal text in Chapter 5, and the challenge of synthesizing findings during an inquiry project in Chapter 6. The next two chapters consider the ways a group of undergraduate preservice social studies teachers in the Midwestern United States and their instructor worked through the five epistemological challenges: defining purposes and launching an inquiry; discerning credibility of textual sources; adjudicating among conflicting claims and evidence in a range of texts; synthesizing findings; and communicating new knowledge. Chapter 7 focuses primarily on the first three challenges, while Chapter 8 addresses the fourth and fifth challenges.

Central to the storylines of Chapters 7 and 8 is collective meaning-making and knowledge-building, as the students worked collaboratively in small groups to investigate issues of capitalism and global trade. While the collective (teachers and groups of students engaged jointly in inquiry) was foundational to Chapters 4, 5, and 6, the next two chapters make more explicit collective knowledge-building and "progressive problem-solving" (Zhang, 2009) as the students and their teacher engage systematically in the five-phase inquiry process. These two chapters also provide an important window into the work of prospective teachers at a crucial time in their professional development. This group of future educators experiences these core challenges as students themselves and then have opportunities to reflect on how they might engage their own future middle-level and secondary school students.

7 Part I: Identifying What We Know and What We Don't Know— Progressive Knowledge-building in an Inquiry Community

With Anne Elsener

This chapter addresses the issue of what knowledge about social studies subject matter a group of undergraduate preservice social studies teachers built through the first three phases of an inquiry project and the ways they developed this knowledge. The setting for this investigation is a reading methods course and our account of what transpired during this course is guided by several questions: What background knowledge do the students access during the first three phases of the inquiry process? What do they identify as knowledge they don't know or need to know? What moves does the teacher make to guide students to access and build upon their background knowledge during these three phases? After a description of the context and goals for the course, we describe the ways Anne designed what she called a Web Inquiry Project[1] and prepared students to work through its first three phases. We then investigate what happened when Anne's students worked in six different disciplinary groups within the social studies (History, Economics, Psychology, Sociology, Government, and Geography) to investigate the topic of capitalism and issues of global trade. We identify the ways her students progressively constructed knowledge during these initial three inquiry phases as well as the ways Anne guided her students to do this challenging work.

CONTEXT OF COURSE

In spring 2009, Anne was the instructor of a reading methods course for preservice social studies teachers. The students travelled as a cohort in this teacher education program; in addition to this reading methods course, they were enrolled in a social studies teaching methods course and a History for Teachers seminar taught by a professor from the History department. In spring 2009, Anne was an advanced student in a literacy and language education doctoral program and this was the fifth time she had taught this reading methods course. The primary goal of this course is for preservice teachers (hereafter called students) to learn how to guide their future middle and high school social studies learners to read, write, and think critically about social studies content. Rooted in the view that reading is an active, constructive process, Anne aims to guide the students to use and then learn how to teach a core set of reading comprehension strategies, which include: making connections, asking questions, making inferences and predictions, summarizing, determining word meanings, and visualizing (Tovani, 2000; Zwiers, 2004). Anne also foregrounded critical literacy in the course, using journal articles (e.g. McLaughlin & DeVoogd, 2004; Pescatore, 2007) and classroom activities to demonstrate what it means to take a critical stance (e.g., questioning techniques used by authors to influence or persuade readers, discerning included and omitted perspectives in a text) while reading a variety of texts, such as political cartoons, newspaper articles, and song lyrics.

Specific learning outcomes, as stated in the course syllabus, include being able to: assess and promote literacy skills in relation to learning in social studies; develop literacy teaching strategies and plans to support literacy learning needs of all students; locate literacy materials of various topics, genres, and reading levels to support social studies curriculum; conduct a web-based inquiry into a social issue and describe how this inquiry process could be implemented in a secondary social studies classroom. This was the second semester the web-based inquiry project had been integrated into this content area literacy course for preservice social studies teachers. A primary goal of the inquiry project was for students to develop content knowledge about globalization and to better understand the literacy strategies necessary to develop this knowledge (e.g., how to select, analyze, and synthesize web-based sources) so the students would be better prepared to guide their future middle school and secondary school social studies learners to do similar work. Although Anne did not have a disciplinary background in social studies, she was becoming more familiar with the practices integral to knowledge production in social studies, especially history, as she learned about historical inquiry (e.g., the three heuristics— sourcing, contextualizing, corroborating—described by Wineburg, 2001) and what this could look like across grade levels. The web-based inquiry was the culminating project in the course and is our focus for the rest of this chapter and Chapter 8.

Launching the Web Inquiry Project

The web inquiry project was designed for the students, as a group, to choose and then investigate an issue pertaining to globalization, what Anne framed as "an issue with local and global concerns." The project began the third week of class with an opportunity for students to identify what they knew about globalization and how global issues are part of social studies education. The students were asked to individually answer three questions on a graphic organizer (a document with a three-column table) that Anne created: 1. What is globalization? 2. What are major issues within globalization? 3. Why does globalization matter to me as a future social studies teacher? Each student then read one article of a set of four. Two of the articles[2] were selected to provide a general overview about globalization issues. The other two articles[3] took a pedagogical look at why issues associated with globalization should be part of social studies education. After the students worked in groups and added ideas to their graphic organizers, Anne used the overhead projector to lead a group discussion and document students' ideas with additions to the graphic organizer. During this discussion students shared ideas about how globalization is making the world smaller and is leading to increased sharing of ideas and goods across far distances. They agreed that globalization would matter to them as social studies teachers because they and their future students would have increased access to information that is constantly changing and conflicting. In addition to building and sharing background knowledge about globalization as inquirers themselves and as future teachers during this initial phase, the class also explored inquiry-based perspectives as a way to support active and meaningful learning.[4] While reading about inquiry-based learning, the students discussed their previous research experiences in school, which focused primarily on individual projects completed in isolated ways. The students did not have school experiences with collaborative inquiry projects where learners develop and jointly research important questions that matter to them.

To support students in moving towards developing their own inquiry questions about globalization, Anne took the students to the computer lab to view the final PowerPoint presentations of the inquiry projects created by students from the previous semester. That class tackled the topic of poverty and Anne highlighted the ways each group developed its own investigative question, articulated its findings, and identified struggles and successes with the research process, which also resulted in advice for future researchers doing similar work. Time dedicated to looking at the previous semester's projects provided the current group of students with an opportunity to see an example of an inquiry project and envision what their own inquiry projects might be like.

It was then time to move explicitly toward Phase 1 of the inquiry process: defining purposes and launching an inquiry with an investigative question. The first challenge the class faced was to narrow the focus to a specific aspect of globalization. To guide this process, Anne suggested that they either build on the previous semester's research into issues of poverty or select their own topic to explore. Several of the students expressed interest in trade issues on local and global levels, which led to one student suggesting that the class focus the inquiry on capitalism as a way to encompass these interests. After the class agreed with this overarching topic focus, students formed small inquiry groups (four to five students) to develop an inquiry question to explore as part of the whole class inquiry into globalization and capitalism. The students decided to break into groups by disciplines within social studies: History, Government,[5] Economics, Sociology, Psychology, and Geography. Anne had suggested this as a possible way to guide the inquiry work of the small groups and connect with the subjects the students could possibly teach as future social studies instructors. The first main task for each group was to engage in a threaded conversation in an online forum to share with their group members what they knew about the topic and might further want to explore for the inquiry. Anne encouraged the students to do some searching on the Internet to help them move towards developing a specific question. For the next class meeting, the students would gather in their inquiry groups to extend their online conversation and develop an inquiry question.

In terms of the design structure for the group work, Anne mostly employed a *fixed small group* design; the different groups collaborated independently on distinct components of the project and then joined forces at the end to assemble their work (Zhang, Scardamalia, Reeve, & Messina, 2009). At times Anne also supported an *interacting groups design*, when she structured opportunities, such as online and in-class discussions, for knowledge-sharing across the groups (Zhang, et. al., 2009).

WEB INQUIRY PROJECT

Phase 1

As the students worked through Phase 1, it was clear that each group possessed some background knowledge about their topic and was at least aware that their disciplinary focus consisted of core concepts, topics, and content. The Sociology group, for example, used the disciplinary concepts of social class, gaps and disparities, and tracking to frame their investigation. The History group considered causal factors and chronology during their initial deliberations, identifying "turning points" over time and issues of continuity, with one student noting how "cultural practices remain dominant and continue to spread." The Geography group referenced their knowledge about maps, places, movement of goods and services, and how companies choose locations based on climate, land, supply of workers, and the ways the forces of globalization have "reshaped land" through irrigation, hydro power, and dams. The Government group discussed their understanding of trade agreements, like the North American Free Trade Agreement (NAFTA), organizations like the World Trade Organization (WTO), and their knowledge of sweatshops and child labor. Some students also referenced what they had learned in other university classes, such as economics.

The online discussion threads enabled each group to identify what they knew about their topics as well as concerns they had about not having adequate background knowledge to best develop their inquiry questions. For example, a member of the Psychology group commented: "Honestly,

I know like nothing about psychology so I have no clue about what we should do" while another member of the same group pointed out: "I don't know a whole lot about psychology but I was thinking maybe we could focus on people's behavior and desires and see how their choices affect others around the world?" As a result, the students were able to build perspective about their topics through an online collaborative exchange of ideas. At times, students would share an information source to build background knowledge, such as a student in the Economics group who posted the following message for her groupmates: "im not sure the difference between a technical sweatshop and child labor but . . . here is the wikipedia definition for sweatshop." Students also identified other potential resources to support them, including a student who suggested: "Maybe we, or at least one of us, could get in touch with the No Sweat group on campus to gather some research, because I am sure that they know a lot more than we do." At other times, students would propose a way to frame their question in relationship to another issue. Another student in the Economics group, for instance, suggested: "I really like the sweatshop idea, I also thought we could incorporate child labor too? I don't really know much about each topic but they seem like they would go hand in hand."

Anne played a pivotal role in this process. For starters, she communicated to the students that the ultimate goal of the project was not to come up with definitive answers to the inquiry questions. Rather, it was to engage in a rigorous and systematic inquiry process in which the likely result would be the identification of new, revised, or more focused questions. In guiding the online deliberations in Phase 1, she told students to develop more background knowledge by "doing some googling." From her own teaching experience, Anne knew that groups needed some time to think about their topics, conduct some initial searches, and discuss ideas with each other in order to develop better investigative questions. She also directed students to the projects completed the previous semester, as the following advice to the geography group demonstrates: "It might be helpful to look at last year's powerpoint from the Geography group. They had some really interesting insights (they might give advice to future researchers on their slides that are useful to you). They looked at poverty maps. You could explore this idea of poverty mapping more. Especially, the idea of how is 'poverty' defined on different maps and in different areas and by different map-makers." Anne also provided explicit advice about how to formulate the investigative questions. She, for example, guided the Government group to modify their question, posting this message: "It may be useful to change the words [to your question] to something like: "how do these organizations affect labor conditions" [because] using the words "lead to" suggests you are building on research showing these organizations do cause labor problems."

As Phase 1 came to a close, the groups came up with the following questions for their projects:

History: In thinking about globalization how do the United States and Asia affect each other?

Government: How do government policies affect outsourcing, tariffs, & labor conditions?

Economics: How do sweatshops affect the global economy?

Sociology: How has globalization expanded the class gap?

Psychology: How does the media portrayal of the ongoing recession affect people's psychological choices and feelings? How do people's feelings and choices influence what the media says?

Geography: How has geography played a role in today's industrial trade relations on a global and local level?

Managing Epistemological Challenge #1– Clarifying Purposes and (Tentatively) Launching an Inquiry

The students accessed what they knew about their topics as a starting point for their investigations. They also knew that they did not know enough about their topics and identified the need for more background knowledge. This was evident with each group's inquiry question, which reflected the broad and general foci for their topics. Nonetheless, the work the students engaged in with Phase 1 remained important, namely because it reflected the work that disciplinary experts do at this stage, such as historians, who place a premium on acquiring as much relevant information as they can about their topic to craft more meaningful and useful investigative questions. We interpret the students' choice of questions as an attempt to cast their nets wide to learn more general information about their topics. One student, in the final reflection after the entire project was completed, even suggested this was an inevitable part of the process, writing: "When addressing an issue through inquiry, students may start out very broad in their understanding of the issue. The general idea becomes the *framework* for the process of inquiry and it is then that a question can be formulated properly."

Looking across the students' work in Phase 1, we can also readily see the significance of collaboration and an emerging sense of individual commitment and responsibility to the community of inquiry and to collective knowledge-building, as the students began to work through ideas in the online discussion forums. In one way, this can be understood as multiple traversals across the terrain; four or five people in each group shared ideas, identified what they knew and didn't know, and moved toward the selection of a group inquiry question. We also can discern the students enacting open and receptive stances, embracing each other's ideas to obtain a "lay of the land." This type of stance reflects the progressive values of care, concern, and connection (Martin, 1994) that are so crucial to cultivating community, and seem especially important at the beginning of a project when much is relatively new and different and the scope and focus of the work is not clear yet. This also helps explain why there is little evidence during Phase 1 of much dialogue across difference. The general process most groups followed could be summarized as one group member introducing a broad topic and then others supporting and adding specificity to begin sharpening the focus. It seems that the need for more background knowledge about a topic might decrease the likelihood of students challenging each other's ideas, one aspect of dialogue across differences. In other words, it is difficult to talk meaningfully across different views if group members are at the early stages of learning about their topics.

With such a complicated topic—capitalism and global trade—and distinct disciplinary foci to frame their work, the groups seemed to adopt a more tentative approach to grapple with the epistemological challenge of defining purposes and launching an inquiry. The groups developed broad questions to frame their investigations, focusing on cultivating more background knowledge about their topic perhaps before moving toward greater specificity as their inquiry proceeded.

Phase 2

The initial focus of Phase 2 was to encourage students to think about the practices they would enact while selecting, analyzing, and synthesizing their sources. To support students in locating useful and reliable sources that they would evaluate and synthesize to answer their inquiry questions, Anne introduced the students to the three heuristics outlined by Wineburg (2001)—sourcing, contextualizing, and corroboration—to demonstrate ways historians engage in historical inquiry. She wanted the students to understand sourcing and contextualizing to critically consider how the time and place a source was written and the author's political, social, and cultural positions shaped the ideas in a text. She also decided it was important in Phase 2 to discuss how judging credibility would be ongoing throughout the inquiry process. This included discussions of how historians also engage in corroboration to compare ideas across texts and how this would become part of their work in Phase 4 as each group synthesized across all the group members' sources. Anne also shared examples from inquiry groups the semester before who expressed how surprised they were when evaluating sources in Phase 3 and synthesizing in Phase 4 led them to question the credibility of sources they had deemed credible in Phase 2.

Anne then led the class to discuss more specifically how to locate useful and reliable web sources to answer their inquiry questions. The students first shared with each other the search engines they most often used for research and how they decided what search terms to type in a search box. Anne extended this discussion by sharing the "topic + focus" keyword search strategy provided by Eagleton & Dobler (2007).[6] The discussion then moved to ways to select a specific site as useful and reliable from a list of search returns.

To evaluate the usefulness of a web resource, the class discussed how this could involve scanning titles and descriptions on the search return page and headings, topic sentences, images, media, and links within specific sites. To evaluate a site's reliability, the students discussed how this could involve considering a site's author and sponsor and what the motivation might be in writing and producing the site and how this motivation could affect what information is and is not shared on the site. The students also pointed out that being aware of a site's URL address is important (i.e., a URL with ".edu" is more credible than one with ".com"). During this conversation Anne referred to the inquiry projects from the preceding semester, indicating that these students had provided tips to future researchers about how to select sites. One piece of advice was to make sure that each group chose sites that represented varying perspectives about the issue, including sites with different domain endings. One group, for example, noted the limitations of selecting all government-sponsored websites. While that group believed this increased the likelihood that the sites would be credible, it restricted the quality of their synthesis because they only worked with government-sponsored web sources.

Anne then asked the students to each choose just one web source to be analyzed for their group's inquiry in Phase 3. Each group was advised to communicate with each other to ensure the sites included content from both local and global perspectives. The students were also encouraged to consider multiple types of texts, including news articles, sites sponsored by different organizations, blogs, as well as video and audio clips. Students posted the URL of the site they selected on an online discussion forum where all group members shared how they found their site (i.e., what search engine and keywords they had used) and explained why they thought the source was useful and reliable.

As the students worked through Phase 2, they recognized the importance of selecting sources to deepen background knowledge, as these two examples from the discussion forums illustrate:

> This website offers different sub-categories: What is a Sweatshop?, What kind of abuses to workers face?, But what kind of jobs?, Sweatshops, the new global economy and the race to the bottom, and NAFTA and the FTAA Sweatshops [categories from her website]. I think all of these categories will be useful to our presentation, because it provides some background information and what is going on today with sweatshops and trade agreements. (Student in Economics group)
>
> I found two sites which give some more simplified explanation of the World Trade Agreement as well as some Myths vs Facts about NAFTA. I think it is necessary for us to explain both these agreements in a more basic form or our audience may lose interest or not understand. (Student in Government group)

Students were also intentional about engaging "difference" as they located sources to be used in Phase 3. The differences were understood, for example, in terms of a need to find a web resource that "provides a new angle on sweatshops that people should be aware of because it may be the truth" (student in Economics group) or in terms of different text genres, as the following example from a student in the Psychology group demonstrates:

> We can use these blogs as a way to get in touch with the common people from around the world and to begin to understand how the recession has hit them and how the media has influenced them. Also the newspapers themselves can be very telling in how they portray different topics.

As with Phase 1, Anne played a key role in the students' decisions about sources. She participated in the online forums for each group and also responded individually to students via e-mail. At times Anne suggested specific search terms to use, such as "effect of media + recession" or pointed out problems with the web resource a group selected. For instance, Anne composed the following message for the History group:

> Your first site provides an interesting look at historical connections between the two countries, however many of the links are dead and I'm not sure the page itself provides enough information to be helpful in answering your inquiry question. The second site seems useful in providing a current look at how the U.S. economy affects Asia.

Anne also encouraged several groups to specify the particular resource within a more comprehensive website. This feedback was primarily because the *Critical Web Reader (CWR)* tools to be used in Phase 3 worked best in guiding readers to evaluate and analyze specific web pages rather than more general websites.

Managing Epistemological Challenge #2– Utility Trumps Credibility

Looking across the students' efforts during Phase 2, they mostly set up broad parameters for their searches, presumably to gather more knowledge about their topic before narrowing their focus. The students were asked to post the URL of a credible and useful web resource, explain why the source was credible and useful, and also explain how it would help answer the group's inquiry question. To build up their knowledge base, they shared useful sources (that provided basic information, defined terms, etc.) and identified the need for an array of perspectives because this could provide a sense of the lay of the land. These more broad or general goals to build background knowledge did pose challenges for some students when it came to selecting their sources, as one student in the Psychology group noted in her end of project reflection: "Looking for sources was the hardest part of the project. I do not know anything about inquiry or psychology really the only thing I brought to the table was that I was a really good consumer, just ask my parents and my credit card bill."

The structure of the assignment for Phase 2 might also have contributed to the challenge of locating web sources. Anne asked the students to each choose just one web source to be analyzed for their group's inquiry in Phase 3. The rationale for this decision was guided by several reasonable assumptions: this would increase the likelihood that each student would carefully adjudicate among a range of sources to choose the best possible source for the group's inquiry; having one source per group member would support close, critical reading and more in-depth analyses of sources in Phase 3; and this approach would help manage and facilitate the flow of students moving from Phase 2 to Phase 3. A larger set of sources to evaluate and analyze would necessitate a more significant time commitment to the project, which was something Anne wanted to contain as much as possible. While these assumptions proved to be true, some students found the limitation of one web source per person to be unnecessarily restrictive. The History group, in particular, expressed how this approach was a problem because it prevented them from conducting a more thorough inquiry.

While the students considered why their chosen sites were useful, they did not substantively address issues of credibility. Anne echoed this finding as she reflected on her own participation in the online discussion forums. She acknowledged dedicating most of her time to suggesting search terms and sharing sources she thought might be useful, but did not comment on or question the students about the credibility of their sources. Put simply, utility trumped credibility at this stage for these students. While this was the case, we know that discerning credibility does not occur solely during Phase 2. We know from doing web-based inquiry projects with students in previous semesters that issues of credibility are part of Phases 3 and 4 when students examine closely each source and then synthesize their findings across all the sources the group examined.

We were concerned with another finding when we looked more closely at what transpired during Phase 2. Although the inquiry project was structured with a framework of new literacies as 21st century social practices, we did not observe the type of collaboration or social practices we anticipated in Phase 2. The students in their groups did not raise many questions of each other about their sources or the reasons given for the selections of sources. At least two factors likely contributed to this result. First, the online forum space did not necessarily promote easy glances across each group member's selected source because students posted their sites in separate discussion threads. It would have been helpful for students to share their selected web sources using a tool where all sites can be seen easily and discussed in one thread (the updated version of the *Critical Web Reader* supports this). This could have facilitated students providing feedback on each other's sources in relation to all the sources the group selected. The second, and likely more significant, factor contributing to the lower level of collaboration in Phase 2 was the issue of background knowledge. The students needed more background knowledge about their topics. As a result, identifying useful and, for the most part, easily digestible sources took precedence over engaging in substantive dialogue with peers about the usefulness and credibility of the sources.

Phase 3

As the class prepared to begin their work on Phase 3 of the inquiry project to analyze the web sources, Anne engaged the students in a class activity to identify and evaluate claims and evidence. The class read an article from the Wall Street Journal entitled "The Trophy Kids Go to Work" (Alsop, 2008) which claimed that individuals born after 1980 (all the students in the class), called the Millennial Generation, have an unreasonable sense of entitlement. The students noticed that evidence provided to support the main claim about entitlement included statistics from a career website and comments from an administrator at Stanford. They also noticed that although the author provided a counter-example in defense of the Millennial Generation, it was from a less credible source, a seemingly random blog. The students engaged in a rather robust discussion about what the author was claiming about their generation and how evidence was purposefully being used to convince readers of this claim.

After the activity, students were invited to consider all the literacy strategies they had used as readers to examine the Trophy Kids text. The class discussed how this involved not only indentifying claims and evidence in a text but also source work (e.g., identifying information about the source itself and the author), questioning the perspectives that were and were not included, and considering how personal beliefs and prior learning influence their reading and evaluation of the claims.

This set the stage for Phase 3 and each group's work with the *Critical Web Reader (CWR)*. Anne introduced the *CWR* to the students and provided on overview of the four primary lenses: descriptive, academic, critical, and reflexive (see Chapter 3). Each student in each group was responsible for examining the web resource s/he selected in Phase 2 along with a source that another group member selected. (This ensured that two people analyzed each web source.) The students completed much of their *CWR* work in the computer lab during one class session with Anne occasionally offering assistance to the students.

While working in Phase 3, the students consistently identified the need to know more about their topics. At times this was cast in more general terms, such as when a member of the History group stated, "It would be nice to have more background information ... even though I am aware of the past relationship [between the US and Asia] from the 80s on, I need a site that shows the relationship." There were also several examples where students referred to the disciplines to frame the need for more knowledge about their topics. A student in the Sociology group stated: "I still need to find more about how sociology applies to these regions" while a Geography group member pointed out: "We have yet to find specific examples of how the actual geography of the land has an effect on industrial trade."

The need for more knowledge about a topic was often framed with specifics in mind, as when a student in the Government group articulated: "I want to know specifically what manufacturing exports reached an all time high of $982 billion compared to the 42% increase b/t 1980–1993, as stated in the NAFTA document." Most of the student groups, in fact, expressed the goal to have more specific details and examples to deepen their investigative work. For instance, a student in the Economics group wanted "more detailed examples of economies that are developed around these [sweat] shops" while a member of the Psychology group intended to find "examples of cases that the media's coverage for the recession has directly affected how people think, feel, and act."

At times the "need to know more" was framed as a need for more perspectives about their topics. Several group members in the History group, for example, noted the need to "find out the Chinese perspective" or "know more about the Asian experience and point of view," including "firsthand accounts" from people "affected by the U.S. influence in Asia." Similarly, the Government group identified the need to obtain Mexican perspectives about NAFTA, as one student pointed out: "I need to get the opinion of the Mexican people. We have only been looking at the NAFTA agreement through the eyes of the United States when Mexico may have a completely different opinion." Some students framed the need for more perspectives as an essential criterion for moving forward with their inquiry, a stance exemplified by one member of the geography group: "I believe we need to better understand the harmful effects of globalization before we advocate for a particular cause. The two websites that I viewed were proponents of globalization and trade, but we need to see other perspectives before we continue onward."

Students also situated their "need to know more" by attending to issues of authorship. One student in the History group wanted to know the editor and "actual owner" of the Christian Science Monitor while a student in the government group found problems with the claim "several studies note that Mexican industries that export or that are in regions with a higher concentration of foreign investment and trade also have higher wages." This student commented: "I want to know what studies state this. If there are several, why are they not cited?"

As the students worked through Phase 3, several groups noted the importance of collaboration and learning with and from each other. A student in the Sociology group acknowledged: "I need to cooraborate with some other members of the group to figure out if they have seen the regional ideas as much as I have" while another member of this group stressed the significance for the group to "sit down and see where everyone is and bounce ideas off of each other."

Managing Epistemological Challenge #3—Adjudicating Among Competing Claims: A Key Initial Step

Overall, there is some evidence of the students involved in the disciplinary practices of sourcing, contextualizing, and corroborating. They responded to the *CWR* questions within the lenses that focus on determining the credibility of a source (e.g., "Who is the author, sponsor, and intended audience of the webpage?"), detecting bias (e.g., "What perspectives are included and omitted in the text?"), evaluating claims and evidence and corroborating across sources (e.g., "Are the claims and evidence convincing? Explain."). Perhaps most significantly, the groups pointed out the need for different perspectives about their topics, the need to hear other voices, especially the voices of those adversely affected by forces of global capitalism and trade, such as people who could provide "firsthand accounts" of being "affected by the U.S. influence in Asia." This type of critical reading—identifying omitted perspectives—is fundamental to Phase 3 (and the focus of the critical lens in the *Critical Web Reader*). Responding to critical questions about authorship and other possible views on a topic also embodies the core practice of "building perspective" where, in order to develop a more sophisticated understanding of an issue, a range of voices must be heard and considered.

The students did work collaboratively in Phase 3. The following discussion posts from the History group highlight this collective meaning-making:

KL: I also think I would like to be able to explore firsthand accounts
JC: Perhaps an interview is the way to go . . . but that's not going to work if we have to keep it to online.
KL: Yay first hand accounts. I think my website is a really great one but I wish it had first hand accounts . . . I would also really like to know how U.S. economy effects the world more too. Maybe I group should have picked the economy!
AB: I have a feeling that firsthand accounts are going to be the only way to see how the US has affected Asia but it seems as though your site is the only one. I wish we could see more of how Asia has affected the US. We are focusing on the history of relationship but it is hard not to include the economy because that's what we want to learn about now.

In this discussion thread we can also see an emerging realization within the group about the interdisciplinary nature of their work. The group began in Phase 1 with the broad inquiry question: *In thinking about globalization how do the United States and Asia affect each other?* Here in Phase 3 we see them striving to further establish the parameters for their inquiry as they consider how economic factors might be entwined with their disciplinary focus in history. With this group and across the other groups, however, there is less evidence of students marshaling the methodological resources of their respective academic disciplines as they worked through Phase 3. For example, the students did not explicitly identify or reflect upon whether or not they were drawing on the methods of historians, psychologists, sociologists, economists, political scientists (government), or geographers in their analysis, evaluation, and interpretation of the web resources.

Looking across the students' efforts in Phase 3, the students clearly continued to identify the need for more background information about their topics. Not possessing this background knowledge, in turn, affected their ability to wrestle with the epistemological challenge of adjudicating among competing claims and evidence. The possession of more substantive background knowledge in many ways is a necessary precursor to skillfully weighing, evaluating, and adjudicating among claims and evidence about a topic. The students, however, did identify omitted perspectives related to their topics and consider the implications of these omissions. This type of reflection is crucial to the inquiry process and is foundational to disciplinary work. We also view this practice as a vital step in the process of adjudicating among competing claims and evidence. A next step is to identify, investigate, and deliberate (in groups and as a whole class) the specific claims and evidence used by different stakeholders, to more fully engage in sourcing, contextualizing, and corroborating (Wineburg, 2001). The students began to do this as they responded to the question prompts in the *Critical Web Reader* but they did not engage in more sustained deliberation and dialogue about their analyses.

CONCLUSIONS

Our goal in this chapter has been to learn more about how students engaged in the inquiry process, how they grappled with the first three epistemological challenges to build knowledge about subject matter, in this case, about capitalism and global trade. We began with an emphasis on what background knowledge the students accessed through the first three inquiry phases and the ways their teacher, Anne, guided them with a collaborative inquiry model. In reflecting on what we have learned, we start with a powerful reminder: every student has a starting point, begins an investigation with understandings and ideas about the content (e.g., capitalism and global trade) and methods to investigate this content. Some of Anne's students professed having little to no background knowledge about their topic (especially when viewed from their disciplinary lens) while other students brought more substantive knowledge to the project. Teachers, in turn, need to begin from this place and provide opportunities for students to identify what they know as well as what they want to know.

Looking across the students' efforts through the first three phases also reaffirms that inquiry-based learning and teaching is highly recursive and iterative. The process of identifying what one does not know to help generate an investigative question does not begin and end in Phase 1. Locating useful resources in Phase 2 and closely analyzing these sources in Phase 3 often leads to revised investigative questions and a commitment to locate and scrutinize additional resources. In this sense, the recursive and iterative qualities of the students' inquiry-based work can be understood as *multiple traversals across a problem space* (an inquiry project), traversals that point to the ways the students were *building perspective* through excavation and elevation practices. The students evaluated the specific background knowledge they brought to the project and examined individual web sources with the *Critical Web Reader* tools (excavation). The students also consistently stepped back from their analysis of specific texts to consider what else they needed to know and how they might acquire this information (elevation).

Across Phases 1, 2, and 3 there is clear evidence of the students and Anne engaged in collective knowledge-building and "progressive problem-solving" (Zhang, 2009). Investigative questions during Phase 1 were forged through online and in-class discussions as the students articulated what they knew and didn't know about their topic and shared ideas about how their own group might best proceed. In Phases 2 and 3 the students wrestled with locating useful resources and then analyzing each web resource with critical questions in mind (*Critical Web Reader*). This enabled students to build their background knowledge about their topics and begin to consider ways to reformulate their inquiry foci.

The collective knowledge-building within this community of inquiry was also bolstered by particular pedagogical processes and technology scaffolds. Anne contextualized each of the first three inquiry phases with whole class introductory activities and guided discussions, each helping to orient the students to the work ahead. She also provided focused and timely feedback that guided each group, and individuals within groups, to clarify, deepen, or extend their thinking. The *Critical Web Reader* set of tools guided students to analyze their web sources—e.g., to evaluate claims and evidence, discern included and omitted perspectives, and consider how people from other backgrounds (cultural, ethnic, religious, gender, economic, etc.) might view the particular web source. These pedagogical moves and technology scaffolds are especially significant in a community of inquiry where the members possess limited knowledge of the content and beginning-level understanding of disciplinary methods of investigation. This was the case in Anne's class.

Through the first three inquiry phases the students, in general, further developed understandings about a complex, multifaceted topic, recognized the challenges of doing this type of inquiry project, and came to value the collective sense-making of their groups. The next chapter considers what happened during the culminating phases of their inquiry projects with an emphasis on the collective knowledge-building within and across the groups as they engaged with the epistemological challenges of synthesizing findings and communicating ideas. The next chapter also considers the work of the students and Anne through the lens of *relational cosmopolitanism*.

8 Part II: Identifying What We Know and What We Don't Know— Progressive Knowledge-building in an Inquiry Community

With Anne Elsener

This chapter considers the ways Anne's students, in an undergraduate content literacy course for preservice social studies teachers, grappled with the two core epistemological challenges that correspond to the fourth and fifth phases of the inquiry process: synthesizing findings and communicating new ideas. We describe the ways Anne prepared her students for these challenges and we explore the work produced by the six groups of students with their different disciplinary foci (History, Economics, Psychology, Sociology, Government, Geography). Similar to Chapter 7, our analysis in this chapter highlights the significance of collective sense-making and "progressive problem-solving" (Zhang, 2009) as the students engaged in the sophisticated tasks of synthesizing findings and devising approaches to communicate, in the most clear and compelling way, the results from their group investigations of capitalism and global trade. Along the way we can see some of the ground they covered (the content of their inquiry), the tools vital to their travels (methods of collaborative inquiry), and their emergent knowledge-building as an inquiry community. Their work also illumines the ways *relational cosmopolitanism* can frame the ways future social studies teachers might be inducted into the profession.

WEB INQUIRY PROJECT

Developing Community of Inquiry Standards for Final Projects

When Anne guided the web inquiry project the previous semester she noted that the groups employed different approaches to conduct their syntheses. Some groups divided the responsibilities and worked independently at separate computers (each student synthesized findings from their one web resource), while other groups sat huddled around one computer to deliberate their ideas and synthesize findings across the individual web sources. In an effort to better support the inquiry groups in this current semester to more collaboratively engage in synthesis across web sources, Anne led a whole class discussion to jointly establish expectations for synthesizing and communicating findings. She began this discussion by inviting the students to consider their previous school experiences synthesizing information as part of group work. The students cited that synthesizing findings was primarily an individual experience with each student working on different tasks to complete the assignment. Anne then led a discussion about what a more collective engagement with synthesis might look like with the current web inquiry investigations of capitalism and global trade. Anne shared her expectation that the final presentation of findings from each group's inquiry in Phase 5 would be a collective synthesis across all the web sources, rather than a site-by-site synthesis of each separate source. Anne then offered Wikipedia, where different authors make distinct contributions to compose an entry, as an example of collective meaning-making. She contrasted this to Encyclopedia Britannica, where collective engagement is less evident.

The students were then given an opportunity to establish the specific criteria for the synthesis each group would create and present with their final projects in Phase 5. Anne guided this process by asking students to consider the following question to develop their criteria: What does it mean to answer our class inquiry question? After exchanging ideas during a whole class discussion, the students settled on three criteria, agreeing that results of the syntheses and answers to the groups' inquiry questions needed to be: 1. Each group's best interpretation of the information; 2. Presented without bias; and 3. Supported by evidence. To reinforce to students that a primary goal of the web inquiry project was not to arrive at definitive answers, Anne added a fourth criterion: identify more questions to pursue. With these working criteria established, Anne asked the students to identify the literacy strategies they would need to successfully synthesize their information from the web sources. The students identified summarizing, making connections with prior knowledge, corroborating (connecting information across sources), questioning what is said and not said, considering multiple viewpoints/perspectives, considering the genre of a source, identifying claims and evidence, and inferring the author's argument.

Developing shared criteria for the final phases of the inquiry project strengthened the classroom community of inquiry. The criteria served as standards and reinforced the perspective that all the students were responsible for advancing community knowledge about capitalism and global trade.

Phase 4

To begin synthesizing their findings, Anne provided three question prompts for the students to respond to in an online discussion forum: 1. What were the most credible claims and evidence from your exploration of your web source? 2. Have you answered the initial questions? 3. What new questions or ideas do you have about the topic? The students were also asked to respond to the posts of their group members. Anne reminded the students how the forums were an important place for groups to begin their collaborative synthesis of information by looking across the claims and evidence each individual group member posted and comparing these to information in their own web source. During the next class meeting, the students then worked as groups in the computer lab to synthesize their findings. While they did this work, Anne encouraged the students to display on their computers their responses saved within the *Critical Web Reader* (CWR) and their recent posts on the online discussion forums.

The online forums and ensuing group discussions in the computer lab were designed to promote collaborative knowledge-building within and across the groups. The quality of this collaborative work, however, differed across the groups. The Economics group, for example, engaged in the type of exchange Anne envisioned for this inquiry phase. Each group member posted the most credible claims and evidence from their individual web source analyses and then each group member compared and contrasted these analyses. The following post from one of the students is representative of the group's work:

> It looks like we have a wide array of answers beginning to pile up. Desiree has found information confirming that the anti-sweatshop movement is helping the worker's conditions in other countries. She has found evidence backing that globalization is furthering these practices. Both Gwen and Lisa were left questioning what the workers think of their working conditions. Some of my information led here as well. These workers are often times working in better conditions than that of others in their countries. BUT does it make it right? No. My information lies somewhere in the middle. Both sides are argued. I think that our best bet for answering "How do sweatshops affect the global economy" would be to present both sides of this, that is the pro's and con's of sweat shop labor and then maybe provide a solution. This might be where we talk about what our University has done to take action against sweatshop labor.

The group members also identified what they deemed to be missing information that might help them answer their question. One student commented: "The two websites I compared showed two opposite viewpoints on sweatshops. I want to know how countries or workers themselves actually feel about sweatshops, if workers themselves are advocating for more workers' rights or not." Another student responded with a more disciplinary emphasis: " . . . We need to find more detailed examples of economies that are developed around these shops. Once we have that specific knowledge we can then apply it to the global economy, and show how these shops are either hurting or helping both the global economy and individual countries." Anne also observed that throughout the project this group questioned their initial stance that sweatshops were unequivocally bad.

In contrast, there was less evidence of the Geography group using the online forum space for "progressive problem-solving" (Zhang, 2009) and collective knowledge-building. The group members posted individual responses based on their web source analyses and they identified what seemed to be needed to answer the inquiry question. They, however, did not engage each other in more substantive discussion. Two group members did ask their peers clarifying questions, but the forum space was not used to jointly compare and contrast the analyses across web sources.

Not surprisingly, the groups who worked diligently to collaboratively synthesize their ideas in the online forums (e.g., Economics group) also produced more meaningful work during the small group discussions during the next class session (as well as stronger final projects). Looking across the groups, the students in general found the *CWR* helpful in guiding their synthesis. The work the students completed with the *CWR* in Phase 3 could be readily accessed (e.g., discernment of main ideas, claims, and evidence) and then shared and discussed with peers in the online discussion forums. The forums then provided a space for the collaborative meaning-making and synthesizing as groups moved toward the creation of their final projects.

Phase 5

In preparing to assemble their work to communicate what they learned during their inquiry, Anne and the students discussed the audience, content, and form for their final projects. In terms of audience, the inquiry projects were to be shared with the whole class as well as future students taking this content literacy course. The content was to include a "research story" (some documentation of the group's process through the five-phase inquiry), the synthesis of information to answer their inquiry question, and advice to future researchers. The students were invited to choose alternative formats for the final projects, such as podcasts or digital video, but each group created a PowerPoint presentation. This was likely due to the time limitations at the end of the semester and because all of the final projects from the previous semester, which Anne showed them, were PowerPoint presentations. The students completed much of the work assembling PowerPoint slides and clarifying ideas for the final projects outside of class.

The final projects and presentations varied in scope. We offer a brief summary of each project and then consider the disciplinary practices and interdisciplinary potential across the projects.

Sociology: In telling a story of their investigation with the inquiry question, "How has globalization affected the poverty gap?," this group discussed the challenge of locating useful web sources (which was surprising because they viewed themselves as "savvy Internet users" who aren't "used to encountering these types of problems." They described that they had figured this would be easy but only a few of the many returns from their Internet searches seemed useful to their research). They synthesized their findings and came up with two main claims they wanted to make, which they supported with statistical evidence: 1. The gap between rich and poor is widening; and 2. There are regional differences based on societal values and political alliances. The group also engaged critically with statistics that demonstrated that poverty levels around the world had decreased in the last decade (ending in 2008). The students pointed out that "this does not mean the gap has not widened." This group concluded their presentation with two important questions. The first concerned disciplinary methods of investigation and spoke to the challenge they experienced locating information sources: "What information do we need and how can we compile it? [because] we need to find a way to put this information together so that the research can be done. The majority of the time was spent chasing down sites and information." The second question of the group charted a path for a more focused inquiry: "It is important to research why globalization has caused the wage gap to widen. In a world where collective effort is becoming the norm wouldn't it make sense that these problems would be addressed better by more countries?"

Psychology: This group discussed their process of choosing two related inquiry questions: "How does the media portrayal of the ongoing recession affect people's psychological choices and feelings? How do people's feelings and choices influence what the media says?" They then outlined four primary challenges they experienced: "It was really difficult to find any answers to our main question; Each of us could give a part of the answer but no one could find the whole answer; Many of our sources were more opinion based rather than research based; Determining the credibility of a source was also difficult." The group came up with a main claim— "The media DOES construct how we see/feel about the current economic situation"—but did not offer any evidence to support this claim. They concluded with advice for the next group of students/researchers in this content literacy course ("Be careful in the sources that you choose as a lot of sources out there are opinion based. Not all opinion based sources are bad some are supported by actual facts!") as well as two questions for further inquiry ("How much is the recession affecting third world countries that have low literacy rates and less resources? What is the difference between how urban and rural dwellers are affected by the recession based on the amount of advertising and news that are present in their lives?").

History: This group investigated the question, "In thinking about globalization, how do the U.S. and Asia affect each other?" Their overarching claim ("The United States and Eastern Asia have affected each other economically, politically, socially, and culturally throughout the course of recent history") was noncommittal (it didn't specify or take a stand on how). But the group did demonstrate their close analysis of each of their four web sources by identifying the main claims and evidence in each source (e.g., "U.S. trade with China impacts China's trade with smaller Asian countries"), which linked to their overarching claim. The group clearly identified the limitations of their work. For example, they noted that they could only use four Internet sources and began with a broad question. During the presentation, they shared that it would have been helpful to narrow their focus at the beginning of the inquiry project because they felt like they were "swimming in information." The group also outlined possible next steps for research, offering a general suggestion (narrowing the focus to one county and a single time in history) and suggesting several questions, including: "How do different nations within Asia affect the US? How does a nation affect a whole continent?" The group also raised a key question about interdisciplinarity, asking "Is anything entirely history or entirely geography, or is overlap unavoidable?"

Economics: This group provided the most comprehensive presentation of their work and ideas. They identified background knowledge and the starting point of their question ("How do sweatshops affect the Global economy?"). They made explicit their moral stance on sweatshops and decided that they wanted their "question not to be biased toward our initial moral values." This group also went beyond stating their inquiry question to clearly articulate what they hoped to learn (national and global legislation pertaining to sweatshops; effects on employees vs. effects on employers; child labor; demographics of sweatshops in US; what can be done to improve or prevent sweatshops; how sweatshops affect us). The group also distinguished itself from the others by documenting their tentative findings *during* the inquiry project. In the early to middle phases of the project, they noted that "sweatshops weren't pure evil" and "actually improved living standards for people in third world countries" and that their university "takes a stance against sweatshops."

The group synthesized claims and evidence made by proponents and opponents of the anti-sweatshop movement, comparing the competing perspectives of economists (e.g., Paul Krugman) and advocacy groups, and they used statistics, charts, graphs, and images as evidence to support their synthesis. While the group did not explicitly take a stand on sweatshops, they posed the following question on one of their concluding PowerPoint slides which suggested an anti-sweatshop stance: "What can you do to stop sweatshops?" The group then concluded their project with a set of recommendations: "Pick a topic that isn't too broad and isn't too specific. THEN, after a little bit of research, choose your question. Choose a website that has multiple perspectives. Be open and willing to listen in the synthesizing portion of the process. This is the most important phase! The better you answer the questions on the *Critical Web Reader*, the easier the synthesizing process will be."

Government: This group investigated the question, "How do government policies affect outsourcing, labor, and tariffs?," with a focus on the North American Free Trade Agreement (NAFTA). To launch the inquiry, the group worked to define globalization and then develop background knowledge about NAFTA. (To highlight the complications of NAFTA, the group began their presentation with a YouTube video clip entitled "The NAFTA Super Highway" from Lou Dobbs Tonight on CNN and a description of the Wikipedia entry on NAFTA). This led to the goal to read and evaluate "specific pieces of NAFTA that represent globalization." The group discussed the challenge of adjudicating among competing perspectives to discern myths versus facts about NAFTA. They found the length of some texts to be "unbearable" (e.g., the NAFTA document itself) and imbued with "confusing" language. Overall, the goals and results of the inquiry focused on learning more about NAFTA; the group did not take a stance on the issue and make its own claims. Similar to the Economics group, however, the Government group addressed local dimensions of the topic, citing the findings of one study about the adverse effects of NAFTA for the local economy where their university is situated. The group posed several questions to guide future work ("Has the agreement benefited Mexico, Canada, and the United States? Did one people, group, or country receive more benefits than others such as, top American businessmen? What can be changed about the agreement to make it better?") and offered research recommendations, which focused on acquiring as much background knowledge as possible about NAFTA before beginning the inquiry, narrowing the inquiry focus, and ensuring the perspectives of relevant stakeholders are considered. The group, for example, noted that their web sources were dominated by United States perspectives; they did not take into account Canadian perspectives and had inadequate representation of Mexican perspectives. One student, in his final reflection, even identified how he needed to broaden his search to include websites written in both Spanish and English to find Mexican viewpoints.

Geography: This group struggled throughout the inquiry project and in their final presentation they pointed out how it was particularly difficult to locate credible sources to answer their question: "How has geography played a role in today's industrial trade relations on a global and local level?" They acknowledged that their goal was "to tie geography, globalization, and poverty together and take a look at how each were interrelated" and that they began with the working assumption that "the globalization of trade would reduce poverty in most of the world's poorest regions by connecting rural and underdeveloped areas to the rest of the world." In constructing their synthesis, the group made a general claim about how developing nations like China "throughout the course of time have relied on waterways and port cities for trade . . . and are continually becoming more globalized to meet the demand of goods and supplies throughout the world." (It bears mentioning that during their class presentation one member stated that while it seemed like a "simple finding" it "took time" to develop). The group considered the concepts of place, movement, and borders in their project, yet there was no evidence of deeper-level engagement with these ideas (e.g., they seemed to have difficulty discerning how a geographic viewpoint could help them understand globalization). The group seemed to focus primarily on developing background knowledge about their topic. The quest for more general information and understanding is also reflected in the following questions they offered as next steps: "What types of problems are associated with globalization? What are the long-term effects of globalization? Is it possible for developing nations to become successful? If so, what does that mean for future world trade relations?"

Relational Cosmopolitanism: Building a Foundation and Charting Next Steps

Relational cosmopolitanism builds from an integrated view of knowledge, embraces core progressive values, such as open-mindedness, public deliberation, dialogue, and critique, and remains committed to understanding and addressing complex problems as a "lived process of ongoing political and ethical action and education" (Mitchell, 2007, p. 717). Anne and her students enacted a stance of *relational cosmopolitanism* through the web inquiry project. We can see this in their disciplinary practices, the emerging interdisciplinarity of their inquiry, and through their "progressive problem-solving" (Zhang, 2009) across the five phases of the project.

Disciplinary Practices

Each group engaged in key disciplinary practices as they synthesized their findings and communicated their ideas through the final projects. The students identified key strategies and standards during the whole class discussion of expectations for synthesizing and communicating findings. They agreed that syntheses and findings should represent their best interpretation of available information, be balanced and presented without bias, and be supported with sufficient evidence. They came to recognize that syntheses are tentative, that it's important to identify gaps or limitations in their findings, and that this results in the emergence of new questions that will need to be addressed to better understand their investigative topics. The students identified key synthesizing strategies, such as summarizing information, making connections with their prior knowledge, corroborating information across sources, identifying the range of claims and evidence made in sources and inferring authors' arguments, and considering multiple viewpoints. In all, each group developed and explored disciplinary questions, concepts, and content, evaluated claims and evidence, synthesized their results, and devised a way to communicate their findings (PowerPoint slides with bulleted lists and images). Most groups demonstrated an awareness that their respective disciplines work with certain kinds of data (e.g., the Sociology group and Economics group selected sources with statistics, graphs, and tables). They also reflected critically on their work and identified what they still needed to know about their topics. Two members of the geography group, for example, articulated the need to "find specific

examples of how the actual geography of the land has an effect on industrial trade" and on how "the particular location of a nation plays a major
role in today's trade market globally."

While all the groups engaged in disciplinary practices, the depth of this
engagement differed by group. The Economics group most skillfully mined
the complexities of their topic by constructing a synthesis that evaluated
and compared claims and evidence of different perspectives (e.g., economists and several advocacy groups). What seemed to distinguish the Economics group was the level of background knowledge they brought to the
inquiry and were able to build upon and access throughout the project. The
groups that began with more background knowledge about their topics,
not surprisingly, produced more developed final projects. The Economics,
History, and Sociology groups stand out in this regard, as each group had
at least one member who possessed some substantive knowledge about the
topic or the discipline in general to help tackle their inquiry topic. One
student in the Sociology group, for example, established himself at the
beginning of the inquiry as a group leader when he informed the group
of his background in sociology (e.g., that he had five or six sociology textbooks), which could help guide the inquiry. This student ended up providing invaluable mentoring, as another group member pointed out: "I learned
that background knowledge was something that was very useful to have
... I did not know a whole lot of information related to globalization, but
Aaron did, and knowing about the subject through background knowledge
really made a difference in the way we thought about globalization." Other
groups began with less background knowledge about their topic and their
academic discipline, which likely contributed to less robust findings. The
Geography group, for example, struggled with how best to proceed with
their inquiry when, in the words of one student, "none of us really knew a
whole lot about geography." The Psychology group also began their work
from a similar place.

Some students framed their desire for more background knowledge
in terms of a need to obtain a more *elevated* or big picture view of the
topic, as a student in the Sociology group demonstrates: "Working to figure out how globalization worked with sociology was challenging. I had
to learn more about both subjects before I could work them together."
Another student in the Sociology group expressed a similar view: "After
uncovering a definition about the concepts of sociology, it made the rest
of the inquiry process much easier as I was then able to have a general
understanding of the claims made by the sources, and how those claims
actually applied to sociology and then globalization." Students also discussed the challenge of achieving sufficient depth in their work, a view
exemplified by a student in the History group who believed the group
did not focus enough on the historical relationship between Asia and the
United States. Other students identified the challenge of finding "concrete
evidence" about their topics.

In many ways, disciplinary experts wrestle with similar challenges. They question themselves about how to best frame an inquiry about a complex issue, about whether their evidence is concrete and compelling, and about whether their findings are deep and robust enough. Unlike Anne's students, disciplinary experts have the experience, the "wisdom of practice" (Shulman, 2004), to navigate these challenges. Nonetheless, Anne's students engaged in comparable practices in response to these challenges, and in so doing, came to cultivate and solidify their membership in a particular "community of practice" (Wenger, 1998). Moreover, while a number of students began their inquiry projects without much knowledge of the academic discipline that framed their inquiry, there was clear evidence that many students advanced their understandings of their respective disciplines through their participation in the web inquiry project. A student in the Geography group stated: "I have never taken a geography course before so it was a new subject for me. I learned more about the relationships between geographical features and how they relate to the economic standing of the country." Another student in the Geography group offered more specificity:

> In terms of geography my thoughts have come a long way since the beginning of the inquiry project on globalization. I just thought of geography as maps and mountains and streams. However, the subject is way broader than just those simple terms. Geography can be thought of in several different ways. In particular I learned about geography in terms of global trade. The causes and effects, and what makes a particular area of the world better economically and logically for trade.

A student from the Sociology group, despite having "no formal instruction" in sociology, described being able to "put together a definition that discusses the core concepts of sociology," a definition stated as "the study of people and their societies, and how societal views influence change, and differences across time and the globe."

Although Anne's students were novices in disciplined inquiry, they were, at minimum, engaged in key approximations of disciplinary work, building a repertoire of practices that will help them more substantively engage with real world and academic problems. Through their participation in the discourse practices of disciplined inquiry, the students were cultivating "conceptual agency" what Greeno & van de Sande (2007) describe as the:

> [S]election, adaptation, and critical judgment about the appropriateness, utility, relevance, and meaning of alternative understandings, strategies, concepts and methods in a domain of activity so that a positive contribution can result in choosing or adapting a method for use in solving a problem or better understanding of a problem or concept. (p. 12)

The students learned to participate in practices that required them to collaboratively identify and evaluate claims and collectively develop their own claims using evidence and elaboration based on their own prior knowledge and information drawn from sources. They considered different perspectives and claims made about capitalism and globalization and negotiated meaning through "interpreting, adapting, questioning, criticizing, and modifying" subject matter (Greeno & van de Sande, 2007, p. 16).

Emerging Interdisciplinarity

Looking across the students' work helps to identify interdisciplinarity as an *elevation* practice, an essential aspect of building perspective as students look across perspectives and disciplines to better understand their topics. The whole class presentation of the final projects was designed to more explicitly enact the interdisciplinary goals of the web inquiry project. After the groups discussed their findings from pursuing a topic through a disciplinary lens within the social studies, they had an opportunity to assemble and jointly assess the overall findings across the disciplinary groups. There was an increased recognition that interdisciplinary perspectives were useful and necessary to engage in an inquiry-based class project like this. The History group, for example, posed the rhetorical question: "Is anything *entirely* history or *entirely* geography, or is overlap unavoidable?" The Psychology and Geography groups in their final projects suggested similar connections to economics.

Interdisciplinary understandings also developed organically as the students worked across the five phases. A student in the History group summed up this sentiment midway through the project: "We are focusing on the history of the relationship [between the United States and Asia] but it is hard not to include the economy because that's what we want to learn about now." Thinking in interdisciplinary ways also was an approach to manage complexity, as a student in the Government group pointed out: "Because our topic was so complex we were all constantly trying to connect what we were reading to other things we had learned about government, the economy, and the relationship between the two." The embrace of interdisciplinarity for the Government group was also likely due to their topic, NAFTA, which seemed inherently more cross-disciplinary. Policy analysis often involves or draws upon, for example, history (e.g., to contextualize the policy), economics (e.g., cost-benefit analysis), and sociology (e.g., examination of how different groups might be affected by a policy's implementation). The Government group also possessed less experience with the methods of the discipline (political science) compared to students in the History and Economics groups.

Progressive Knowledge-building

Progressive knowledge-building was integral to the students' work across Phases 4 and 5. Each group synthesized findings through online and in-class discussions, decided how best to communicate these findings, and then assembled and communicated their ideas as PowerPoint presentations to the class. In doing this collaborative work, we see examples of multiple and repeated traversals through the problem domains central to their investigative questions, dialogue around different ideas, claims, and perspectives they encountered, and efforts to build perspective, especially during the process of completing their final projects. As with Phases 1, 2, and 3 (as described in Chapter 7), a central aspect of the knowledge-building for each group was identifying what they did not yet know or needed to know. This was especially salient at the conclusion of this inquiry project. Given the project limitations (e.g., few sources examined, time restrictions) it was not expected that students would make strong, unequivocal claims supported with conclusive evidence. What was important to Anne was for students to deepen their appreciation and understanding of inquiry as an iterative and recursive process, dynamic and ongoing, rather than as a pathway to a final, definitive destination. She also wanted students to have "sustained, incremental gains in knowledge" (Zhang, 2009, p. 274). The project was designed for students to work in the disciplines in authentic ways (enacting or at least approximating the practices of disciplinary experts) to investigate a complex, multifaceted issue: the forces of capitalism and global trade. The students proceeded with limited background knowledge and little to no experience with disciplinary methods of investigation. Each student and each group needed to figure out, with Anne's support, how to negotiate challenges each step of the way.

Progressive problem-solving and collective knowledge-building is also based on the idea that higher-level goals can emerge when initial knowledge problems are addressed (Zhang, 2009). As a result, the students' work during the synthesizing and sharing findings phases was shaped by the ways they engaged in progressive questioning and sustained knowledge advancement during early phases of the inquiry process. Several groups alluded to this when they shared the "stories of their research" during the presentations. As they moved into the synthesizing and sharing phases of their work they became more aware of some of the problems they were having with their inquiry questions and the limited available resources, perspectives, and knowledge claims they could work with. As a result, some groups had to adjust and reformulate the goals of their project in order to make tentative claims in response to their research questions.

Critical Self-reflection

Critical self-reflection is a crucial practice of *relational cosmopolitanism*, so we do that here to review what transpired during the project. Overall, Anne was pleased with the level and quality of the students' work with the web inquiry project. Given time and resource constraints, she was pleased that her students had the opportunity to move systematically through an inquiry project and grapple with core epistemological challenges. Reflecting on the experience with a critical lens, with a "willingness to the doubt the goodness of one's own way" (Nussbaum, 1997, p. 62), also charts a path of potential next steps for teachers like Anne. These steps include Anne continuing to fortify her own knowledge of disciplined inquiry in the social studies, collaborating with colleagues in social studies education and across campus in the History, Economics, Sociology, Geography, Sociology, Political Science, and Psychology departments, and rethinking some pedagogical moves to more successfully guide students through the inquiry phases.

For starters, it is important to note that Anne guided the web inquiry project with an inquiry stance herself as a teacher. She intended to explore and examine what happened when this project was introduced and carried out in her content reading course. Her own inquiry question could be summed up as: *What happens when a web inquiry project is implemented in such a way that shifts the focus in the course from more general literacy strategies (i.e. making connections, asking questions, making inferences and predictions, etc.) to using and thinking about literacy strategies specific to academic disciplines, where learners are supported in not only learning content but also how literacy practices are an essential part of producing knowledge in a discipline* (e.g., Moje, 2008; Shanahan & Shanahan, 2008)? As part of her own practitioner inquiry, Anne read the work of historians engaged in historical inquiry as well as how historical inquiry could be implemented across grade levels. Anne also recognized the need to step outside her literacy and language education department to more purposefully collaborate with the instructor of the social studies methods course, a senior faculty member and accomplished scholar and teacher. Because they shared the same students, Anne was able to sit in on his classes to observe their discussions of historical inquiry and to exchange resources about social studies education related to inquiry and reading practices in the discipline. This enabled Anne to be more deliberate in connecting her content literacy course with the other courses the students were taking as a cohort in the social studies education program. Further, Anne felt better equipped to guide students through the web inquiry project to develop content knowledge and understandings about literacy strategies, which she viewed to be integral to their future as social studies teachers.

During this semester, Anne was also reaching out to faculty members across campus in the History, Economics, Sociology, Geography, Sociology, and Political Science departments. She joined an interdisciplinary study group of faculty and graduate students committed to improving the intellectual quality of undergraduate teacher preparation for social studies teachers. Through conversations with these colleagues Anne has learned distinctions between historical and ahistorical claims, enriched her understanding about bias, and learned how to teach particular target skills in history.

The inquiry into her own practice has also led Anne to rethink some of her teaching moves. After the final project presentations Anne invited students to share what they noticed about the presentations. A common theme the students noticed was the challenge of narrowing an inquiry question. The class discussed how the process of narrowing the question can be overwhelming without background knowledge of the topic. It was clear that more scaffolding is needed to support students in identifying, gathering, and sharing information needed to develop an inquiry question. This finding is now leading Anne in subsequent semesters to increase the amount of time dedicated to developing the inquiry questions and to design opportunities for students to more intentionally explore their topics before drafting an inquiry question.

Anne has also realized the need to be more strategic in promoting collaborative knowledge-building and "making collective cognitive responsibility a social norm" (Zhang, 2009, p. 36). As suggested in Chapter 7, web-based tools are needed to better support students to deliberate the selection of specific web sources for the inquiry project. Individuals posting sites within their own discussion threads did not sufficiently promote collaboration. Further, Anne was the key person giving feedback about the usefulness of the sites selected. This responsibility could be shared with students, especially if Anne guides them in this process.

Collective knowledge-building is especially important in the latter phases of inquiry as students are synthesizing findings and preparing to communicate ideas. The class time when students worked in inquiry groups to synthesize findings allowed Anne important opportunities to check in with each group, identify their needs, and offer a few suggestions about how to move forward, but this time was too brief and limited. In future semesters, time needs to be structured for each group to meet with Anne after they post and discuss their claims from individual web sources in the forums. This will help each group of students evaluate their progress towards answering their inquiry question and identify necessary next steps in their work.

Another way Anne could revise her approach to bolster collective knowledge-building would be to experiment with different design models to organize the group work. For this web inquiry project Anne primarily employed a *fixed small group* design structure (Zhang, Scardamalia, Reeve, & Messina, 2009) in which groups worked independently on distinct components of the project and then combined forces at the end to assemble their work. At times Anne also used an *interacting groups* design by structuring opportunities for collaboration across groups, such as offering prompts for online forum discussions and guiding discussions in-class. Both of these design approaches embody a more centralized framework, where the teacher plays a more authoritative and directive role throughout the project. A different approach with a more distributed framework is also possible. Zhang et. al. (2009) describe a *flexible, opportunistic collaboration* design in which there is more fluidity to group work, where participants assume responsibilities to form and disband groups according to their needs as a project evolves, rather than solely or primarily in response to a teacher's plans. This responsibility necessitates "collaborative improvisation" (p. 13)—anticipating, identifying, and solving problems as they emerge and monitoring, adjusting, and reformulating goals of a project as they evolve. Zhang et al. (2009) go on to describe three requirements of teachers interested in *flexible, opportunistic collaboration*. Teachers must possess a deep trust in student agency and possess the conviction that students can and will create knowledge; teachers must value "working with emergence" and embrace the shift from factory models to organic models of teaching and learning; and, similarly, teachers must understand and enact "progressive curriculum" by maintaining a commitment to guiding the evolution of students' ideas and ensuring that these ideas are engaged with in "the community space" (p. 38). In many ways, a flexible, opportunistic design aligns with the *relational cosmopolitanism* we describe and call for in this book. There is undeniably an improvisational quality to the type of intellectual work required when participants pose and pursue questions that aim to understand and address complex, multifaceted problems. Teachers and students need to flexibly adapt to every shifting problem space, be able to skillfully interpret and work with a range of texts, discern and adjudicate among competing perspectives, and engage in "a community of reason" (Nussbaum, 1997, p. 25) to deliberate and make informed decisions (Parker, 2006). For teachers and students this involves a continual process of thinking and rethinking what topics to investigate, ways to conduct the investigations, and what to do with knowledge learned.

In the next chapter, which concludes the book, we use the idea of *rethinking* to look across the key ideas of the book and reconsider what should be taught, why it should be taught, how it should be taught, and how these decisions get made (Eisner, 1997). We believe the time is especially ripe for this rethinking.

Part III
Synthesis and Implications

9 Social Studies as New Literacies
Relational Cosmopolitanism in the Classroom

Our aim is this book has been to develop a viable vision of an inquiry-based social studies education in which students engage in new literacies to understand and address complex multifaceted problems. We have advocated a vision of social studies as new literacies because so much of what we know about and do in the world is mediated through texts, technologies, and media. In turn, we believe inquiry approaches can help students best navigate new and emerging global landscapes and transnational flows. Social studies as new literacies for understanding and addressing multifaceted problems can direct teachers and students toward what Dewey (1935) referred to as a "method of intelligence"– the critical capacities to analyze social problems and participate actively in improving social conditions (Stanley, 2010). Developing these capacities prepares students to engage in logical analysis, test the range of beliefs and claims they encounter (including their own and those commonly accepted) for justification, validity, and consistency, and construct and effectively communicate their own claims about the social world. This type of education is absolutely critical for helping students confront ideological fundamentalisms, dogmatic rigidity, intolerance, and the fear of uncertainty. Students develop the confidence to deal with increasing complexity, novelty, diversity, and ambiguity amidst rapidly changing social conditions. This type of education is integral to cultivating *relational cosmopolitanism* in the classroom.

We have two primary goals with this culminating chapter: to look across the previous chapters to synthesize key ideas about what we have learned from examining classroom enactments of social studies as new literacies; and to appeal to social studies and literacy educators to rethink content and curriculum and teaching and learning in order to take greater control of education in the global age. With these goals in mind, we created two figures. The first synthesizes the features of a conceptual landscape in which transnational flows and global "scapes" (Appadurai, 1996) necessitate practices of excavation and elevation, including multiple traversals across a problem space, dialogue across difference, and building perspective. The second figure is an image and description designed to depict the multifaceted work that students and teachers in a classroom community can do with complex texts and technologies. These two figures are fundamentally about meaning-making and each provides a snapshot of the complexity of meaning-making in a global age. Figure 9.1 focuses on macro-level features of the global landscape and core practices to engage with these features while Figure 9.2 addresses implications at the micro-level of the classroom, what we identify as six dimensions of *inquiry in use.*

KEY FEATURES OF CONCEPTUAL LANDSCAPE

Figure 9.1 provides a model of how transnational flows and global "scapes" (Appadurai, 1996) define a complex landscape in which social studies and literacy are conceptualized as inquiry-based social practices. At the base of the model, transnational flows of goods, people, and ideas, new identity movements, new technologies, fast capitalism, etc. intersect with global "scapes"– *technoscapes, financescapes, mediascapes, ideoscapes,* and *ethnoscapes.* As discussed in Chapter 1, these "scapes" help paint broad brushstrokes of the larger terrain, providing a sense of the intersections, connectivity, and multidimensionality of this ever-shifting landscape. Situated on this base is a globe that outlines the core practices that are necessary for understanding and participating within these "scapes" and flows. The complexity of this multidimensional space requires the use of disciplinary, interdisciplinary, and transdisciplinary tools and resources to help students understand and participate in new global landscapes. These tools include the substantive knowledge (paradigms, concepts, frameworks, and canons of accumulated evidence) and the syntactic knowledge (methods of inquiry, procedures for truth claims, and norms of evidentiary warrants) of different disciplines along with the ways interdisciplinary and transdisciplinary approaches can be leveraged to understand and address problems. These tools and resources support the core practices of multiple traversals across problem spaces, dialogue across difference, and the building of perspective. Similarly, these core practices enable students to develop greater facility with disciplinary, interdisciplinary, and transdisciplinary tools and resources. Two metaphors, excavation and elevation, frame these practices and the different lines within the globe emphasize iterative and recursive qualities of meaning-making.

Figure 9.1 also suggests a fluidity of movement between excavation and elevation practices and the potential of moving quickly between each. Excavation involves analysis and evaluation, attending closely to the particulars of text (e.g., discerning fact from opinion, detecting bias, evaluating claims and evidence, and identifying persuasion techniques employed by authors). Elevation involves contextualizing and corroborating, such as considering when, where, and why a text was produced and what else was happening within the immediate and broader contexts when the text was produced and distributed. Both excavation and elevation practices benefit immensely from diverse perspectives by helping students consider different ways of seeing and thinking about information sources, by helping them consider connections (with other texts, experiences, issues, knowledge, etc.), and by helping them become more aware of their own perspectives. Progressive problem-solving and collective knowledge-building are fundamental to this effort and new media and technologies support these practices by offering opportunities for varied and multiple representations of content and dialogue with others who may have different perspectives.

The fluid movement among these practices suggested by the circles within the globe also helps break down rigid conceptions of boundaries and borders between nations, academic disciplines, the world of work and civil society (Shaker & Heilman, 2008), the child and curriculum, and between school and society (Dewey, 1900/1990; Mitchell, 2007). Katharyne Mitchell (2007), drawing on Beck (2000), argues that disrupting our allegiance to boundaries is crucial because "the boundaries associated with territories, disciplines, institutions, and ideas can no longer be considered fixed or pregiven but rather must be understood as constantly reworked in specific contexts" (p. 707). We see examples of traditional boundaries being disrupted in the classrooms highlighted in Chapters 4–8 as teachers and students moved fluidly across boundaries to develop more integrated understandings of multifaceted issues. In Chapter 4, Rindi and her group of young students disrupted the subject matter boundaries of science and social studies and the boundary between teacher and students as they worked collaboratively to develop shared criteria and tools to guide a class inquiry into the destruction and preservation of rain forests. In Chapter 5, Mark and his ninth grade students engaged in "postdisciplinary conversation" where the goal wasn't to sustain knowledge stratification of institutional imperatives but to deliberate publicly about a complicated text (Dimitriadis & McCarthy, 2001). In Chapters 7 and 8, Anne worked with small groups of students in an undergraduate course for prospective social studies teachers as they came to recognize the salience of interdisciplinary inquiry in their investigations. Across these chapters we see students working across boundaries vis-à-vis emergent and expansive (rather than prescriptive) curricula as they pursued issues, questions, sources of information, and representations of learning that mattered to them.

Figure 9.1 aims to depict how flows and forces intersect with "scapes" in dynamic, multidimensional ways, which, in turn, necessitate particular meaning-making practices. We frame these practices with the metaphors of excavation and elevation. The dynamism of these flows, forces, and meaning-making practices also permeates spaces at the micro-level of particular classrooms in interrelated ways that require what we call *inquiry in use*.

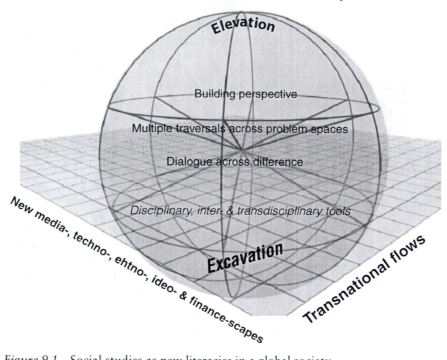

Figure 9.1 Social studies as new literacies in a global society.

A MODEL OF INQUIRY IN USE: RELATIONAL COSMOPOLITANISM IN THE CLASSROOM

Leander and Rowe (2006) note how challenging it is to capture and represent "literacy in use," especially the diverse and innovative ways students make connections across texts and perform identities. In this book we have made a case to see "literacy in use" in social studies as inquiry-based social practices for understanding and addressing complex, multifaceted problems. As we look across previous chapters and reflect on the complex meaning-making work of the teachers and students, we propose a model of "inquiry in use" as an attempt to capture this complexity.

To represent and understand "inquiry in use," we created Figure 9.2 by turning to an image of Calabi-Yau shapes (Funch, 2006). These six-dimensional geometric shapes represent multidimensional spaces in theoretical physics, string theory in particular. Calabi-Yau spaces "are tremendously complicated and are not completely understood," yet physicists are finding them useful as they attempt to explain additional spatial dimensions in the universe (Susskind, 2003). Classrooms, especially those committed to web-based inquiry projects, are also complicated and "not completely understood." We address this complexity by employing the concept of a six-dimensional Calabi-Yau image to help us identify six dimensions that we think best represent the dynamic, interrelated, and multidimensional nature of teaching and learning in a classroom committed to web-based inquiry. We also posit these six dimensions as the core components of *relational cosmopolitanism* for the classroom. No dimension is more important than the next and all overlap and are mutually reinforcing. These six dimensions include:

- Resources of participants
- Relational knowing
- Rigorous content and curricula
- Facility with key tools and resources
- Dialogic, problem-solving pedagogies
- Transformative goals and outcomes

Figure 9.2 is depicted as a classroom inquiry community that is embedded in and shaped by the myriad flows and forces of larger contexts (institutional, cultural, local, regional, national, global, etc.). The six dimensions of Figure 9.2 also define the contours of what constitutes *relational cosmopolitanism* in classrooms.

Resources of Participants

This dimension begins with a deep recognition that it matters what participants, primarily teachers and students, bring to the classroom. They are

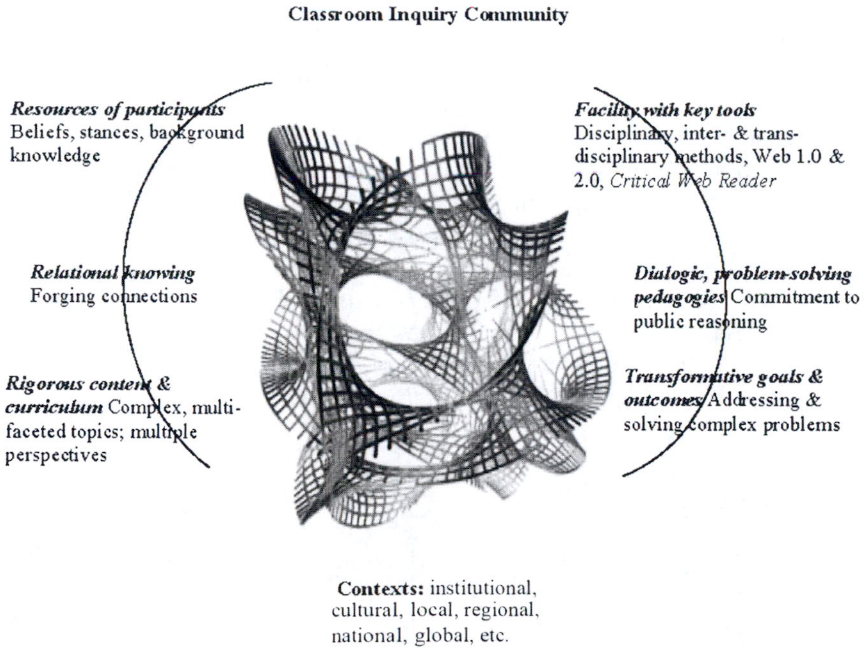

Classroom Inquiry Community

Resources of participants
Beliefs, stances, background knowledge

Facility with key tools
Disciplinary, inter- & transdisciplinary methods, Web 1.0 & 2.0, *Critical Web Reader*

Relational knowing
Forging connections

Dialogic, problem-solving pedagogies Commitment to public reasoning

Rigorous content & curriculum Complex, multifaceted topics; multiple perspectives

Transformative goals & outcomes Addressing & solving complex problems

Contexts: institutional, cultural, local, regional, national, global, etc.

Figure 9.2   Inquiry in use: *relational cosmopolitanism* in the classroom

not *tabula rasa* devoid of knowledge and experience. Rather, they come to classrooms with beliefs, values, stances, and background knowledge, which all factor into the ways they engage with content, view teaching and learning, approach curriculum, and understand broader purposes of education. Moreover, the resources that students and teachers bring to the classroom are especially salient when curriculum is conceptualized in terms of complex, multifaceted problems of global and local significance, such as climate change, pollution, war, disease, and poverty. Students and teachers in all contexts have, to some extent, understandings of and experience with these problems, and these understandings can be brought to bear in inquiry projects. Students and teachers can also access their knowledge and expertise with technology tools to more skillfully engage with and enact new literacies in their investigations.

Students and teachers also mobilize in different ways what they bring to the classroom. In a study that examined the ways students in an international school in Taiwan evaluated competing websites about the Taiwan Straits, two colleagues joined us to discern how the students mobilized their cultural and contextual knowledge related to living in Taiwan to identify two authorial techniques, *disputable historical facts* and *emotional appeals*, that were used in the text written from a Mainland China perspective (Damico, Baildon, Exter, & Guo, 2009). After using the *Critical Web Reader (CWR)*, the students in this study also became more aware of what they brought to this reading task because they were prompted to think about questions like "What affects the way I read this site?" and "How might people with different backgrounds, experiences, and beliefs read this site?"

We can see similar work being done in Chapters 4–8 as the students mobilized their background knowledge, beliefs, and stances in their meaning-making. In Chapter 4, the children accessed their knowledge about the tsunami photo to impugn the photo's authenticity; in Chapter 5, the students drew upon what they knew about the September 11th attacks to challenge the truth claims in the video, *Loose Change*; in Chapter 6, one of the students, Stan, shaped his inquiry through his strong stance and identity as a pirate; and the students in Chapters 7 and 8 had ongoing opportunities to access and build upon their background knowledge through each phase of the inquiry process. It is also essential to note that in each of these classrooms, the teacher honored what the students brought with them to the inquiry projects.

Relational Knowing

Inquiry in use is at heart relational. Students investigate significant problems and teachers play the crucial role of guiding and facilitating these investigations. In other words, producing knowledge is inherently "a relational act" with teachers "sensitive to the actual historical, social and cultural conditions that contribute to the forms of knowledge and meaning that students bring to school" (Freire & Macedo, 1987, p. 15). Knowing is essentially "a relational process between the knower and the known" (Thayer-Bacon, 2003, p. 48), a process that involves students *relating* what they know (e.g., background knowledge) to new ideas, concepts, etc. and forging new understandings in and through collaboration with others. The term *relational knowing* also suggests fluid and dynamic qualities of knowledge-building as opposed to *relational knowledge*, which connotes stability and permanence (Gallego, Hollingsworth, & Whitenack, 2001).

Relational knowing is foundational to a view of literacy as socially situated practices (New London Group, 2000, Street, 2003). In his argument that reading is a social process, Bloome (1985) describes how reading entails relationships among teachers, students, parents, and authors along with the ways groups are established, status and social positions are gained and maintained, and how "culturally appropriate ways of thinking, problem-solving, valuing and feeling" are acquired (p. 134).

A stance of relational knowing has curricular implications. Rather than view curriculum in terms of rigid, inflexible borders and boundaries, a relational epistemology leads to a more multidisciplinary curriculum where there is great value placed on overlap, association, the forging of connections, and integration along with a concern for and commitment to curricular depth (Thayer-Bacon, 2003). Each of Chapters 4–8 in this book highlights this concern and commitment and depicts relational knowing in action. Rindi and her young students in Chapter 4 forged understandings about rain forests, along with understandings of disciplinary methods of investigation, through collaborative inquiry. Mark and his students in Chapter 5 jointly grappled with issues of credibility as they viewed and discussed the complicated digital video, *Loose Change*. While the focus in Chapter 6 was individual case studies, these three students developed and refined their ideas within a classroom inquiry community. And collaborative and progressive problem-solving was integral to all the work Anne and her students completed in Chapters 7 and 8.

Rigorous Content and Curriculum

As we described in the introduction to this book, a number of seminal scholars have advocated (and some have created) curricula aimed to guide students and teachers to identify and investigate important social problems or controversial issues. Our goal has been to add to this noteworthy historical lineage, and this led us to make a case to conceptualize social studies as *inquiry-based social practices for understanding and addressing complex, multifaceted problems*. Chapters 4–8 highlight the ways several teachers and their students wrestled with some of these problems: the destruction and preservation of rain forests in Chapter 4, terrorism with September 11th in Chapter 5, intellectual property rights and national sovereignty (Taiwan) in Chapter 6, and the effects of capitalism and global trade in Chapters 7 and 8. Inquiry in use requires that students have opportunities to investigate these kinds of problems and then to generate and apply knowledge to address them.

These investigations can best take place within a curriculum that views knowledge not as an end in itself but as a resource for deeper and richer understandings of the world. For curriculum to be rigorous, students need opportunities for multiple traversals across the subject or problem and skillful guidance to work through problems they encounter. Students need opportunities to make meaningful connections between personal and social experience, between past and present (e.g., to apply past lessons to a contemporary issue), across disciplines, between self and others, and between the local and global. In this way, rigorous content and curricula is marked by a "connection code" rather than a "collection code" approach to knowledge (Luke, 2003).

Rigorous content and curricula is also shaped by an ethic of care, concern, and connection (Martin, 1994) as well as critique. Care, concern, connection, and critique are only possible through a focused curriculum in which students "immerse themselves in a problem and address it with compassion, rather than try to solve a great many problems at a superficial, surface level" (Thayer-Bacon, 2003, p. 265). Rigorous content and curriculum focus on relationships, connections, interactions, interrelationships, and patterns of change that cut across particular nations, cultures, and societies (Dunn, 2010). This would include, for example, issues that are central to transnational flows and "the powerful effects of transregional and global historical processes such as large-scale migrations, cross-cultural trade, biological diffusion, technological transfers, and cultural exchanges in world history" (Bentley, 2005, pp. 62–63).

Rather than view subject matter content as a body of fixed, inert, and static knowledge to be attained, new landscapes require that content and curricula be seen "as resources for 'pursuing performativity' . . . the ability to take elements from one knowledge system, put them together with elements from another *different* knowledge system, rearranging them to do something new and different. It involves *doing things with knowledge*: going beyond the mastery of existing knowledge to the generation of new knowledge" (Gilbert, 2007, italics in original, p. 120). According to Gilbert (2007), such knowledge "develops on an *as-and-when-needed* basis" (italics in original, p. 119).

We see examples of rigorous content and curriculum and knowledge being produced on an "as-and-when needed basis" in Chapters 4–8. In Chapter 4 a teacher and her young students investigated rain forest destruction and preservation by collaboratively developing a set of criteria and research tools to guide the careful and systematic appraisal of information sources in terms of their reliability, readability, and utility. In Chapter 5 we see attentive deliberation focused on the credibility as well as the claims and evidence of a sophisticated digital text. In Chapter 6, we see three of Mark's students engaged with a range of web-based sources of information to critically evaluate claims, systematically synthesize their findings, and develop their own interpretive accounts of complex multifaceted issues (intellectual property rights, Internet piracy, national sovereignty). In Chapters 7 and 8, we see Anne and her students tackle the challenging topic of capitalism and global trade through different disciplinary perspectives (history, economics, sociology, psychology, political science or government, and geography).

Facility with Key Tools and Resources

In Chapter 2 we offered a way of thinking about disciplinary, interdisciplinary, and transdisciplinary perspectives as valuable meaning-making tools and resources (e.g., organizing themes and "big ideas" as well as methods of investigation). In Chapter 3 we considered web-based resources to help manage five core epistemological challenges of inquiry-based social studies education. We argued that to best manage these and other related challenges stemming from new global and knowledge landscapes, students and teachers need to develop greater facility with key tools and resources. A primary point in this concluding chapter is to stress the importance of understanding that this facility, especially with new and emerging technologies, is deeply integrated with the other dimensions in our *inquiry in use* model.

There is evidence of this facility across the classrooms in Chapters 4–8. In Chapter 4, Rindi accessed web resources (e.g., from Alan November's website) to help frame the class investigation. She and the students then worked collaboratively to develop criteria to discern the readability, trustworthiness, and usefulness of a text. The result was the creation of an inquiry tool, the "Research Resource Guide," which became a focal point for the class deliberations. In Chapter 5, the class investigation of the digital text, *Loose Change*, led Mark to create two new *Critical Web Reader* lenses with target questions for the critical evaluation of a video. In Chapter 6, Mark and his colleagues modified the existing *Critical Web Reader* lenses to guide his students through the trajectory of their inquiry projects. In Chapters 7 and 8, Anne guided her students through each phase of the small group inquiry projects with a range of tools, such as the guiding questions, tips, and suggestions from the *Critical Web Reader* toolset and the use of online discussion forums for small group and whole class deliberations. In each of these classrooms, technology tools (or tools to address technology related challenges, such as reading websites) were used strategically to promote public reasoning and deliberation around important issues, to cultivate dialogue across difference, and to build perspective.

Dialogic, Problem-solving Pedagogies

Dialogue is necessary to manage the five central epistemological challenges that correspond to the inquiry phases. It is through dialogue that teachers and students manage the challenges of asking good investigative questions, locating relevant and useful sources of information, considering issues of reliability and credibility, evaluating claims and evidence, synthesizing findings, and generating and communicating new ideas. A dialogic approach requires time and space for teachers and students to both "plumb the world deeply" toward an "enlarged understanding of the text *and* one another" as well as choose courses of action after appraising alternatives (Parker, 2006, p. 12, italics in original). Dialogue requires that students and teachers collectively address learning tasks, listen to each other, share ideas, and consider alternative viewpoints in a supportive, caring environment (Alexander, 2008). Having time for this work is essential because, as Oliver and Shaver (1966) have argued, issues- and inquiry-centered social studies hinges on a willingness to explore ideas, tolerate ambiguity, and have "an intelligent, open, inquiring and imaginative mind" (p. 240).

The teachers in Chapters 4–8 employed dialogic approaches with their students. In Chapter 4, Rindi posed questions to connect with students' prior knowledge and experiences and then guided her students through a range of activities that required dialogue and deliberation as they jointly developed criteria and approaches to evaluate the readability, trustworthiness, and utility of websites. In Chapter 5, Mark facilitated a whole class viewing and discussion of the complicated digital video, *Loose Change*, in which he and the students jointly identified and talked through the challenges of reading and discerning the credibility of this text. In Chapter 6, a dialogic pedagogy served as a crucial foundation for the individual students' inquiry investigations. Throughout the year, Marked worked to cultivate a "community of reason" in the classroom through a range of activities, and the three students highlighted in this chapter were able to build from this foundation in their inquiry pursuits. In Chapters 7 and 8, Anne created opportunities for students, in small groups and as a whole class, to manage and solve problems with each phase of the inquiry process. In these classrooms there is evidence of the ways that, through dialogue, teachers and students can "become knowers" as "social beings-in-relation-with-others" (Thayer-Bacon, 2003, p. 247)

Transformative Goals and Outcomes

The preservation and maintenance of the status quo amidst wide-scale social, political, and economic problems in the world is simply not an option. Building on the work of influential social studies and literacy educators, this book is based on a view that an understanding of social studies as new literacies entails a pedagogical commitment and a corresponding set of practices in which students investigate and address these complex, multifaceted problems with transformative goals and outcomes in mind. Chapters 4–8 highlight this commitment and set of practices in action. In Chapter 4, Rindi and her students investigated rain forest destruction, a social and ecological crisis that transcends boundaries, to learn how humans cause this destruction and the consequences of this destruction on societies throughout the world. In Chapter 5, Mark and his students took on the topic of terrorism, and mined some of the complexities involved in determining the credibility of claims and evidence of a politically charged text about September 11th. In Chapter 6, the three featured students investigated intellectual property rights, Internet piracy, and national sovereignty to begin building deeper understandings of the social and political consequences of these issues. In Chapters 7 and 8, Anne and her students tackled the weighty topic of capitalism and global trade to examine the widening gap between the rich and poor, competing arguments about sweatshop labor, the impact of the media, and components of NAFTA. In each of these classrooms, the teachers and students were enriching their understandings about these complex topics in ways that could better prepare them to address these problems.

This dimension, transformative goals and outcomes, compels us to think about consequences, "trac[ing] out in the imagination the conceivable practical consequences" of a particular concept or action (Peirce, 1905/1984 in Cherryholmes, 1999, p. 26), in this case an inquiry project, to imagine before an inquiry begins what the consequences of a particular pedagogical pathway might be and to reflect critically on the consequences of how a classroom community travels down a pathway. An emphasis on consequences leads to questions like: *what work in the world does or can this inquiry do?* (Damico, Campano, & Harste, 2009), which involves addressing and using all the dimensions in the *inquiry in use* model (Figure 9.2) to offer a response to this question. An "ends-in-view" emphasis also embodies the emergent, improvisational, and organic qualities of teaching, where curriculum is a "living verb" (Doll, 2002) so that "ends arise and function within action . . . they are terminals of deliberation, and so turning points *in* activity" (Dewey, 1923/1974, p. 70). In this sense, the goal of an inquiry project is not necessarily attained definitively. Rather, it is often an ongoing struggle toward a "social imaginary" where "the common good [is] a vanishing point, something that we must constantly refer when we are acting as citizens" (Mouffe, 1992, p. 379).

Summary

The six dimensions help define the contours of *relational cosmopolitanism* in the classroom. Figure 9.2 depicts the six dimensions as interrelated, mutually reinforcing, and dynamic. The shapes in the figure suggest fluidity among the dimensions with each at play transacting simultaneously with each other.

Acknowledging the resources that participants bring to classrooms acknowledges each individual's integrity and worth and communicates that she or he has something to contribute based on her or his particular background, experiences, knowledge, perspectives, and skills. Relational knowing places greater emphasis on learning and problem-solving as shared and collective enterprises; that others help us learn about ourselves and the world in ways that we, in general, are not capable of doing well on our own. Rigorous curriculum acknowledges and helps frame the complexity of multifaceted problems that confront all of us and points to the available knowledge and intellectual resources in, across, and even outside of academic disciplines that we need to adequately address these problems. Since so much is mediated by new technologies and media, new digital tools and resources must be powerfully harnessed in inquiry classrooms to understand and address fundamental problems and challenges facing humanity. Facility with these tools enables fuller and more effective participation in increasingly technological and mediated social contexts. Dialogic problem-solving approaches emphasize the role of talk and interaction since societies need people who can argue, reason, question, challenge, evaluate alternatives, and take judicious action (Alexander, 2008). These approaches prepare students to participate in social institutions and communities of reason at local, national, regional, or global levels. And an inquiry in use model shifts education goals from the maintenance of knowledge stratification and institutional imperatives to educational practices as transformative, reflective, and public intellectual activity (Dimitriadis & McCarthy, 2001).

Taken together, the six dimensions of inquiry in use support a notion of civic education that consists of commitments to justice, connection, concern, and care for people within and outside of the nation-state, coupled with informed social action to address issues that are no longer solely national in scope, such as poverty and inequality, disease and health care, war and violence, and sustainability and climate change.

IMPLICATIONS OF SOCIAL STUDIES AS NEW LITERACIES

Core ideas in this book, as depicted in Figures 9.1 and 9.2, have implications for how to think in general about educational reform. These ideas rest on a relational view of educational reform, as Gallego, Hollingsworth, and Whitenack (2001) describe:

> [P]roductive and lasting educational reform requires not only attention to standards, but resources and structures to establish critical relationships which enable educators to learn about themselves as they learn with others, thereby creating the opportunity for the understanding and development of different perspectives. (2001, p. 241)

This sits in stark contrast to externally imposed reform initiatives, as Dewey pointed out approximately a century ago:

The vice of externally imposed ends has deep roots. Teachers receive them from superior authorities; these authorities accept them from what is current in the community. The teachers impose them upon children. As a first consequence, the intelligence of the teacher is not free; it is confined to receiving the aims laid down from above. (Dewey, 1916/2004, p. 104)

Externally imposed ends and attempts to enforce them often create an overly bureaucratic and conservative climate for schooling that emphasizes the status quo, curriculum coverage, and control and order in classrooms (Cornbleth, 2001), a climate in which teachers tend to self-censor and engage in over-simplification and defensive teaching (McNeil, 1986), where deficit views of students are more likely to persist, and, in more recent times, where standards and accountability movements are dominated by high-stakes testing and public school rankings (Madaus, 1999; Shaker & Heilman, 2008). In contrast, *relational cosmopolitanism*, and the core practices of multiple traversals across a problem space, dialogue across difference, and building perspective, begin with the premise that standards, criteria, goals, and norms are worked out through deliberation in a community of reason that considers the full range of ends that constitute human striving and fulfilment (Nussbaum, 2006; Sen, 1999).

Teachers play a crucial role in this community of reason and we believe any educational reform initiative must come with a commitment to create the conditions for teachers to be *relational cosmopolitans* and participate fully in communities of reason. For starters, these conditions include time, space, and resources for teachers to collaborate with each other and dialogue across different perspectives about curriculum, teaching, and learning– for opportunities to scan the horizon for emerging trends and developments between academic subjects (within and across the disciplines) and contemporary life, identify significant issues for study, and persistently strive to educate themselves so they can guide students to investigate complex, multifaceted problems. Creating conditions for teacher communities of reason can support teachers who are committed to social studies as new literacies for living in global society be more aware of the social and intellectual demands made by globalization, the increasing social and cognitive complexity based on the need to address pressing global issues that are affecting communities everywhere, new forms of labor in the global knowledge-based economy, the need to effectively and productively use new and emerging technologies, and the need to understand difference and actively participate in civil society at local, national, and global levels. Teachers can situate their own learning and teaching within and across contexts as they prepare young people to be critical and creative thinkers with capacities to participate more fully in society.

Teachers, of course, are not the sole participants in communities of reason and a stance of *relational cosmopolitanism* helps ensure that discussions and decisions about any education reform initiatives take into account a range of different perspectives from diverse stakeholders, including but not limited to the perspectives of teachers, students, administrators, government officials, university researchers and teacher educators, business leaders (e.g., from textbook and educational software companies, among others), parents, community groups, etc. Ben-Peretz (2009) makes a similar argument, outlining a holistic, ecological model for policy-making that "involves representatives of the dimensions of global changes cooperatively in the deliberations that lead to a coordinated policy statement" (2009, p. 134). We see the three core practices—multiple traversals across a problem space, dialogue across difference, and building of perspective– playing a pivotal role in the model that Ben-Peretz offers. Multiple traversals and dialogue across difference are central to what Ben-Peretz outlines as first, second, and third deliberation phases, which then leads to the building of perspective as a range of representatives contribute to the formation of policy, with a crucial factor for success of any new policy being a synergy among these different stakeholders (Ben-Peretz, 2009, p. 149). Excavation and elevation practices are also foundational to doing this work. Excavation involves careful reading and analysis of key texts related to a reform initiative, while elevation practices include cultivating an awareness of the many factors that shape an initiative, especially the relations of power among stakeholders. For example, power can be exercised by prominent politicians, the media, teacher organizations, parental and religious organizations, or industry sectors in ways that influence policy-making. The potential as well as the lived consequences of the ways power is exercised needs to be considered during deliberations (Ben-Peretz, 2009).

CONCLUDING THOUGHTS

We believe the core practices outlined in Figure 9.1– multiple traversals across a problem space, dialogue across difference, and building perspective along with the "inquiry in use" model in Figure 9.2 can help us collectively respond to the "chores of complexity" (Wieseltier, 2010) that are part and parcel of living in an increasingly information and media saturated world brought on by new digital technologies. In this book we have made a case for teachers working with young people through and toward a stance of *relational cosmopolitanism* to create communities of reason that deliberate, develop, and implement criteria and standards that guide collaborative intellectual work, especially investigations of complex social realities and problems. These types of criteria and standards are guided by goals of sustainability, justice, and equity through an ethic of care, concern, and connection. Working out such standards and criteria requires commitments and capacities in which all participants in a community listen to each other and deliberate the consequences of ideas and undertakings in order to build perspective and choose optimal courses of action. Individual growth along with the well-being and sustainability of our global society depend on our ability to create and live out such conditions in and outside of classrooms.

Notes

NOTES TO CHAPTER 2

1. It bears noting that viewers are not necessarily conscious of making these kinds of decisions. Psychological beliefs, which typically don't operate in the foreground of our consciousness, can propel people toward information that conforms to their views (Manjoo, 2008, p. 175).

NOTES TO CHAPTER 7

1. The term "Web Inquiry Project" is used by others and is even the name of a website (http://webinquiry.org/). Anne's use of the term here reflects an attempt to concisely name the class assignment based on the five-phase inquiry model described in Chapter 3.
2. The articles were "What is Globalization?" from the Carnegie Endowment for International Peace (http://www.globalization101.org/What_is_Globalization.html) and the "Globalization" entry from Wikipedia (http://en.wikipedia.org/wiki/Globalization).
3. These texts were the National Council of Social Studies (NCSS) position statement, "Preparing Citizens for a Global Community" (http://www.social-studies.org/positions/global) and the MercyCorps web page: "For Teachers: Why Teach Globalization?" (http://www.globalenvision.org/teachers).
4. The class read the chapter: Wilhelm, J. D., & Smith, M. W. (2007). Making it matter through the power of inquiry. *Adolescent Literacy: Turning Promise into Practice* (231–242). Portsmouth: NH: Heinemann.
5. While political science would be the disciplinary designation at the university, the term government was used because this is what the course is often titled in most US high schools where the students were planning to teach.
6. To model this strategy, Anne explained that if she was searching for information on content area literacy (topic) in social studies (focus) she would use the following keywords: content area literacy + social studies.

References

Agger, B. (1989). *Fast capitalism: A critical theory of significance*. Urbana, IL: University of Illinois Press.

———. (2004). *Speeding up fast capitalism: Culture, jobs, families, schools, bodies*. Boulder, CO: Paradigm.

Albrow, M. (1996). *The global age: State and society beyond modernity*. Palo Alto, CA: Stanford University Press.

Alexander, R. (2008). *Essays on pedagogy*. London: Routledge.

Allen, J. (2003). *Lost geographies of power*. Oxford: Blackwell.

Allen, T.J. (2006). The 9/11faith movement. *Alternet*. Retrieved July 29, 2006, from http://www.alternet.org/story/37647/

Alsop, R. (2008). "The 'Trophy Kids' Go to Work". *Wall Street Journal*. Retrieved December 28, 2009, from http://online.wsj.com/article/SB122455219391652725.html

Alvermann, D.E., Swafford, J., & Montero, M.K. (2004). *Content area literacy instruction for the elementary grades*. Boston, MA: Pearson.

Anderson, B. (1983), *Imagined communities: Reflections on the origin and spread of nationalism*. New York: Verso.

Anstey, M. (2002). "It's not all black and white": Postmodern picture books and new literacies. *Journal of Adolescent and Adult Literacy*, 45(6), 444–457.

Appadurai, A. (1996), *Modernity at large: Cultural dimensions of globalization*. Minneapolis: University of Minnesota Press.

Appiah, K. (1997). Cosmopolitan patriots. *Critical Inquiry* 23(Spring 1997), 617–39.

———. (2006). *Cosmopolitanism: Ethics in a world of strangers*. New York: W.W. Norton.

Ashburn, E., Baildon, M., Damico, J., & McNair, S. (2006). The landscape of teaching: Mapping the terrain of teaching for meaningful learning using technology in social studies. In E. Ashburn, & R. Floden (Eds.), *Teaching for meaningful learning using technology: Knowledge, skills and leadership* (117–140). New York: Teachers College Press.

Baildon, M. (2009). "Being rooted and living globally": Singapore's imagined communities and identities through the prism of educational innovation. In R. Ismail, B. Shaw, & G.L. Ooi (Eds.), *Southeast Asian Culture and Heritage in a Globalising World* (9–78). Surrey, U.K.: Ashgate.

Baildon, M., & Damico, J. (2006). "We have to pick sides": Students wrestle with counterclaims while reading Web sites. *Social Education*, 70(3), 158–161.

———. (2008). Negotiating epistemological tensions in thinking and practice: A case study of a literacy and inquiry tool as a mediator of professional conversation. *Teaching & Teacher Education*, 24(6), 1645–1657.

————. (in press). Judging credibility on the Internet: The case of 911 and Loose Change. *Social Education*, 74(3).

Baildon, M., & Sim, J.B.-Y. (2009). Notions of criticality: Singaporean teachers' perspectives of critical thinking in social studies. *Cambridge Journal of Education*, 39(4), 407–422.

Bain, R. (2006). Rounding up unusual suspects: Facing the authority hidden in history textbooks and teachers. *Teachers College Record*, 108(10), 2080–2114.

Bakhtin, M. (1973). *Problems of Dostoevsky's poetics*. Trans. R.W. Rotsel. Ann Arbor, MI: Ardis.

Ball, A. (2000). Empowering pedagogies that enhance the learning of multicultural students. *Teachers College Record*, 102(6), 1006–1034.

Banks, J.A. (2004). Teaching for social justice, diversity, and citizenship in a global world. *The Educational Forum*, 68(4), 296–305.

Barton, D., & Hamilton, M. (1998). *Local literacies: Reading and writing in one community*. London, Routledge.

Basch, L., Schiller, N.G., & Szanton Blanc, C. (1994). *Nations unbound: Transnational projects, postcolonial predicaments, and deterritorialized nation-states*. London: Routledge.

Baudrillard, J. (2001). *Selected writings*. In M. Poste (Ed.), *Jean Baudrillard: Selected writings*. 2nd edition, revised and expanded. Cambridge, UK: Polity.

Bauman, Z. (1998), *Globalisation: The human consequences*. New York: Columbia University Press.

Beal, C., Bolick, C.M., & Martorella, P.H, (2009) *Teaching social studies in middle and secondary schools* (5th ed). Boston, MA: Pearson.

Beck, U. (2000). The cosmopolitan perspective: sociology of the second age of modernity. *The British Journal of Sociology*, 51(1), 79–105.

Ben-Peretz, M. (2009). *Policy-making in education: A holistic approach in response to global changes*. Lanham, MD: Rowman & Littlefield Publishers.

Benkler, Y. (2006). *The wealth of networks: How social production transforms markets and freedom*. New Haven, CT: Yale University Press.

Bentley, J.H. (2005). *Shapes of world history in twentieth-century scholarship*. Washington, DC: American Historical Association.

Bernstein, R. (1992). *The new constellation: The ethical-political horizons of modernity/postmodernity*. Cambridge, MA: The MIT Press.

Best, S., & Kellner, D. (1997). *The postmodern turn*. New York: The Guilford Press.

Bhavani, K. (2005). Email reply to Mr. Au regarding government policy titled, *MICA Connects*. Retrieved April 20, 2009, from http://www.yawningbread. org/arch_2005/yax-446.htm

Bizar, J. (1998). Expert profiles Juarez killers. San Antonio Express News. Retrieved June 22, 2010, from http://officialcoldcaseinvestigations.com/showthread. php?t=6408.

Black, R.W. (2009). Online Fanfiction, global identities, and imagination. *Research in the Teaching of English*, 43(4), 397–425.

Bloome, D. (1985). Reading as a social process. *Language Arts*, 62(4), 134–142.

Boix-Mansilla, V., Miller, W. C., & Gardner, H. (2000). On disciplinary lenses and interdisciplinary work. In S. Wineburg, & P. Grossman (Eds.), *Interdisciplinary curriculum: Challenges to implementation* (17–38). New York: Teachers College Press.

Boli, J., & Thomas, G.M. (1997). World culture in the world polity: A century of international non-governmental organization. *American Sociological Review*, 62(2), 171–190.

Bono/U2 (2000). Elevation. *All that you can't leave behind*. Island Records.

Boorstin, D. (1985). *The discoverers*. New York: Random House.

Bowers (2002) Computers, culture, and the digital phase of the Industrial Revolution: Expanding the debate on the educational uses of computers, Retrieved March 18, 2009, from http://www.cabowers.net/pdf/computers_colonizingtech.pdf

Boyle-Baise, M., & Goodman, J. (2009). What would he say? Harold O. Rugg and contemporary issues in social studies education. *Interchange,* 40(3), 269–293.

Bransford, J.D., Brown, A.L., & Cocking, R.R. (2000). (Eds.), *How people learn: Brain, mind, experience, and school.* Committee on Developments in the Science of Learning and Committee on Learning Research and Educational Practice, Commission on Behavioral and Social Sciences and Education, National Research Council. Washington, DC: National Academy Press.

Brown, P., & Lauder, H. (2001). *Capitalism and social progress: The future of society in a global economy.* Basingstoke: Palgrave.

Bruce, B.C., & Bishop, A.P. (2002). Using the Web to support inquiry-based literacy development. *Journal of Adolescent and Adult Literacy,* 45(8), 706–714.

———. (2008). New literacies and community inquiry. In J. Coiro, M. Knobel, C. Lankshear, & D.J. Leu, Jr. (Eds.), *Handbook of research on new literacies* (699–742). New York: Lawrence Erlbaum Associates.

Bruner, J. (1960). *The process of education.* Cambridge, MA: Harvard University Press.

Buck, P.S. (1931/2005). *The Ggood Eearth.* New York: Simon & Schuster.

Burbules, N.C. (1993). *Dialogue in teaching: Theory and practice.* New York: Teachers College.

———. (2001) Paradoxes of the Web: The ethical dimensions of credibility, *Library Trends,* 49(3), 441–453.

Burbules, N.C., & Callister, T.A., Jr. (2000). *Watch IT: The promises and risks of new information technologies for education.* Boulder, CO: Westview Press.

Burke, J. (2002). The Internet reader. *Educational Leadership,* 60(3), 38–42.

Carnegie Endowment for International Peace. (n.d.). What is globalization? Retrieved January 27, 2009, from http://www.globalization101.org/What_is_Globalization.html

Carr, N. (2008). Is Google making us stupid? *The Atlantic.* Retrieved March 22, 2010, from http://www.theatlantic.com/magazine/archive/2008/07/is-google-making-us-stupid/6868/.

Castells, M. (1996). *The rise of the network society.* Oxford: Blackwell Publishers.

———. (1999). Flows, networks, and identities: A critical theory of the informational society. In M. Castells, R. Flecha, P. Freire, H. Giroux, D. Macedo, & P. Willis (Eds.), *Critical education in the new information age* (pp. 37–64). Lanham, MA: Rowman & Littlefield Publishers, Inc.

———. (2004). *The network society: A cross-cultural perspective.* Northampton, MA: Edward Elgar Publishing.

Cervetti, G., Pardales, M.J., & Damico, J.S. (2001). A tale of differences: Comparing the traditions, perspectives, and educational goals of critical reading and critical literacy. *Reading Online,* 4(9). Retrieved January 9, 2010, from http://www.readingonline.org/articles/cervetti/

Chan, S.L. (2005). Singapore's biotechnology push: Stem cells and urine power hint at innovations under way. *International Herald Tribune.* Retrieved June 22, 2009, from http://www.iht.com/articles/2005/09/19/bloomberg/sxsing.php.

Cherryholmes, C. (1999). *Reading pragmatism.* New York: Teachers College Press.

Christensen, L. (2000). *Reading, writing, and rising up: Teaching about social justice and the power of the written word.* Milwaukee, WI: Rethinking Schools.

Coiro, J. (2003). Reading comprehension on the Internet: Expanding our understanding of reading comprehension to encompass new literacies. *Reading Teacher*, 56(5), 458–464.

Coiro, J., & Dobler, B. (2007). Exploring the online reading comprehension strategies used by sixth-grade skilled readers to search for and locate information on the Internet. *Reading Research Quarterly*, 42(2), 214–257.

Comber, B., & Simpson, A. (2001). (Eds.), *Negotiating critical literacies in classrooms*. Mahwah, NJ: Lawrence Erlbaum Associates.

Cope, B., & Kalantzis, M. (2000). (Eds.), *Multiliteracies: Literacy learning and the design of social futures*. London: Routledge.

Cormode, G., & Krishnamurthy, B. (2008). Key differences between Web 1.0 and Web 2.0 *First Monday* [Online], 13(6) (25 April 2008). Retrieved May 4, 2009, from http://firstmonday.org/htbin/cgiwrap/bin/ojs/index.php/fm/article/view/2125/1972

Cornbleth, C. (2001). Climates of constraint/restraint of teachers & teaching. In W. Stanley (Ed), *Critical issues in social studies research for the 21st century* (pp. 73–95). Greenwich, CT: Information Age Publishing.

Cuban, L. (1986). *Teachers and machines: The classroom use of technology since 1920*. New York: Teachers College Press.

———. (2001). *Oversold and underused: Computers in classrooms*. Cambridge, MA: Harvard University Press.

Damico, J.S., & Baildon, M. (2007). Reading web sites in an inquiry-based literacy and social studies classroom. In D.W. Rowe, R.T. Jiménez, D. Compton, D.K. Dickinson, Y. Kim, et al. (Eds.), *Yearbook of the National Reading Conference* (204–217). Oak Creek, WI: National Reading Conference.

Damico, J.S., Baildon, M., & Campano, G. (2005). Integrating literacy, technology and disciplined inquiry in social studies: The development and application of a conceptual model. *Technology, Humanities, Education and Narrative*. 2(1). Retrieved March 22, 2008, from http://thenjournal.org/feature/92/

Damico, J.S., Baildon, M., Exter, M., & Guo, S. (2009). Where We Read From Matters: Disciplinary literacy in a 9th grade social studies classroom. *Journal of Adolescent and Adult Literacy*, 53(4), 325–335.

Damico, J.S., Campano, G., & Harste, J. (2009). Transactional and critical theory and reading comprehension. In S. Israel & G. Duffy (Eds.), *Handbook of Research on Reading Comprehension* (177–188). Mahwah, NJ: Lawrence Erlbaum Associates.

Damrosch, D. (1995). *We scholars: Changing the culture of the university*. Cambridge, MA: Harvard University Press.

Dede, C. (2008). Theoretical perspectives influencing the use of information technology in teaching and learning. In J. Voogt & G. Knezek (Eds.), *International handbook of information technology in primary and secondary education* (43–62). New York: Springer.

Dede, C. (2009). Comments on Greenhow, Robelia, and Hughes: Technologies that facilitate generating. *Educational Researcher*, 38(4), 260–263.

Delandshire, G. (2002). Assessment as inquiry. *Teachers College Record*, 104(7), 1461–1484.

Dewey, J. (1900/1990). *The school and society*. Chicago, IL: The University of Chicago Press.

———. (1916/2004). *Democracy and education*. Mineola, NY: Dover Publications.

———. (1923/1974). The nature of aims. In R.C. Archambault (Ed.) *John Dewey on education: Selected writings*. New York: Random House.

———. (1934). *Art as experience*. New York: G.P. Putnam's Sons.

———. (1935). The need for orientation. *Forum*, 93(6), 334.

Dimitriadis, G., & McCarthy, G. (2001). *Reading and teaching the postcolonial: From Baldwin to Basquiat and beyond.* New York: Teachers College Press.

Doll, W.E., Jr. (1993). *A post-modern perspective on curriculum.* New York: Teachers College Press.

———. (2002). Ghosts and the curriculum. In W.E. Doll, Jr., & N. Gough (Eds.), *Curriculum visions* (23–70). New York: Peter Lang.

Douglas, M. (1986). *How institutions think.* Syracuse, NY: Syracuse University Press.

Drèze, J., & Sen, A. (2002). *India: Development and participation.* New Delhi: Oxford University Press.

Duke, N. (2004). The case for informational text. *Educational Leadership,* 61(6), 40–44.

Dunn, R.E. (2010). The two world histories. In W. Parker (Ed.), *Social studies today: Research and practice* (183–195). New York: Routledge.

Durrant, C., & Green, B. (2001). Literacy and the new technologies in school education: Meeting the L(IT)eracy challenge. In H. Fehring & P. Green (Eds.), *Critical literacy: A collection of articles from the Australia Literacy Educators' Association* (142–164). Newark, DE: International Reading Association.

Eagleton, M., & Dobler, E. (2007). *Reading the Web: Strategies for Internet inquiry.* New York: Guilford Press.

Eagleton, T. (1996). *The illusions of postmodernism.* Oxford and Cambridge: Blackwell.

Edelsky, C. (1999). On critical whole language practice: Why, what, and a bit of how. In C. Edelsky (Ed.), *Making social justice our project: Teachers working toward critical whole language practice* (7–36). Urbana, IL: National Council of Teachers of English.

Eisenstein, Z. (1998). *Global obscenities: Patriarchy, capitalism and the lure of cyberfantasy.* New York: New York University Press.

Eisner, E.W. (1997). *The enlightened eye: Qualitative inquiry and the enhancement of educational practice.* New York: Merrill Publishing Company.

———. (1997). Who decides what schools teach? In D. Flinders, & S.Thornton (Eds.), *The curriculum studies reader* (337–341). New York: Routledge.

Engeström, Y. (2008). *From teams to knots.* New York: Cambridge University Press.

Engle, S.II., & Ochoa, A.S. (1988). *Educating citizens for democracy: Decision making in social studies.* New York: Teachers College Press.

Fabos, B. (2008). The price of information: Critical literacy, education, and today's Internet. In J. Coiro, M. Knobel, C. Lankshear, & D. J. Leu, Jr. (Eds.), *Handbook of research on new literacies* (839–870). New York: Lawrence Erlbaum Associates.

Fairclough, N. (1989). *Language and power.* Harlow, UK: Pearson Education Ltd.

Foucault, M. (1973). *Madness and civilization: A history of insanity in the age of reason.* New York: Vintage Books.

Freire, P., & Macedo, D.P. (1987). *Literacy: Reading the word and the world.* Westport, CT: Bergin & Garvey.

Friedman, T. (1999). *The lexus and the olive tree.* London: Harper Collins.

Fukuyama, F. (1992). *The end of history and the last man.* New York: Free Press.

Funch, F. (2006). A quick tour of ten dimensions. Retrieved April 25, 2007, from Flemming Funch's NewsLog, Ming the Mechanic Web site http://ming.tv/flemming2.php/__show_article/_a000010–001672.htm

Gallego, M.A., Hollingsworth, S., & Whitenack, D. (2001). Relational knowing in the reform of educational cultures. *Teachers College Record,* 103(2), 240–266.

Gallo, D. (1994). Educating for empathy, reason, and imagination. In K.S. Walter (Ed.), *Re-thinking reason: New perspectives in critical thinking* (43–60). Albany, NY: State University of New York Press.

Gardner, H. (2006). *Five minds for the future.* Boston: Harvard Business School Press.

Gaudelli, W. (2003). *World class: Teaching and learning in global times.* Mahwah, NJ: Lawrence Erlbaum Associates.

Gee, J.P. (2007). *What video games can teach about learning and literacy.* New York: Palgrave Macmillan.

Gee, J.P., Hull, G.A., & Lankshear, C. (1996). *The new work order: Behind the language of the new capitalism.* Boulder, CO: Westview Press.

Geertz, C. (1983). *Local knowledge: Further essays in interpretive anthropology.* New York: Basic Books.

Gilbert, J. (2007). Knowledge, the disciplines, and learning in the digital age. *Educational Research for Policy and Practice,* 6(2), 115–122.

Gill, J.H. (1993). *Learning to learn: Toward a philosophy of education.* Atlantic Highlands, NJ: Humanities Press.

Giroux H. (1988). *Teachers as intellectuals: Toward a critical pedagogy of learning.* South Hadley, MA: Bergin & Garvey.

Globalization. (n.d.) In *Wikipedia.* Retrieved January 27, 2009, from http://en.wikipedia.org/wiki/Globalization

Goh, C.T. (1996). *National Day Rally speech.* Retrieved April 5, 2010, from http://www.moe.gov.sg/corporate/contactonline/pre-2005/rally/speech.html.

———. (1997). *Shaping our future: Thinking Schools, Learning Nation.* 7ᵗʰ International Conference on Thinking. Singapore. Retrieved April 5, 2010, from http://www.moe.gov.sg/media/speeches/1997/020697_print.htm.

———. (1999). Prime Minister's National Day Rally Speech, 1999: *First-World Economy, World-Class Home.* Speech-Text Archival and Retrieval System. Retrieved April 5, 2010, from http://stars.nhb.gov.sg/stars/public/viewHTML.jsp?pdfno=1999082202.

———. (2002). *National Day Rally Address* by Prime Minister Goh Chok Tong at the University Cultural Centre, NUE, on Sunday, 18 August 2002: Remaking Singapore—Changing Mindsets. Speech-Text Archival and Retrieval System. Retrieved April 5, 2010, from http://stars.nhb.gov.sg/stars/public/viewHTML.jsp?pdfno=2002081805.

Goodman, J. (1992). *Elementary schooling for critical democracy.* Albany, NY: State University of New York Press.

Gopinathan, S. (2007). Globalisation, the Singapore developmental state and education policy: A thesis revisited. *Globalisation, Societies and Education,* 5(1), 53–70.

Grant, S.G. (2010). High-stakes testing: How are social studies teachers responding? In W. Parker. (Ed.), *Social studies today: Research and practice* (43–52). New York: Routledge.

Green, B. (1988). Subject-specific literacy and school learning: A focus on writing. *Australian Journal of Education,* 32(2), 156–179.

Greenhow, C., Robelia, B., & Hughes, J. (2009). Web 2.0 and classroom research: What path should we take *now?* *Educational Researcher,* 38(4), 246–259.

Greeno, J.G., & van de Sande, C. (2007). Perspectival understanding of conceptions and conceptual growth in interaction. *Educational Psychologist,* 42(1), 9–23.

Greider, W. (1997). *One world ready or not: The manic logic of global capitalism.* San Francisco, CA: Jossey-Bass Publishers.

Griffin, D.R. (2004). *The new Pearl Harbor: Disturbing questions about the Bush administration and 9/11.* Northampton, MA: Interlink Publishing.

Gunn, G. (2006). *Global and international studies at UCSB.* Retrieved January 21, 2008, from http://www.global.ucsb.edu/programs/gs/gs.html.

Gutmann, A. (1993). The challenge of multiculturalism in political ethics. *Philosophy and Public Affairs*, 22(3), 171–206.

Hagood, M.C. (2000). New times, new millennium, new literacies. *Reading Research and Instruction*, 39(4), 311–328.

Hall, K. (1998). Critical literacy and the case for it in the early years of school. *Language, Culture and Curriculum*, 11(2), 183–194.

Hall, S. (1989). The meaning of new times. In S. Hall, & M. Jacques (Eds.), *New times* (116–133). London: Lawrence and Wishart.

Harari, J.V. & Bell, D.F. (1982) Introduction: Journal a plusieurs voies. In M. Serres (Ed.), *Hermes: Literature, science, philosophy* (ix–xl). Baltimore, MD, Johns Hopkins University.

Hardt, M., & Negri, A. (2000). *Empire*. Cambridge, MA: Harvard Press.

Harste, J. (2010). E-mail communication to authors.

Heath, S.B. (1983). *Ways with words: Language, life, and work in communities and classrooms*. New York: Cambridge University Press.

Heim, M. (1993). *The metaphysics of virtual reality*. New York: Oxford University Press.

Hess, D. (2009). *Controversy in the classroom: The democratic power of conversation*. New York: Routledge.

Hill, I. (2002). The history of international education: An international baccalaureate perspective. In M. Hayden, J. Thompson, & G. Walker (Eds.), *International education in practice: Dimensions for national and international schools* (18–29). Sterling, VA: Stylus Publishing.

Hirsch Hadorn, G., Hoffmann-Riem, H., Biber-Klemm, S., Grossenbacher-Mansuy, W., Joye, D., Pohl, C., Wiesmann, U., & Zemp, E. (2008). (Eds.), *Handbook of transdisciplinary research*. Swiss Academies of Arts and Sciences: Springer.

Hodge, R., & Kress, G. (1988) *Social semiotics*. Ithaca, NY: Cornell University Press.

Hofstadter, R. (1964). The paranoid style in American politics. *Harper's Magazine*, November 1964, 77–86. Retrieved March 27, 2005, from Centre for Research on Globalisation Web site: http://karws.gso.uri.edu/JFK/conspiracy_theory/the_paranoid_mentality/The_paranoid_style.html

Hogan, D. (2007). *Centre for Research in Pedagogy and Practice Conference keynote speech*. National Institute of Education, Singapore.

Holmes, D.R. (2000). *Integral Europe: Fast-capitalism, multiculturalism, neofascism*. Princeton, NJ: Princeton University Press.

Hunt, M.P., & Metcalf, L.E. (1955/1968). *Teaching high school social studies*. New York: Harper and Row.

Huntington, S.P. (1993). The clash of civilizations? *Foreign Affairs*, 72(3), 22–49.

Jäger, J. (2008). Foreward. In G. Hirsch Hadorn, et. al. (2008). (Eds.), *Handbook of transdisciplinary research*. Swiss Academies of Arts and Sciences: Springer.

Jamieson, K.H., & Cappella, J. A. *Echo chamber: Rush Limbaugh and the conservative media establishment*. Oxford: Oxford University Press.

Janks, H. (2000). Domination, access, diversity, and design: A synthesis for critical literacy education. *Educational Review*, 52(2), 175–186.

Jaspers, K. (1955). *Vom ziel und ursprung der geschichte*. Frankfurt/Main: Fischer.

Jenkins, K. (1991). *Re-thinking history*. New York: Routledge.

Keen, A. (2008). *The cult of the amateur: How blogs, MySpace, YouTube, and the rest of today's user-generated media are destroying our economy, our culture, and our values*. New York: Doubleday.

Kellner, D. (2002). Theorizing globalization. *Sociological Theory*, 20(3), 285–305.

Keohane, R.O., & Nye, J.S. (2001). *Power and interdependence.* New York: Addison Wesley Longman.

Kincheloe, J. (2001). *Getting beyond the facts: Teaching social studies/social sciences in the twenty-first century.* New York: Peter Lang Publishing.

Klein, J.T. (1996). *Crossing boundaries: Knowledge, disciplinarities, and interdisciplinarities.* Charlottesville, VA: University Press of Virginia.

Knobel, M., & Lankshear, C. (2008). Remix: The art and craft of endless hybridization. *Journal of Adolescent and Adult Literacy,* 52(1), 22–33.

Koh, A. (2002). Toward a critical pedagogy: Creating "Thinking Schools" in Singapore. *Journal of Curriculum Studies,* 34(3), 255–264.

———. (2004). Singapore education in "New Times": Global/local imperatives. *Discourse: Studies in the Cultural Politics of Education,* 25(3), 335–349.

———. (2007). Living with globalization tactically: The metapragmatics of globalization in Singapore. *Sojourn: Journal of Social Issues in Southeast Asia.* 22(2), 179–201.

———. (2008). Progressive education: Why it's hard to beat, but also hard to find. *Independent School,* Spring 2008. Retrieved January 7, 2010, from http://www.alfiekohn.org/teaching/progressive.htm.

Kress, G. (2003). *Literacy in the new media age.* New York: Routledge.

Krishna, S. (2009). (Ed.) *Globalization and postcolonialism: Hegemony and resistance in the twenty-first century.* Lanham, MD: Rowman & Littlefield.

Kristeva, J. (1980). *Desire in language: A semiotic approach to literature and art.* New York: Columbia University Press.

Kuhn, D. (2003). Understanding and valuing knowing as developmental goals. *Liberal Education,* 89(3). Retrieved April 10, 2009, from http://www.aacu.org/liberaleducation/le-su03/le-su3feature.cfm

Kuiper, E., Volman, M., & Terwel, J. (2005). The web as an information resource in K-12 education: Strategies for supporting students in searching and processing information. *Review of Educational Research,* Fall 2005, 75(3), 285–328.

Kumashiro, K. (2001). "Posts" perspectives on anti-oppressive education in social studies, English, mathematics, and science classrooms. *Educational Researcher,* 30(3), 3–12.

Lakoff, G. (1996). *Moral politics: How liberals and conservatives think.* Chicago, IL: University of Chicago Press.

Lakoff, G. (2004). *Don't think of an elephant!: Know your values and frame the debate.* White River Junction, VT: Chelsea Green Publishing.

Lakoff, G., & Johnson, M. (1980). *Metaphors we live by.* Chicago, IL: The University of Chicago Press.

Lamont, M. (2009). *How professors think: Inside the curious world of academic Jjudgment.* Cambridge, MA: Harvard University Press.

Lanham, R.A. (1994). *The economy of attention.* Chicago, IL: University of Chicago Press.

Lankshear, C., & Knobel, M. (2003). *New literacies: Changing knowledge and classroom learning.* Buckingham: Open University Press.

———. (2006). *New literacies: Everyday practices & classroom learning.* New York: Open University Press.

Lankshear, C., & McLaren, P. (1993). (Eds.), *Critical literacy: Politics, praxis, and the postmodern.* Albany, NY: State University of New York Press.

Lankshear, C., Peters, M., & Knobel, M. (2000). Information, knowledge and learning: Some issues facing epistemology and education in a digital age. *Journal of Philosophy of Education,* 34(1), 17–39.

Larreamendy-Joerns, J., & Leinhardt, G. (2006). Going the distance with online education. *Review of Educational Research,* Winter 2006, 76(4), 567–605.

Lasch, C. (1984). *The minimal self: Psychic survival in troubled times.* New York: Norton.

Leander, K., & Rowe, D. (2006). Mapping literacy spaces in motion: A rhizomatic analysis of a classroom literacy performance. *Reading Research Quarterly*, 41(4), 428–460.

Lee, H.L. (2006). Transcript of Prime Minister Lee Hsien Loong's National Day Rally English Speech on Sunday, 20 August 2006 at National Cultural Centre. Speech-Text Archival and Retrieval System. Retrieved April 5, 2010, from http://stars.nhb.gov.sg/stars/public/viewHTML.jsp?pdfno=2006082010.

Leu, D.J., Jr. (2000). Literacy and technology: Deictic consequences for literacy education in an information age. In M.L. Kamil, P. Mosenthal, P.D. Pearson, & R. Barr (Eds.), *Handbook of reading research* (Vol. III, 743–770). Mahwah, NJ: Lawrence Erlbaum Associates.

Leu, D.J., Jr., & Kinzer, C. K. (2000). The convergence of literacy instruction with networked technologies for information and communication. *Reading Research Quarterly*, 35(1), 108–127.

Leu, D.J., Jr., Kinzer, C.K., Coiro, J., & Cammack, D. (2004). Toward a theory of new literacies emerging from the Internet and other information and communication technologies. In R. B. Ruddell, & N. Unrau (Eds.), *Theoretical models and processes of reading* (1570–1613). Newark, DE: International Reading Association.

Leu, D.J., Jr., Leu, D.D. & Coiro, J. (2004). Teaching with the Internet: New literacies for new times (4th ed.). Norwood, MA: Christopher-Gordon.

Leu, D. Jr., O'Byrne, W.I., Zawilinski, L., Greg McVerry, G., & Everett-Cacopardo, H. (2009) Expanding the new literacies conversation: Comments on Greenhow, Robelia, and Hughes. *Educational Researcher*, 38(4), 264–269.

Leu, D.J., Jr., Zawilinski, L., Castek, J., Banerjee, M., Housand, B. Liu, Y., & O'Neill, M. (2007). What is new about the new literacies of online reading comprehension?. In L.S. Rush, A.J. Eakle, & A. Berger (Eds.), *Secondary school literacy: What research Reveals for classroom practice* (pp. 37–68). Urbana, IL: National Council of Teachers of English.

Levstik, L. & Barton, K. (2006). *Doing history: Investigating with children in elementary and middle schools.* Mahwah, NJ: Lawrence Erlbaum Associates.

Lewison, M., Leland, C. & Harste, J. C. (2008). *Creating critical classrooms: K–8 reading and writing with an edge.* Mahwah, NJ: Lawrence Erlbaum Associates.

Luke, A. (2002). Curriculum, ethics, metanarrative: Teaching and learning beyond the nation. *Curriculum Perspectives*. Retrieved April 2, 2008, from http://wwwfp.education.tas.gov.au/English/luke.htm.

Luke, A., & Freebody, P. (1997). The social practices of reading. In S. Muspratt, A. Luke, & P. Freebody (Eds.), *Constructing critical literacies: Teaching and learning textual practice* (185–226). Cresskill, NJ: Hampton Press.

Luke, A. & Woods, A. (2009). Critical literacy in schools: A primer. *Voices in the Middle.* 17(2), 9–18.

Luke, C. (2003). Pedagogy, connectivity, multimodality, and interdisciplinarity. *Reading Research Quarterly*, 38(3), 397–403.

Madaus, G.F. (1999).The influence of testing on the curriculum. In M.J. Early & K.J. Rehage (Eds.), *Issues in curriculum: A selection of chapters from past NSSE yearbooks* (Part II, pp. 73-111). Chicago: University of Chicago Press.

Mander, J., & Goldsmith, E. (1996). *The case against the global economy and for a turn to the local.* San Francisco, CA: Sierra Club Books.

Manjoo, F. (2008). *True enough: Learning to live in a post-fact society.* Hoboken, NJ: John Wiley & Sons.

Martin, J.R. (1994). *Changing the educational landscape: Philosophy, women, and curriculum.* New York: Routledge.

Martorella, P.H., Beal, C., & Bolick, C.M. (2008). *Teaching social studies in middle and secondary schools* (5th ed.). Columbus, OH: Merrill Prentice Hall.

Massey, D. (1994). *Space, place, and gender.* Minneapolis, MN: University of Minnesota Press.

Massialas, B., & Cox, B. (1966). *Inquiry in social studies.* New York: McGraw-Hill.

McIntosh, P. (2005). Gender perspectives on educating for global citizenship. In N. Noddings (Ed.), *Educating citizens for global awareness* (22–39). New York: Teachers College Press.

McLaughlin, M., & DeVoogd, G. (2004). Critical literacy as comprehension: Expanding reader response. *Journal of Adolescent and Adult Literacy,* 48(1), 52–62.

McNeil, L.M. (1986). *Contradictions of control: School structure and school knowledge.* New York: Routledge.

Media Development Authority. (2003). Retrieved December 10, 2009, from http://www.mda.gov.sg/wms.www/thenewsdesk.aspx?sid=674.

MercyCorps. (n.d.). Why teach globalization? Retrieved January 27, 2009, from http://www.globalenvision.org/teachers

Merryfield, M.M. (2001). Moving the center of global education: From imperial world views that divide the world to double consciousness, contrapuntal pedagogy, hybridity, and cross-cultural competence. In W.B. Stanley (Ed.), *Critical issues in social studies research for the 21st century* (179–208). Greenwich, CT: Information Age Publishing.

Meyssan, T. (2002). *911: The big lie.* London: Carnot Publishing, Ltd.

Mitchell, K. (2003). Educating the national citizen in neoliberal times: From the multicultural self to the strategic cosmopolitan. *Transactions of the Institute of British Geographers,* 28(4), 387–403.

Mitchell, K. (2007). Geographies of identity: The intimate cosmopolitan. *Progress in Human Geography,* 31(5), 706–720.

Moje, E. (2008). Foregrounding the disciplines in secondary literacy teaching and learning: A call for change. *Journal of Adolescent & Adult Literacy,* 52(2), 96–107.

Molebash, P.E. (2004). Web historical inquiry projects. *Social Education,* 68(3), 226–229.

Molebash, P.E., Dodge, B., Bell, R.L., Mason, C.L., & Irving, K.E. (n.d.). Promoting student inquiry: WebQuests to Web inquiry projects. Retrieved February 5, 2010, fromhttp://webinquiry.org/WIP_Intro.htm

Morgan, W. (1997). *Critical literacy in the classroom: The art of the possible.* New York: Routledge.

Morrell, E. (2004). *Becoming critical researchers: Literacy and empowerment for urban youth.* New York: Peter Lang.

———. (2008). *Critical literacy and urban youth: Pedagogies of access, dissent, and liberation.* New York: Routledge.

Morris-Suzuki, T. (2000). For and against NGOs: The politics of the lived world. *New Left Review,* 2, 63–84.

Mouffe, C. (1992). Feminism, citizenship and radical democratic politics. In J. Butler, & J.W. Scott (Eds.), *Feminists theorize the political* (368–384). New York: Routledge.

National Council for the Social Studies. (2001). Preparing citizens for a global community. Retrieved May 10, 2008, from http://www.socialstudies.org/positions/global

National Council of Social Studies and Partnership for 21ˢᵗ Century Skills, The. Retrieved May 15, 2009, from http://www.21stcenturyskills.org/documents/ss_map.pdf

New London Group. (1996). A pedagogy of multiliteracies: Designing social futures. *Harvard Educational Review,* 66(1), 60–92.

New London Group. (2000). A pedagogy of multiliteracies. In B. Cope, & M. Kalantzis (Eds.), *Multiliteracies: Literacy learning and the design of social futures* (9–37). London: Routledge.

Nixon, H. (2003). New research literacies for contemporary research into literacy and new media? *Reading Research Quarterly,* 38(3), 386–413.

Noddings, N. (2005). Global citizenship: Promises and problems. In N. Noddings (Ed.), *Educating citizens for global awareness* (1–21). New York: Teachers College Press.

Nokes, J.D., Dole, J.A., & Hacker, D.J. (2007). Teaching high school students to use heuristics while reading historical texts. *Journal of Educational Psychology,* 99(3), 492–504.

Nussbaum, M. (1986). *The fragility of goodness: Luck and ethics in Greek tragedy and philosophy.* Cambridge: Cambridge University Press.

Nussbaum, M.C. (2006). *Frontiers of justice: Disability, nationality, species membership.* Cambridge, MA: Harvard University Press.

Nussbaum, M. (1997). *Cultivating humanity: A classical defense of reform in liberal education.* Cambridge, MA: Harvard University Press.

Oliver, D.W., & Shaver, J.P. (1966). *Teaching public issues in the high school.* Boston, MA: Houghton Mifflin.

Ong, A. (1999). *Flexible citizenship: The cultural logics of transnationality.* Durham, NC: Duke University Press.

———. (2006). *Neoliberalism as exception: Mutations in citizenship and sovereignty.* Durham, NC: Duke University Press.

Ooi, G.L., & Shaw, B.J. (2004), *Beyond the port city: Development and identity in 21st century Singapore.* Singapore: Prentice Hall.

Packard, V. (1957). *The hidden persuaders.* New York: David McKay Company.

Parker, W. (2006). Public discourses in schools: Purposes, problems, possibilities. *Educational Researcher,* 35(8), 11–18.

Parker, W. (2010). Idiocy, puberty, and citizenship: The road ahead. In W. Parker (Ed.), *Social studies today: Research and practice* (247–260). New York: Routledge.

Parker, W., Nonomiya, A., & Cogan, J. (1999), Educating world citizens: Toward multinational curriculum development. *American Educational Research Journal,* 36(2), 117–46.

Pearson, P.D., Roehler, L.R., Dole, J.A., & Duffy, G.G. (1992). Developing expertise in reading comprehension. In S.J. Samuels & A.E. Farstrup (Eds.), *What research has to say about reading instruction* (145–199). Newark, DE: International Reading Association.

Peirce, C.S. (1905/1984). Review of Nichols' A Treatise on Cosmology, The Monist, XV (April, 1905). In H.S. Thayer, (1984), (Ed.), *Meaning and action: A critical history of pragmatism* (494–495). Indianapolis, IN: Hackett Publishing Company.

Pescatore, C. (2007). Current events as empowering literacy: For English and social studies teachers. *Journal of Adolescent and Adult Literacy,* 51(4), 326–339.

Pinar, W.F. (2004). *What is curriculum theory?* Mahwah, NJ: Lawrence Erlbaum Associates.

Polimeni, J. (2006). Transdisciplinary research: moving forward. *International Journal of Transdisciplinary Research,* 1(1), 1–3.

Prensky, M. (2001). *Digital game-based learning.* New York: McGraw Hill.

Quah, J.S.T. (2000). Globalisation and Singapore's search for nationhood. In L. Suryadinata (Ed.), *Nationalism and globalisation: East and west* (71–101). Singapore: Institute of Southeast Asian Studies.

Reporters Without Borders (2007). Singapore: Annual Report, 2007. Retrieved December 10, 2008, from http://www.rsf.org/article.php3?id_article=20796.

Rommetveit, R. (1987). Meaning, context, and control. *Inquiry*, 30(1), 77–99.

Rorty, R. (1986). *Contingency, irony, and solidarity*. Cambridge: Cambridge University Press.

Rosenzweig, R. (2003). Scarcity or abundance? Preserving the past in a digital era. *The American Historical Review, 108*(3). Retrieved February 23, 2010, from http://www.historycooperative.org/journals/ahr/108.3/rosenzweig.html

Roth, W-M., & Duit, R. (2003). Emergence, flexibility, and stabilization of language in a physics classroom. *Journal of Research in Science Teaching*, 40(9), 869–897.

Roy, K. (2005). The Politics of freedom: A Spinozian critique. *Journal of Curriculum   Theorizing*, 21(3), 86–115.

Rugg, H. (1921). On reconstructing the social studies: Comments on Mr. Schafer's letter. *Historical Outlook*, 12(7), 249–252.

Sachs, J. (2008). *Common wealth: Economics for a crowded planet*. New York: Penguin Books.

Said, E. (1993). Culture and imperialism. The T.S. Eliot Lectures at the University of Kent l985. New York: Knopf/Random House.

Sales, N.J. (2006). Click here for conspiracy. *Vanity Fair*. Retrieved February 3, 2008, fromhttp://www.vanityfair.com/commentary/content/printables/060717 roco02?print=true

Sanchez, C.A., Wiley, J., & Goldman, S.R. (2006). Teaching students to evaluate source reliability during Internet research tasks. In S.A. Barab, K.E. Hay, & D.T. Hickey (Eds.), *Proceedings of the seventh international conference on the learning Ssciences* (662–666). Mahwah, NJ: Lawrence Erlbaum Associates.

Sassen, S. (2001). *The global city*. New York: Princeton University Press.

———. (2005). The repositioning of citizenship and alienage: Emergent subjects and spaces for politics, *Globalizations*, 2(1), 79–94.

Saye, J.W., & Brush, T. (2006). Comparing teachers' strategies for supporting student inquiry in a problem-based multimedia-enhanced history unit. *Theory and Research in Social Education*, 34(2), 183–212.

Schwab, J. (1978). *Science, curriculum, and liberal education: Selected Eessays*. Chicago, IL: The University of Chicago Press.

Schweber, S. (2010). Holocaust fatigue in teaching today. In W. Parker (Ed.), *Social studies today: Research and practice* (151–162). New York: Routledge.

Seah, C. N. (2005). Old formula losing impact in new world. *The Star Malaysia*, October 23. Retrieved March 31, 2009, from http://www.singapore- window. org/sw05/051023st.htm

Segall, A. (1999). Social stdies education: A re-conceptualized framework. Project Time Occassional Paper No. 1. Retrieved June 3, 2007, fromhttp://www.projecttime.org/resources/paper.taf .

———. (2006). What's the purpose of teaching a discipline, anyway? The case of history. In A. Segall, E.E. Heilman, & C.H. Cherryholmes (Eds.), *Social studies—The next generation: Re-searching in the postmodern* (125–139). New York: Peter Lang.

Segall, A., & Gaudelli, W. (2007). Reflecting socially on social issues in a social studies methods course. *Teaching Education*, 18(1), 77–92.

Segall, A., Heilman, E.E., & Cherryholmes, C. (2006). (Eds.), *Social studies—The next generation*. New York: Peter Lang.

Sen, A. (1999). *Development as freedom*. New York: Anchor Books.

———. (2002). How to judge globalism. *The American Prospect*, 13(1). Retrieved March 31, 2009, from http://www.prospect.org/cs/articles?article=how_to_ judge_globalism.

———. (2009). *The idea of jjustice*. London: Penguin Books.

Seuss, D. (1971). *The lorax*. New York: Random House.

Shaker, P., & Heilman, E.E. (2008). *Reclaiming education for democracy: Thinking beyond No Child Left Behind*. New York: Routledge.

Shannon, P. (1990). *The struggle to continue: Progressive reading instruction in the United States*. Portsmouth, NH: Heinemann.

Shanahan, T., & Shanahan, C. (2008). Teaching disciplinary literacy to adolescents: Rethinking content area literacy. *Harvard Educational Review*, 78(1), 40–61.

Shulman, L. (2004). *The wisdom of practice: Essays on teaching, learning, and learning to teach*. San Francisco, CA: Jossey-Bass.

Sipe, L. (1998). How picture books work: A semiotically framed theory of text-picture relationships. *Children's Literature in Education*, 29(2), 97–108.

Slotta, J.D., & Linn, M.C. (2009). *WISE Science: Web-based inquiry in the classroom*. New York: Teachers College Press.

Spiro, R.J., Collins, B.P., Thota, J.J., & Feltovich, P.J. (2003). Cognitive flexibility theory: Hypermedia for complex learning, adaptive knowledge application, and experienceacceleration. *Educational Technology*, 43(5), 5–10.

Spiro, R.J., Coulson, R.L., Feltovich, P.J., & Anderson, D. (2004). Cognitive flexibility theory: Advanced knowledge acquisition in ill-structured domains. In R. B. Ruddell (Ed.), *Theoretical models and processes of reading* (5th ed., 602–616). Newark, DE: International Reading Association.

Stanley, A. (2008). TV panders to the Gilded Age. *International Herald Tribune*. Retrieved December 21, 2009, from http://www.iht.com/articles/2008/09/09/arts/gossip.php.

Stanley, W. (1992). *Curriculum for utopia: Social reconstructionism and critical pedagogy in the postmodern era*. New York: State University of New York Press.

Stanley, W. (2010). Social studies and the social order: Transmission or transformation? In W. Parker (Ed.), *Social studies today: Research and practice* (17–24). New York: Routledge.

Stiglitz, J.E. (2006). *Making globalisation work*. New York: W.W. Norton.

Stone, M., & Parker, T. (2006). *South Park: Mystery of theurinal deuce*. [Television series]. Accessed at www.vidpeek.com (first aired October 11, 2006).

Street, B. (1984). *Literacy in theory and practice*. Cambridge: Cambridge University Press.

———. (2003). What's "new" in New Literacy Studies? Critical approaches to literacy and practice. *Current Issues in Comparative Education*, 5(2), 1–14.

Sunstein, C.R. (2001). *Republic.com*. Princeton, NJ: Princeton University Press.

Susskind, L. (2003, November). Superstrings. *Physics World*. Retrieved May 11, 2007, from http://physicsweb.org/articles/world/16/11/8/1

Swan, K.O., & Hicks, D. (2007). Through the democratic lens: The role of purpose in leveraging technology to support historical inquiry in the social studies classroom. *International Journal of Social Education*, 21(2), 142–168.

Swan, K.O., & Hofer, M. (2008). Technology and social studies. In L.S. Levstik, & C.A. Tyson, (Eds.), *Handbook of research in social studies education* (307–326). New York: Routledge.

Tan, E. (2004). "We, the citizens of Singapore . . . ": Multiethnicity, its evolution and its aberrations. In L.A. Eng (Ed.), *Beyond rituals and riots: Ethnic pluralism and social cohesion in Singapore* (65–97). Singapore: Eastern Universities Press.

Tan, J., & Gopinathan, S. (2000). Education reform in Singapore: Towards greater creativity and innovation? *NIRA Review*, 7(3), 5–10.

Tharman, S. (2004). Leading schools in a broad-based education. Singapore Government Press Release. Speech by Mr. Tharman Shanmugaratnam. Retrieved

March 21, 2009, from http://www.moe.gov.sg/speeches/2004/sp20040410a. htm.

———. (2007). Why National Education matters more now. Speech at the Network Conference, Singapore. Retrieved March 21, 2009, from http://www.singaporeunited.sg/cep/index.php/web/News-Room/Why-National-Education-Matters-more-now.

Thayer-Bacon, B.J. (2003). *Relational (e)pistemologies*. New York: Peter Lang Publishing, Inc.

Tierney, R. (2008). The agency and artistry of meaning makers within and across digital spaces. In S.E. Israel, & G.G. Duffy (Eds.), *Handbook of research on reading comprehension* (261–288). New York: Routledge.

Tovani, C. (2000). *I read it but I don't get it: Comprehension strategies for adolescent readers*. Portland, ME: Stenhouse.

Vasquez, V. (2004). *Negotiating critical literacies with young children*. Mahwah, NJ: Lawrence Erlbaum Associates.

Wallace, R.M. (2004). A framework for understanding teaching with the Internet. *American Educational Research Journal*, 41(2), 447–488.

Wallerstein, I. (1999). *The end of the world as we know it: Social science for the twenty-first century*. Minneapolis: University of Minnesota Press.

Wenger, E. (1998). *Communities of practice: Learning, meaning, and identity*. Cambridge: Cambridge University Press.

Werner, W. (2002). Reading visual texts. *Theory and Research in Social Education*, 30(3), 401–428.

Wieseltier, L. (2010). Intellectuals and their America. *Dissent*, 57(1), 25–42.

Wiggins, G., & McTighe, J. (1998). *Understanding by design*. Alexandria, VA: Association for Supervision and Curriculum Development.

Wiley, J., & Voss, J.F. (1999). Constructing arguments from multiple sources: Tasks that promote understanding and not just memory for text. *Journal of Educational Psychology*, 83(1), 301–311.

Wilhelm, J.D., & Smith, M.W. (2007). Making it matter through the power of inquiry. *Adolescent literacy: Turning promise into practice* (pp. 231–242). Portsmouth: NH: Heinemann.

Willinsky, J. (1998). *Learning to divide the world: Education at empire's end*. Minneapolis, MN: University of Minnesota Press.

Windschitl, M. (2002). Framing constructivism in practice as the negotiation of dilemmas: An analysis of the conceptual, pedagogical, cultural, and political challenges facing teachers. *Review of Educational Research*, 72(2), 131–175.

Wineburg, S. (2001). *Historical thinking and other unnatural acts: Charting the future of teaching the past*. Philadelphia: Temple University Press.

Wolf, M., & Barzillai, M. (2009). The importance of deep reading. *Educational Leadership*, 66(6), 32–37.

Zhang, J. (2009). Comments on Greenhow, Robelia, and Hughes: Toward a creative social web for learners and teachers. *Educational Researcher*, 38(4), 274–279.

Zhang, J., Scardamalia, M., Reeve, R., & Messina, R. (2009). Designs for collective cognitive responsibility in knowledge building communities. *Journal of the Learning Sciences*, 18(1): 7–44.

Zhao, Y., & Frank, K.A. (2003). Factors affecting technology uses in schools: An ecological Perspective. *American Educational Research Journal*, 40(4), 807–840.

Zinn, H. (1980). *A people's history of the United States*. New York: Harper Collins.

Zwiers, J. (2004). *Building reading comprehension habits in grades 6–12: A toolkit of classroom activities*. International Reading Association: Newark, DE.

WEBSITES REFERENCED

Chapter 3 Websites

Accuracy.org: http://accuracy.org/
Animemusicvideos.org: http://www.animemusicvideos.org/home/home.php
Bob Bain: http://www-personal.umich.edu/~bbain/display/talkingpoints.htm
University of California, Berkeley, Library: http://www.lib.berkeley.edu/instruct/
    guides/evaluation.html
The Center for Media Literacy: http://www.medialit.org/reading_room/article227.html
Cornell University: http://www.library.cornell.edu/olinuris/ref/webcrit.html
Critical Web Reader: http://cwr.indiana.edu
William Cronon: http://www.williamcronon.net/researching/index.htm; http://
    www.williamcronon.net/researching/questions.htm
David Darts: CT4CT: Creative Tools for Critical Times: http://ct4ct.com/index.
    php?title=Main_Page
Dispute Finder: http://disputefinder.cs.berkeley.edu/
Factcheck.org: http://www.factcheck.org/
Fanfiction.net: http://www.fanfiction.net/
Historical Inquiry: Scaffolding Wise Practices in the History Classroom: http://
    www.historicalinquiry.com/index.cfm
History Matters: http://historymatters.gmu.edu/
Inquiry Chart: http://forpd.ucf.edu/strategies/stratIChart.html
Knowledge Forum: http://www.knowledgeforum.com/
Library of Congress' "The Learning Page": http://lcweb2.loc.gov/ammem/ndlpedu/
    lessons/psources/pshome.html
machinima.com: http://machinima.com/
University of Maryland Library: http://www.lib.umd.edu/UES/webcheck.html
Meaningful Learning Toolbox: http://mltoolbox.org/about.asp
Media Watch: http://mediawatch.com/about.html
Mixter.org: http://mixter.org/
National Archives and Records Administration's Digital Classroom: http://www.
    archives.gov/education/lessons/index.html
National Council of Social Studies and Partnership for 21st Century Skills Map:
    http://www.21stcenturyskills.org/images/stories/matrices/ICTmap_ss.pdf
National History Project: http://www.history.ilstu.edu/nhp/terminology.html
Newgrounds.com: http://www.newgrounds.com/
Alan November—November Learning: http://novemberlearning.com/; http://
    novemberlearning.com/resources/information-literacy-resources/
Persistent Issues in History Network: http://dp.crlt.indiana.edu
Propaganda Critic: http://www.propagandacritic.com/
Kathy Shrock: http://school.discoveryeducation.com/schrockguide/eval.html
Smashing Magazine: http://www.smashingmagazine.com/2007/08/02/data-visual-
    ization-modern-approaches/; http://www.smashingmagazine.com/2008/01/14/
    monday-inspiration-data-visualization-and-infographics/
Snopes.com: http://www.snopes.com/.
Southern Poverty Law Center: http://www.tolerance.org/teach/web/site_check/
    index.jsp
Splicemusic.com: http://www.splicemusic.com/
Stanford Persuasive Technology Lab: http://captology.stanford.edu/; http://cred-
    ibility.stanford.edu/guidelines/index.html
Swift River: http://swift.ushahidi.com/.

Web Inquiry Projects: http://webinquiry.org/overview.htm; http://webinquiry.org/
    WIP_Intro.htm
WebQuest: http://webquest.org/

Chapter 4 Websites

November, A. *The Pacific Northwest Tree Octopus*: http://zapatopi.net/treeocto-
    pus/. Retrieved August 7, 2008, from *November Learning* website: h t t p : / /
    novemberlearning.com/resources/information-literacy-resources/.
Save the Orangutan: www.savetheorangutan.com
snopes.com: http://ww.snaopes.com/photos/tsunami/tsunami2.asp#photo

Chapter 5 Websites

911 Research: www.911research.wtc7.net
911 Truth.Org: http://www.911truth.org/
911 Truth Movement.Org: http://www.911truthmovement.org/
Alternet: www.alternet.org
Google video site: http://video.google.com/videoplay?docid=-8260059923762628848
The Journal of 911 Studies: http://www.journalof911studies.com/
Loose Change: http://www.loosechange911.com/
Screw Loose Change: http://screwloosechange.blogspot.com/).
Zogby News: http://www.zogby.com/search/ReadNews.dbm?ID=855

Chapter 6 Websites

Business Software Alliance site: http://www.bsa.org/usa/antipiracy
Chaos Computer Club: www.ccc.de/campaigns/boycott-musicindustry
Creative Commons: http://www.creativecommons.org
Global Security Organization: http://www.globalsecurity.org/wmd/libaray/news/
    taiwan/2004/taiwan-040219-cna04.htm
Government Information Office of Taiwan: www.gio.gov.tw
Motion Picture Association of America: http://www.mpaa.org/home.htm
Taiwan's International Legal Position: http://www.taiwanadvice.com/ustaiwan/

Chapter 7 Websites

"What is Globalization?" from the Carnegie Endowment for International Peace:
    http://www.globalization101.org/What_is_Globalization.html
"Globalization" entry from Wikipedia: http://en.wikipedia.org/wiki/Globaliza-
    tion
National Council of Social Studies (NCSS) position statement, "Preparing Citizens
    for a Global Community" http://www.socialstudies.org/positions/global
MercyCorps webpage: "For Teachers: Why Teach Globalization?" http://www.
    globalenvision.org/teachers

Index